Philosophy, Science and Religion for Everyone

Philosophy, Science and Religion for Everyone brings together these great truth-seeking disciplines and seeks to understand the ways in which they challenge and inform each other.

Key topics and their areas of focus include:

- Foundational Issues – why should anyone care about the science-and-religion debate? How do scientific claims relate to the truth? Is evolution compatible with design?
- Faith and Rationality – can faith ever be rational? Are theism and atheism totally opposed? Is God hidden or does God simply not exist?
- Faith and Science – what provides a better explanation for the origin of the universe – science or religion? Faith and physics: can they be reconciled? Does contemporary neuroscience debunk religious belief? Creationism and evolutionary biology – what constitutes science and what constitutes pseudo-science?
- Practical Implications – is fundamentalism just a problem for religious people? What are the ethical implications of the science-and-religion debate? Do logic and religion mix?

This book is designed to be used in conjunction with the free 'Philosophy, Science and Religion' MOOC (massive open online course) created by the University of Edinburgh and hosted by the Coursera platform (www.coursera.org). This book is also highly recommended for anyone looking for a concise overview of this fascinating discipline.

Mark Harris, Duncan Pritchard, James Collin, David de Pomerai, Michael Fuller, David Fergusson, Emma Gordon, Sarah Lane Ritchie, S. Orestis Palermos, Alasdair Richmond, Katherine Snow, and **Till Vierkant** all teach and research in Philosophy, Science and Religion at the University of Edinburgh, UK. **J. Adam Carter** teaches Philosophy at the University of Glasgow, UK, and **Ian Church** teaches Philosophy at Hillsdale College, USA, while **Jeremy Kidwell** teaches theological ethics at the University of Birmingham, UK.

Philosophy, Science and Religion
Free Online Course Series

This completely free and open online course series introduces you to some of the main debates at the intersection of philosophy, science, and religion, and is designed to be used in conjunction with *Philosophy, Science and Religion for Everyone*. Each week a distinguished guest lecturer talks you through some of the most important questions and issues in their area of expertise. The series is split into three courses: Science and Philosophy, Philosophy and Religion, and Religion and Science, each of which is introduced by instructors from the University of Edinburgh. No prior knowledge is required. Students who successfully complete the course are eligible for a certificate from the University of Edinburgh.

This Massive Open Online Course (MOOC) series has been created by the University of Edinburgh's *Eidyn* research centre (www.eidyn.org), thanks to generous support from the John Templeton Foundation, and is offered by Coursera.

Watch an introductory video
and sign up for the courses at:
www.coursera.org/learn/philosophy-science-religion-1

Taught by Dr J. Adam Carter, Dr Mark Harris, Dr S. Orestis Palermos, Prof Duncan Pritchard, Dr Mog Stapleton, Dr James Collin

Prof Martin Kusch, Prof Tom McLeish, Prof Michael Murray, Prof Conor Cunningham, Prof Stathis Psilos, Prof John Schellenberg, Prof Justin Barrett, Prof John Greco, Dr Rik Peels, Prof John Evans, Prof Mark Alfano, Prof Tim Maudlin, Prof Al Mele, Dr Kevin Scharp, Prof David Clough, Prof Simon Conway Morris, Prof Michela Massimi, Dr Bethany Sollereder, and Prof Graham Priest.

Philosophy, Science and Religion for Everyone

Edited by Mark Harris
and Duncan Pritchard

Routledge
Taylor & Francis Group

LONDON AND NEW YORK

First published 2018
by Routledge
2 Park Square, Milton Park, Abingdon, Oxon OX14 4RN

and by Routledge
711 Third Avenue, New York, NY 10017

Routledge is an imprint of the Taylor & Francis Group, an informa business

© 2018 Mark Harris, Duncan Pritchard with J. Adam Carter, Ian Church, James Collin, David de Pomerai, Michael Fuller, David Fergusson, Emma Gordon, Jeremy Kidwell, Sarah Lane Ritchie, S. Orestis Palermos, Alasdair Richmond, Katherine Snow, and Till Vierkant

British Library Cataloguing-in-Publication Data
A catalogue record for this book is available from the British Library

Library of Congress Cataloging-in-Publication Data
A catalog record has been requested

ISBN: 978-1-138-23415-4 (hbk)
ISBN: 978-1-138-23421-5 (pbk)
ISBN: 978-1-315-10247-4 (ebk)

Typeset in Times New Roman
by Apex CoVantage, LLC

Contents

Introduction

Mark Harris and Duncan Pritchard

The science-and-religion discourse is so significant that it's hardly possible to live in the Western world and not hold an opinion on it. The discourse is, however, almost universally construed in terms of a 'debate', and a debate that's characterised by 'conflict' above all. The fact that the discourse underlies some highly volatile social and political disagreements adds fuel to the fire (and these disagreements are especially live in North America, especially concerning climate change, the place of **evolution** versus creation' in high school education, and in bioethics concerning 'pro-life versus pro-choice'). Arguably, there's too much heat and little light in these disagreements. Adding philosophy to the mix ('Philosophy, Science, and Religion'), this book takes the view that the science-and-religion debate can move beyond hostility to become a major force behind a new kind of intellectual enlightenment in modern culture.

At present, it's possible to see the science-and-religion debate as a near-perfect example of C. P. Snow's famous *Two Cultures* idea, that there's an intellectual gulf between the natural sciences and humanities subjects so deep that meaningful dialogue is almost impossible. We are all too familiar with the many inexpert and over-confident commentators on both sides of the science-and-religion divide who weigh in blithely, with the effect that all too often the misunderstanding and hostility are entrenched due to a poor grasp of the issues at stake. The new **atheism** debate and the creation versus **evolution** debate are good examples of areas dominated by clashes of ideologies rather than the productive exchange of ideas. As a result, the *conflict hypothesis* – that science and religion are irreconcilably at war with each other – looks set to be perpetuated indefinitely. And yet, the academic discipline of philosophy, science, and religion, which brings together thousands of scientists, philosophers, historians, and theologians (among other kinds of scholars), has demonstrated again and again the superficiality of the view that science and religion have to be completely at loggerheads.

Why, then, is the conflict hypothesis so pervasive? Partly it's because the conflict story 'sells' in the popular media, and partly it's because it suits the agendas of the vocal few on the extreme sides of the debate. More importantly, though, it's because the conflict hypothesis is a 'social construct', an idea that seems so obvious that a society will largely believe it without question, because that idea supports (or legitimates) a widespread assumption of that society. In this case, that assumption is what's known as the 'secularisation thesis', the idea that traditional religious beliefs and practices must inevitably decline in the face of modern scepticism and relativism, with a special emphasis on the superiority of modern science and technology for providing essential knowledge and truths.

It's not our purpose to investigate the rights and wrongs of the secularisation thesis, nor the ways in which it entwines with ideologies and practices at the heart of Western culture, such as neo-liberalism and different forms of democracy and social welfare. All of these are hotly disputed by academics in the social sciences, not to mention public figures such as politicians, journalists, and religious leaders. Instead, we want to point the way to the new kind of intellectual enlightenment that we mentioned above, where the gulf between the 'Two Cultures' is bridged by the medium of philosophy. This book sets out some of the main parameters at play in bridging that gulf. The book accompanies the University of Edinburgh's freely-available MOOC ('Massive Open Online Course') in Philosophy, Science, and Religion (available from www.coursera.org), but it can also be read in its own right as a stand-alone introduction to the field.

The philosophy, science, and religion field of scholarship has always held questions of ultimate meaning and purpose to its heart; not only does the field embrace all of such big questions asked by science and by religion, but in allowing philosophy to take the lead in showing how the different sciences and religions can come together, the field introduces big questions of its own concerning the nature of knowing, the nature of seeking, and the nature of enquiry. Clearly, the potential questions that can be asked and tackled here are enormous, both in magnitude and in number, and we've needed to be selective in compiling this book. Chapters that address the central philosophical questions of how the sciences and religions relate to the concepts of truth, **logic**, free will, and reason are centre-stage in the book (Pritchard and Orestis, Collin, Pritchard, Carter, Church, Vierkant), along with the general question of how and why the science-and-religion debate is important in the first place (Fuller). But the book also looks at issues arising from specific sciences. The natural sciences where science-and-religion questions most frequently arise – physics (Harris), biology (Richmond), and the neurosciences (Ritchie) – are mined, especially for their ability to shed light on religious claims. Moreover, chapters covering the formidable debates of our times – especially concerning **fundamentalism** (Gordon), evolution and creationism (de Pomerai and Harris), creation and cosmology (Fergusson and Snow), and the ethical implications of the science-and-religion debate (Kidwell) – appear. Each chapter includes a set of study questions directly related to the text, which could be used (for instance) in a discussion group, or to provide inspiration for student essays or dissertations in the area. Importantly (since this book is intended merely as a starting point for a rich field of further research), each chapter has a short list of suggested reading if you're interested in taking things further, which is divided into introductory and more advanced texts (along with some suggestions for internet resources). The book closes with a glossary of key terms throughout, so that you can't get lost working your way through these issues. The result is a book that we hope offers an enlightening, while also accessible, overview of the Philosophy, Science, and Religion debate.

Mark Harris and Duncan Pritchard
Edinburgh, April 2017

1 How do scientific claims relate to the truth?

S. Orestis Palermos and Duncan Pritchard

Scientific realism

Often we refer to claims as being "scientifically proven." For example, that the earth revolves around the sun, that in the centre of our galaxy there is a black hole, that water is H_2O, and so on. "Scientifically proven" claims are taken to constitute paradigmatic instances of knowledge and they are held to be indubitable or absolute truths. A corollary assumption is that scientific knowledge is a cumulative body of knowledge, which grows simply by adding new theories to the existing body of "scientifically proven" theories. On this view, scientific knowledge steadily progresses towards greater levels of understanding, bringing the human intellect ever closer to the *true* nature of the world.

Within **philosophy of science**, this view is known as **scientific realism**. It holds that well-confirmed scientific theories are approximately true and that the aim of science is to give a literally true account of the world. It is perhaps the most widely held view of the scientific progress, with part of its appeal coming from the fact that, if true, it would elegantly explain the success of the scientific enterprise. Yet the history and philosophy of science demonstrate that arguing in its support may not be as easy as one would have hoped for.

Logical empiricism

The first philosophers of science who attempted to argue that science is a cumulative body of proven knowledge that approximates truth are known as the **logical empiricists**. They were a group of young intellectuals, including Philipp Frank for physics, Hans Hahn for mathematics, Otto Neurath for economics, and the philosophers Moritz Schlick (who joined the group in 1922) and Rudolf Carnap (who joined in 1926). According to their view, scientific knowledge follows the method of **inductivism**: in this view, scientific theories are confirmed by inductive inferences (see **induction**) from an increasing number of positive instances to a universally valid conclusion. For example, Newton's second law seems confirmed by many positive instances from the pendulum to harmonic oscillators and free fall, among others. We can think of scientific theories as sets of laws of nature. Laws of nature are sentences that express true universal generalizations, and they take the form, 'For all objects x, if Fx then Gx' (e.g., Newton's second law would read as follows: if an external force acts on a body of mass m, then the body will accelerate).

The logical empiricists held that true universal generalizations are confirmed when a sufficiently large number of positive instances (and no negative instances) have been found for them. In other words, induction was at the heart of the logical empiricists' criterion of verification (which is why proponents of this view are sometimes known as *verificationists*): a claim or statement is scientific if there is a way of empirically verifying it (i.e., if there is a way of finding positive **empirical** instances confirming that claim or statement).

The inductive methodology, however, is problematic on two grounds. First, it is too liberal as a method for demarcating good science from pseudo-science. Political theories such as Marxism or Freud's psychoanalysis would equally meet the requirements of inductivism. A Freudian psychoanalyst could appeal to plenty of positive instances of people's dreams that can confirm the **validity** of Freud's analysis of the Oedipus complex, for example. But is this sufficient to license the scientific status of Freud's psychoanalysis? Similarly, people that read horoscopes can claim that there are positive instances in their monthly working schedule confirming the horoscope's warning that it is going to be a very demanding working month for Aquarians! Does this mean that horoscopes are scientific?

Second, induction, although it may be a good mechanism for drawing inferences, falls short of supporting the logical empiricists' claim that scientific theories and the claims they support amount to proven knowledge. The problem is that induction cannot be given a non-circular justification. This is known as the **problem of induction**. Induction cannot be justified via **deduction**, since although a large observed sample (e.g., that every swan observed so far is white) might imply that the corresponding universal claim is true (e.g., that every swan is white), it does not deductively entail it (i.e., there might nonetheless be, say, a black swan). But one cannot non-deductively justify induction, either. Induction allows us to form beliefs about unobserved matters of fact on the basis of evidence provided by past and present observations. But in order for such inferences to be rational – such that they can amount to proven knowledge in the way the logical empiricists suggested – we need the further assumption that the future will resemble the past. The problem, however, is that this further assumption is circular, in that it relies for its support on induction itself. It is not a matter of **logic** that the future resembles the past, after all, and our only rational basis for this claim is that the future has previously resembled the past, but of course this basis is itself an inductive reason. Therefore, given that circular reasoning does not justify, there is no way of justifying our use of induction.

Against the backdrop of these doubts against the inductive methodology, logical empiricism appeared to lose the battle of demonstrating how science might amount to a cumulative body of proven knowledge that approximates truth.

Falsificationism

Not all was lost for the idea that scientific knowledge is a cumulative body of knowledge that gets closer to truth, however. Karl Popper – undoubtedly one of the most influential philosophers of science – attempted to demonstrate how the scientific method may still be deductively valid. He argued that, despite the apparent prevalence of induction within science, the validity of scientific theories does not originate from the validity of the inductive method but instead from what he called **falsificationism**.

Contra the logical empiricists, Popper thought that the distinctive method of science does not consist in confirming hypotheses, but in falsifying them, looking for one singular crucial piece of negative evidence that may refute the whole theory. According to Popper, science proceeds by a method of conjectures and refutations: scientists start with bold (theoretically and experimentally unwarranted) conjectures about some phenomena, deduce novel undreamt-of predictions, and then go about finding potential falsifiers for those predictions. Currently accepted scientific theories have passed severe tests and have survived, without being falsified yet. If a theory does not pass severe tests, and/or if there are no sufficient or suitable potential falsifiers for it, the theory cannot be said to be scientific. The history of science is full of theories that enjoyed a relative period of empirical success until they were eventually falsified and rejected: from the caloric theory of Lavoisier (which regarded heat as an imponderable fluid) to Stahl's phlogiston theory in the eighteenth century, and to Newton's ether theory. Science has grown across centuries by dismantling and rejecting previously successful theories – scientific progress is characterized and made possible by falsification.

According to Popper, falsificationism is the distinctive method of science. It is a deductive (instead of inductive) method, whereby scientists start with bold conjectures, and deduce novel predictions, which then they go about testing. If the predictions prove wrong, the conjecture is falsified and replaced with a new one. If the predictions prove correct, the conjecture is corroborated and will continue to be employed to make further predictions and pass more tests, until proven wrong. In this sense, the logical validity of scientific theories does not originate from confirmation they receive from evidence but from surviving the empirical tests that could refute them. So long as a theory survives such tests, scientists may take their theory to be valid. If it fails, they can take it to be conclusively false. According to Popper, then, science does not approximate truth by having its theories confirmed, but by rejecting theories that have been proven wrong. In this sense, science tends to truth by avoiding falsity.

This was an ingenious attempt to save scientific realism. Reality, however, turned out to be much more complex than Popper's simple deductive scheme. In daily laboratory situations, scientists never test a scientific hypothesis or conjecture by itself. Nor can they deduce any empirical consequence out of any bold conjecture either. This problem, known as the **problem of auxiliary hypotheses**, is the topic of the next section.

The problem of auxiliary hypotheses

Before Popper developed falsificationism as the method of science, the French physicist and scientist Pierre Duhem had already realized that no scientific hypothesis can be tested in isolation, but only in conjunction with other main theoretical hypotheses, plus some auxiliary ones. Consider Newton's law of gravity. Scientists never test the hypothesis of gravitation by itself, but always in conjunction with other theoretical hypotheses H1, H2, H3 (e.g., Newton's three laws of motion) plus some auxiliary hypotheses A1, A2, A3 (e.g., A1 says that the mass of the sun is much bigger than the mass of other planets; A2 says that no other force apart from the gravitational one is acting on the planets; A3 reports that planetary attractions are weaker than attractions between the sun and the planets). Now, suppose we deduce from this set of main and auxiliary hypotheses some observable evidence *e* and we proceed to test whether *e* occurs or not in nature:

$$\text{H \& H1 \& H2 \& H3 \& A1 \& A2 \& A3} \rightarrow \text{evidence } e$$

Suppose we find that *e* does not occur (or that the measured value for *e* is not what one would expect from this set of hypotheses). This would only indicate that there must be something wrong with the whole set of hypotheses:

$$\frac{\text{H \& H1 \& H2 \& H3 \& A1 \& A2 \& A3} \rightarrow \text{evidence } e \text{ not } e}{\text{Then not-(H \& H1 \& H2 \& H3 \& A1 \& A2 \& A3)}}$$

But we do not know whether it is H or H1 or H2 or H3 or A1 or A2 or A3, or any combination of any of these main and auxiliary hypotheses, which is refuted by the negative evidence.

Given this holistic picture, the process of refutation of a hypothesis can no longer be regarded as a one-to-one comparison between the hypothesis and a piece of evidence. Instead, it takes place through a variety of direct and indirect links across the entire web of knowledge. Thus, suppose again we get a piece of negative evidence. How can we know which element of the web, which particular belief, this negative piece of evidence is going to refute? If there is leeway in the way evidence relates to any particular belief in the web, how do we know what to change in the web itself?

The problem of auxiliary hypotheses presented a serious concern against Popper's attempt to demonstrate how scientific knowledge may progress in a deductively valid manner. While Popper's falsificationism provided an elegant solution to the problem of induction that was facing logical empiricism, the complexity of scientific theories and their interconnectedness with auxiliary hypotheses as well as other theories makes it impossible to apply the falsificationist method in a clear-cut manner. And even if it were assumed that elaborating further on falsificationism could provide a solution out of this problem, such that scientists could direct counterevidence to isolated hypotheses and selectively refute them, the emerging field of the history of science demonstrated that falsification hardly ever occurs in practice.

The structure of scientific revolutions

Problems such as the above made apparent the limits of experimental evidence and the impossibility of the very idea of a 'crucial experiment', able to establish one way or another the fortunes of any theory. Against this backdrop, in 1962, the US historian and philosopher of science Thomas Kuhn offered a highly influential, radically new conception of how science grows and unfolds, in a seminal book entitled *The Structure of Scientific Revolutions*.

Both the logical empiricists and Popper had thought of scientific knowledge as a largely incremental affair. As scientific inquiry proceeds, and new evidence is found, our scientific knowledge accumulates (by either inductively confirming or deductively falsifying theoretical hypotheses). In this way, we gradually acquire better and better scientific knowledge. Scientific progress would be secured by the right scientific method, which would deliver theories more and more likely to be true.

However, on the basis of his historical analysis, Kuhn argued that neither logical empiricism nor falsificationism work in practice. He noted that every scientific theory is born in an ocean of counterevidence and that it is only through time that novel theories produce corroborating evidence. If Popper's falsificationism were correct, such that theories should be rejected as soon as they are met with counter-evidence, then science as we know wouldn't have existed.

Kuhn began his career in physics and attempted to provide a more realistic picture of the scientific progress that chimed with the historical data. During a postdoctoral position at Harvard, he had the chance to study and teach a course in the history of science dedicated to Aristotelian physics. The difficulty encountered in making sense of outmoded lines of reasoning had a profound influence in the way Kuhn came to rethink scientific inquiry as a non-cumulative process of knowledge acquisition, with no distinctive (inductive or deductive) method. Most importantly, it reshaped radically Kuhn's view of scientific progress by rescinding the link between progress and truth, understood as the ability of a theory to capture things correctly.

Instead, Kuhn suggested that science is characterized by three-stage cycles of normal science, crises, and scientific revolutions. During normal science, a scientific community works on a well-defined scientific paradigm. Although Kuhn never defined exactly the notion of 'scientific paradigm', he thought a scientific paradigm (or what he later called a 'disciplinary matrix') would typically include the dominant scientific theory, the experimental and technological resources, no less than the system of values of the community at a given time (e.g., how the community may value judgements of simplicity, accuracy, plausibility, and so on). In addition, a scientific paradigm includes also what Kuhn called 'exemplars', i.e., concrete solutions to problems that students encounter from the early stages of their scientific education, whether in laboratories, on examinations, or at the ends of chapters in science texts (1962/1996, Postscript, p. 187). Any scientific community in periods of normal science acquires its identity by working on an accepted textbook (be it Ptolemy's *Almagest*, or Newton's *Principia*) and solving well-defined problems or puzzles within a well-defined textbook tradition. No attempt to test, falsify, or refute the accepted paradigm takes place during periods of normal science.

Only when a sufficiently large number of anomalies – which cannot be done away with – accumulate does the accepted paradigm undergo a period of crisis. In periods of crises, a new paradigm may come to the fore, and the crisis resolves into a scientific revolution when the scientific community decides to abandon the old paradigm and shift consensus around the new paradigm. Kuhn stressed how theory choice in these cases is not determined by the alleged superiority of the new paradigm over the old one. The consensus-gathering process is not determined by the new paradigm being more likely to be true or correct than the old one, but by the increase in the puzzle-solving power of the new paradigm. The new paradigm should be able to solve more puzzles than the old one, and thus Kuhn redefined scientific progress in terms of increased puzzle-solving. But this shift of focus from Popper's falsification to Kuhn's puzzle-solving has far-reaching implications for the rationality of theory choice.

Kuhn famously claimed that scientific paradigms (say, Ptolemaic astronomy and Copernican astronomy) are *incommensurable*. **Incommensurability** meant lack of a 'common measure' to evaluate two paradigms – in other words, lack of a common measure for rational choice between paradigms. Different paradigms use different scientific concepts, methodology, resources, and even systems of values. For example, competing paradigms may use the same word to refer to the same aspect of the world but mean entirely different things. 'Mass' in Newtonian physics is conserved, whereas in Einsteinian mechanics 'mass' is convertible with energy. 'Gravity' in Newtonian physics is a force that is innate to the objects, whereas, according to Einstein, 'gravity' is the effect of curvature in space-time. Paradigms also define methods, problem-fields, and standards of solution. As a result, the reception of a new paradigm often necessitates a redefinition of the corresponding science. Old problems may be declared unscientific (e.g., what is the special weight of phlogiston?) while problems that that were previously non-existent or trivial may become the very archetypes of significant scientific achievement (e.g., is gravity just a force that is innate in every object, should we try to explain it in terms of particle exchanges, or is it the curvature of space-time?).

Because of such incommensurable features between paradigms, Kuhn noted that paradigm shifts resemble psychologists' Gestalt switches rather than rational, objective decision-making processes. His radical conclusion was that 'although the world does not change with a change of paradigm, the scientist afterward works in a different world' (1962/1996, p. 121).

Seen from the point of view of scientific realism, the above analysis is highly problematic. First, it has the unwelcome consequence that science, far from being a cumulative body of knowledge that tends to truth, is instead interrupted and revolutionary. Due to the phenomenon of incommensurability, it might be impossible to find connections between the new and the old theory. If scientific revolutions involve radical theoretical change, then the new scientific knowledge that accrues after the scientific revolution is unlikely to incorporate the body of scientific knowledge constituted by the old scientific theory. What was 'known' before is not supplemented with additional scientific knowledge, but rather replaced in its entirety with a completely new body of scientific knowledge. New theories do not grow on top of the old ones but next to them. Second, Kuhn's appeal to the notion of incommensurability does not only render science a non-cumulative body of knowledge. It also presents a deeper, perhaps more worrying concern: if it is impossible to compare the content, methodologies, and standards of evaluation of different scientific theories, then scientists are facing the possibility of **scientific relativism** – the idea that any theory could be valid from within its own point of view, with no way of comparing the relative validity of competing theories.

Scientific relativism

The possibility of scientific relativism was an unwelcome result of Kuhn's view and immediately attracted criticism. To solve this problem, Kuhn suggested that scientists could compare scientific paradigms on the basis of epistemic norms such as simplicity, predictive accuracy and broad scope. It soon transpired, however, that such criteria would not promote rational paradigm choice. The way such epistemic norms may be interpreted and the weight that might be ascribed to them depend, in fact, on the very paradigm that they are called to assess. Simplicity might mean one thing for proponents of quantum mechanics and quite another for proponents of Einsteinian mechanics. And while simplicity might be of paramount importance to proponents of Einsteinian mechanics, proponents of quantum mechanics might first and foremost focus on predictive accuracy.

To save science from the threat of relativism, Imre Lakatos attempted to provide a rational reconstruction of the scientific progress on the basis of a view that he called **sophisticated falsificationism.** Lakatos disagreed that scientific theory choice is irrational, although he agreed with Kuhn that falsificationism "cannot kill" as fast as Popper thought. Once faced with counterevidence, scientists rarely, if ever, abandon their theories. Instead, they attempt to make adjustments to them by adding auxiliary hypotheses. For example, if the trajectory of a planet deviates from what was estimated by Newtonian mechanics, scientists do not thereby abandon the Newtonian paradigm. Instead, they postulate an explanation for the observed deviation by adding an auxiliary hypothesis – for example, that there might be a second, so far unobserved planet that perturbs the trajectory of the first planet. Lakatos' historical data indicated that this is standard practice within science. He also argued that it is a perfectly acceptable practice, so long as the additional auxiliary hypothesis that is invoked to save the initial version of the theory generates new expectations that can themselves be empirically tested. For example, it wouldn't do if scientists postulated that the second planet had some special properties that would prevent any available or future technological equipment from ever detecting it. But it would be perfectly acceptable if scientists used Newtonian mechanics to esti-mate the mass and position of the second planet such that they could devise an experiment to confirm or disconfirm whether a planet with the expected proper-ties exists. Lakatos thought that so long as scientists modify their theories in a way that creates new expectations, their theories will qualify as 'theoretically progressive' such that they may count as scientific. Lakatos, of course, further noted that *good* scientific theories must be both 'theoretically' and 'empirically progressive,' meaning that some of their predictions are corroborated – i.e., turn out to agree with the facts. However, so long as a theory is theoretically progres-sive, it can at least qualify as scientific such that its proponents can keep having faith in it.

There is a potential problem with Lakatos' sophisticated falsificationism, how-ever. The problem stems from the fact that it is always possible for scientists to turn a stagnant scientific theory into an empirically progressive one. Think, for example, of Heliocentricism. Heliocentricism was first proposed by Aristarchus of Samos in the 3rd century BC. As soon as it was put forward it was faced with overwhelming counterevidence, while none of its predictions could become cor-roborated. Nevertheless, in the sixteenth century, Copernicus took up Heliocentri-cism again and, by proposing a predictive mathematical model of the heliocentric system, he generated predictions that were subsequently corroborated. Eventually Heliocentricism became the accepted view within astronomy.

According to Paul Feyerabend – a friend and colleague of Imre Lakatos – this possibility to turn a stagnant theory into an empirically progressive one meant that scientists, from their point of view, could stay with any scientific theory even if it is facing counterevidence or suffers from a lack of corroborating instances. According to Feyerabend, neither lack of empirical content nor conflict with exper-imental results makes it irrational for scientists to retain and elaborate a point of view that pleases them.

Employing such a liberal approach to scientific theory choice may initially seem counterintuitive and counterproductive. Feyerabend, however, noted that it actu-ally has a particularly positive epistemic effect. Following Kuhn, Feyerabend noted that reality is, in Williams James' words, a "blooming buzzing confusion" or, in Benjamin Whorf's words, a "kaleidoscopic flux of impressions." In the absence of any background theories or assumptions, we would be at a loss about how to perceive the world in a meaningful way. Consider, for example, an ultra-sound scan at the early stages of a pregnancy. In the beginning, the parents-to-be look at the doctor's screen, but they have no clue about what they are looking at. On the contrary, the doctor's training and experience allows her to clearly perceive some of the baby's anatomical features and direct the future parents' attention to them. This phenomenon, whereby one's previous training and experience allows one to perceive the world in specific ways is known as the **theory-ladenness of observation**, and it is widely pervasive within science, constantly affecting scien-tists' interpretation of almost every experimental result. But while the theory-laden nature of observations is particularly helpful with respect to making any scientific observations at all, Feyerabend noted that it also has a negative effect. It may make proponents of a given paradigm blind to evidence that could potentially go against their own paradigm.

Feyerabend argued that the only way for scientists to avoid this negative effect of the theory-ladenness of observation, such that they could have access to as much evidence as possible, would be for them to 'think outside the box' with the help of alternative paradigms. Therefore, Feyerabend thought that Lakatos' sophisticated falsificationism, which suggested that scientists could stay with any scientific theory, was a welcome result, because it encouraged the proliferation of scientific point of views that could reveal each other's weaknesses.

On the whole, scientific relativism denies that science is a cumulative body of knowledge or that there exists a rational criterion for telling which scientific theories better approximate truth. At the same time, however, scientific relativism does not present science as an arbitrary practice. So long as a theory is theoretically progressive – meaning that new modifications lead to novel predictions – scientists can rationally stay with the theory even if none of its predicted expectations becomes corroborated (we previously considered the example of Heliocentricism). On the one hand, this may disallow proponents of a given theory to tell whether their theory approximates truth but, on the other hand, it allows science to progress as a whole. The constant proliferation of theories allows scientists to explore all possible scientific hypotheses, while maximizing the evidence they can use in order to test them and subsequently improve them. In this sense, while it is impossible to tell whether scientific theories are true, science as a whole progresses faster as it retains only those theories that can successfully withstand the criticism provided by the maximum amount of rival theories and the evidence they collectively generate.

It should be noted, however, that scientific relativism remains a controversial thesis with only a few philosophers of science siding with it. Amongst the many objections raised against the view, a central worry concerns the notion of incommensurability. As we have seen, the threat of incommensurability lies at the core of the claim that it is impossible to compare the validity of competing paradigms, thereby making it impossible to rationally choose between them. Scientists and philosophers of science, however, argue that incommensurability is an obscure theoretical notion with few practical consequences. While competing paradigms may indeed be incommensurable in some ways, the phenomenon is not as pervasive as Kuhn and other philosophers of science (most notably Feyerabend) have suggested. It is argued that, so far, it has always been possible to compare between competing paradigms, and this raises doubts about the relativist nature of science and its inability to approximate truth.

Chapter summary

- We began with scientific realism, which is the view that well-confirmed scientific theories are approximately true and that the aim of science is to give a literally true account of the world.

- Next we looked at logical empiricism. This attempts to offer an account of scientific knowledge in terms of whether the scientific claim in question can be supported by empirical evidence. In this proposal, the scientific method is essentially inductive.
- This commitment to induction at the heart of the scientific method is problematic, however, for at least two reasons. The first is that it may end up treating lots of theorizing that we would not regard as scientific as genuine scientific theory. The second is that induction is itself problematic, since it seems to lack any justification.
- One response to these problems is to appeal instead to falsifiability as an account of the scientific method, whereby we seek out evidence which decisively falsifies a bold scientific conjecture. Falsificationism has the advantage of making the scientific method deductive rather than inductive.
- Falsificationism is itself problematic, however, in that scientific hypotheses are never tested in isolation, but rather as part of a wider whole which includes other relevant theoretical claims and auxiliary hypotheses. When faced with counterevidence, it is thus not straightforward which scientific claim should be rejected, and so falsification is undermined.
- We then looked at Kuhn's account of scientific progress. Rather than treating such progress as being a gradual expansion of scientific knowledge, he instead argued that such progress in fact occurs when a new scientific paradigm replaces an older paradigm. Crucially, he argued that the new paradigm may well be incommensurable with the old paradigm, such that rather than scientific progress involving the accumulation of scientific knowledge, it instead involves a radical replacement of the old scientific knowledge with the new.
- Finally, we looked at scientific relativism, which is the idea that any scientific theory could be valid from within its own point of view, with no way of comparing the relative validity of competing scientific theories. We noted how some aspects of Kuhn's account of scientific paradigms, particularly the idea that different scientific paradigms could be incommensurable with one another, could provide support for scientific relativism. We also considered some other potential sources of support, such as the theory-ladenness of observation.

Study questions

1. What is scientific realism? Try to express the proposal in your own words.
2. What is the difference between an inductive inference and a deductive inference?
3. What is logical empiricism, and what account of the scientific method does it offer?
4. What is the problem of induction, and how does this create difficulties for logical empiricism?

5. What is falsificationism? Why is this account of the scientific method deductive rather than inductive?
6. What is the problem of auxiliary hypotheses, and why does it pose particular difficulties for falsificationism?
7. What is a scientific paradigm? What does Kuhn mean when he says that different scientific paradigms can be incommensurable with each other?
8. What is scientific relativism, and how might the incommensurability of scientific paradigms lend support to this view?
9. What is the theory-ladenness of observation, and how might it lend support to scientific relativism?

Introductory readings

Achinstein, Peter (2010). 'Scientific Knowledge', *Routledge Companion to Epistemology*, S. Bernecker and D. H. Pritchard (eds.), chapter 32 (London: Routledge). [A fairly comprehensive introductory overview of the main issues regarding scientific knowledge, written by an expert in the field.]

Chalmers, A. F. (1999). *What Is This Thing Called Science?* (3rd Ed.) (Milton Keynes: Open University Press). [One of the most widely used contemporary introductions to philosophy of science, and for good reason, as it is a superb outline of the main issues in this area: accessible, authoritative, and very readable.]

Ladyman, J. (2002). *Understanding Philosophy of Science* (London: Routledge). [One of the best introductory textbooks of the past two decades. Accessible, well-written and informative.]

Advanced readings

Gillies, Donald (1993). *Philosophy of Science in the Twentieth Century* (Oxford: Blackwell). [An excellent, if intellectually demanding, account of contemporary themes in the philosophy of science. See especially the chapter on logical empiricism and Popper.]

Goldacre, Ben (2009). *Bad Science* (London: Harper Collins). [We can't recommend this book highly enough. Although it is not a text on the philosophy of science, reading this book will give you a fantastic introduction to the scientific method and why it is so important.]

Internet resources

Anderson, Hanne and Hepburn, Brian (2015). 'Scientific Method', *Stanford Encyclopedia of Philosophy*, E. Zalta (ed.), https://plato.stanford.edu/entries/scientific-method/. [An excellent overview of the main philosophical issues with regard to scientific methodology.]

Chakravarty, Anjan (2011). 'Scientific Realism', *Stanford Encyclopedia of Philosophy*, E. Zalta (ed.), https://plato.stanford.edu/entries/scientific-realism/. [An insightful survey of philosophical work on scientific realism, written by one of the leading figures in the debate.]

Hansson, Sven Ove (2014). 'Science and Pseudo-Science', *Stanford Encyclopedia of Philosophy*, E. Zalta (ed.), https://plato.stanford.edu/entries/pseudo-science/. [A useful overview of the main issues regarding the philosophical question of how best to demarcate science from pseudo-science.]

Niiniluoto, Ilkka (2015). 'Scientific Progress', *Stanford Encyclopedia of Philosophy*, E. Zalta (ed.), https://plato.stanford.edu/entries/scientific-progress/. [A comprehensive, if rather technical in places, survey of the main philosophical accounts of scientific progress.]

2 Faith and physics
Can they be reconciled?

Mark Harris

Introduction

This chapter takes an unconventional approach in order to cut to the chase. There are plenty of comprehensive presentations of the opportunities and challenges that physics poses for Christian theology. **Cosmology** and quantum physics always feature prominently, but are not themselves crucial for deciding the relationship between physics and religious faith. The Big Bang theory, for instance, is used by both theists and atheists alike as evidence for and against (respectively) belief in a Creator God. And on the other end of the length scale, the indeterminacy of quantum mechanics is invoked by many theologians to support their belief that the universe is open to God's action in the world, while sceptics cite the amazing success of the very same quantum mechanics as proof that there's no need to believe in such a God. But the experiments and theories themselves are silent on such higher-order interpretations. Hence, this chapter will take a quite different angle. The primary factor in assessing the relationship between physics and faith, I'll suggest, is not the physics of the unimaginably big and the unfeasibly small – fascinating and counter-intuitive as it may be – but the elusive concept of **worldview**.

There's a widespread assumption today that science and religion are locked in conflict. While this assumption rings true in specific cases such as the creation-evolution debate, it's far from being universally valid. Take the case of fundamental physics. For sure, many physicists would answer the question in this chapter's title with an emphatic 'no'. But for myself – a physicist-turned-theologian who's had strong religious beliefs for as long as I can remember – my reaction would be an equally-emphatic 'yes'. And I know other physicists who'd say much the same. Clearly, then, the issue isn't as straightforward as a blanket assumption that there must always be conflict between science and religion: the answers given are as much dependent on the individual as on the physics, or, to be precise, as much on the individual's *worldview* as on the interpretation of scientific evidence. For it makes a difference what are our individual predispositions and presuppositions, especially those more intangible beliefs that we often take for granted because they inform our entire view of the world. Some of those beliefs might be religious, but many are not; the point is that few of them are subject to scientific scrutiny in the way that **empirical** evidence and hypotheses are, *although these intangible beliefs inform our view of science nonetheless.*

Surely one of the most umbrella-like of all terms, worldview is as difficult to define as 'faith'. An individual's worldview must include their beliefs as to how physics relates to the other natural sciences and to the reality of the natural world, as well as how the natural world might relate to other potential realities, such as the supernatural. Physics, as an empirical science, cannot by its own means test these beliefs: they are *metaphysical* (literally 'beyond physics'). Some of these metaphysical beliefs are religious in nature and concern the entirely otherworldly, but many are not (e.g. varieties of **realism, determinism** and **reductionism**). The fact that some of these latter beliefs are virtually the consensus in physics doesn't make them any less metaphysical. My point is that, whether we're religious believers, agnostics or atheists, our physics is done within a wider matrix of basic metaphysical beliefs which (because of their worldview character) we often take for granted and can't test empirically (i.e. scientifically), even if we're conscious of them. These beliefs inform the ways that we interpret our science conceptually – sometimes dominating the direction of whole research fields – but we can't work in the opposite direction, using the science to evaluate our metaphysical beliefs in any direct way. We can argue that physics is more consistent with this or that metaphysical position, but we can't test our argument empirically. And if this is true of a widespread metaphysical assumption in physics such as reductionism, it must also be true of those religious (or anti-religious) interpretations of physics that inspire such controversy. Hence, while some, such as myself, will maintain that physics is fully compatible with religious faith, others will insist upon the exact reverse. Who is right? The physics itself is compatible with both approaches.

We can take this further by looking at scientific method in physics.

Metaphysics and method

Physics is widely said to have a unique ability to shine light on physical reality at its most fundamental level. But in order to do so, physicists must make many assumptions. Indeed, the widespread assumption that physics is the most fundamental of the natural sciences, and that all others relate to it, is a consequence of *reductionism*, a metaphysical belief which can't itself be established empirically in any direct way. Moreover, whether theorists or experimentalists, most physicists assume a form of *realism* – in spite of the fact that quantum physics has led to various anti-realist challenges – and a strong belief in the *uniformity of nature*, that physical reality is systematic, regular and patterned everywhere, and that these patterns may be understood rationally (the idea that is often expressed as the 'laws of nature/physics'). This requires reliance on physical *models* to explain or summarise observations. A model is effectively a scientific metaphor, or an analogy, a way of explaining something we don't understand in terms of something we do. A classic example is the billiard ball model of a gas, which assumes that gas molecules in a container bounce around like tiny billiard balls. Whether the gas molecules really are like tiny billiard balls is another question: the point is that the model makes the analogy sufficiently well that we can successfully predict experimental observations on the gas (within limits). The next assumption is that the uniform patterns we think we see in nature, which we try to describe using models, are *universal*. This means that we can eliminate local variables. For instance, in an experiment we discard the vast array of data we observe which are not universally systematic in favour of those (usually much sparser) data that are. Note that this means that we inevitably bring theoretical expectations to the lab: we can't perform an experiment without having a pre-conceived theoretical framework already in place. This is often summarised by the famous phrase of N. R. Hanson that, 'All data are theory-laden'. In other words, our observations come with theoretical baggage which already goes some way towards interpreting them.

By and large, these assumptions seem to hold up when they can be tested. But notice that, in order to test them, we need to assume them. This circularity is an inherent weakness in the empirical method, identified by **David Hume** in his famous *Enquiry Concerning Human Understanding* of 1748. It has a devastating consequence for a natural science like physics, since this circularity means that we can never know for sure that our experiments and theories truly reveal reality as it is in itself. We can perform experiments, and we can construct models and theories to explain them, but we have no way of knowing how good their purchase is on 'reality' except by performing more experiments, constructing more theories and so on. Even when we seem to make advances in our understanding, we can't rest secure that we've achieved the final, most definitive answer. Scientific knowledge is inherently provisional, which is why both religious and anti-religious rhetoric that make metaphysical claims on the basis of science (e.g. about the existence of God) can't be supported directly by the science itself. This also means that reality claims made from science are metaphysical, going beyond what science can demonstrate in and of itself. This may sound incredible (given the predominantly realist assumptions in science), but to say, for instance, that electrons really exist, is to go beyond what physics or chemistry can actually demonstrate of themselves using their own empirical methods (although it's true that the existence of electrons as real entities is consistent with a vast body of science when interpreted using realist **metaphysics**). The point is that an anti-realist belief in the electron – where the electron is a kind of convenient fiction to make the theories work – would satisfy the empirical science just as well.

Physics has varied in its commitment to realist versus anti-realist interpretations of its theories, especially since the advent of quantum mechanics in the early twentieth century. One individual physicist may take a different metaphysical stance from another, often depending on what particular problem in physics they're thinking about. In other words, the metaphysical assumptions that underpin the practice of physics infiltrate every aspect of the science, and they're subtle and complex. It's hardly surprising, then, if the relationship between physics and faith turns out to be equally subtle and complex. To see this more clearly, it's worth looking at the historical dimension.

The historical dimension

In any historical discussion of the science-faith relationship, conflict attracts special interest. In the biological sciences, the religious debates surrounding the reception of **Darwin**'s theory of evolution – still as furious today as at any time in the past – are the most obvious cases in point, while in the physical sciences attention tends to focus on events such as the 1633 trial of Galileo. Here, Galileo was condemned by the Roman Catholic Church for teaching the Copernican cosmology and was required to recant. The popular perception of such stories today is that they demonstrate that science and religion are engaged in a fight to the death over fundamental matters of truth. However, modern historians (e.g. Brooke) studying the Galileo affair argue that this conclusion misunderstands the dispute by attempting to force unsustainable polarities between science and faith into the story. For it seems that many of the most notable early modern scientists working in what we now call physics (including Galileo) were not only religious believers themselves, but were able to integrate their science with the widespread religious beliefs of their time. Indeed, there's a case for saying that, far from being inimical to early modern science, Christianity in fact provided a fertile ground for the intellectual planting and growth of scientific method.

It's certainly true that Galileo made explicit use of theology from time to time to support his science, especially regarding the sensitive question of whether his work went against biblical teaching. A particular bone of contention concerned biblical passages like Joshua 10:13 ('and the sun stood still, and the moon stopped'), which, taken literally, indicated (against Copernicus) that the sun went around the earth. Galileo engaged with this challenge in various ways, but it's especially worth noting his use of the ancient 'two books' metaphor, whereby God's purposes were said to be disclosed both by Scripture (the book of God's words), and by nature (the book of God's works). This meant that biblical interpretation could be understood to complement, not conflict with, natural philosophy (i.e. science). In his *Letter to the Grand Duchess Christina* (1615), Galileo answered his critics by contending that

> to prohibit the whole science [of astronomy, including Copernicus' theory of heliocentricity] would be to censure a hundred passages of holy Scripture which teach us that the glory and greatness of Almighty God are marvellously discerned in all his works and divinely read in the open book of heaven.

Galileo's point was that the relevant biblical passages agree with the science that God's glory is revealed in nature. A prohibition of the new science would therefore be an indirect censure of the Bible itself.

Galileo was certainly not the first to make use of the 'two books' analogy, and neither was he the last, but he did provide an important twist on it which echoed perhaps the most significant conceptual advance in the history of physics, namely the realisation that physical law could be expressed in mathematical terms. In his work, *The Assayer* (1623), Galileo explained that the 'grand book' of the universe was written in the 'language of mathematics', and that we'd wander in a 'dark labyrinth' if we couldn't understand this language. His point was that traditional theological and philosophical reasoning were no longer sufficient for understanding nature: new tools must be brought to bear, especially mathematical tools. Nowadays, mathematics is so basic to the physical sciences that it's easy to miss the novelty of this point, but the development of physics as an 'exact' science would have been impossible without such a move by Galileo (and others, such as Kepler, Descartes and Newton) to connect physical reality directly to mathematics. It hardly needs saying that it's a metaphysical move; significantly, it was legitimated by the essentially religious conviction that nature was governed by mathematical laws of nature given by God, the divine Lawgiver who was a mathematician at heart. The religious context of the time was a help, not a hindrance, here, since it provided the metaphysical justification for this key advance in scientific method.

Many other scientists of the period saw their science in religious terms. Newton is notable, not least for the theological background to his view that space and time form a fixed and absolute frame of reference for all entities and events. The significance of this view can hardly be understated, since it forms the backbone of the Newtonian deterministic universe which held sway until Einstein's discovery of relativity in the twentieth century, and it still informs a great deal of (non-relativistic) physics. Newton's critics complained that his conception of space as unchangeable, infinite and eternal was practically divine: was Newton exalting space to become God, or was Newton reducing God to space? Newton was in fact doing neither, since he didn't see space as a thing which existed in its own right. Instead, Newton believed that space arises where any being exists, even an insubstantial being like God. Space is infinite, eternal and absolute precisely because God is everlasting and omnipresent: space is an 'emanative effect of God', as Newton explained in his *De Gravitatione*. Time, likewise, is absolute and infinite in extent, arising from the eternal existence of God: 'he [God] constitutes Duration and Space' (General Scholium to the *Principia*). Famously, Newton also described space as the 'sensorium' of God: the realm of God's activity, where the divine will is played out. This provided Newton with a theological justification for his radical claim that the laws of motion and gravitation were universal: since space was the sensorium of God, and since the laws of nature were the outworkings of God's will in space, then the laws must be universal in extent and influence.

Nowadays, we take Newton's achievements in physics so much for granted that they are virtually physics 'common sense'. So it's worth remembering that, not only were these achievements not common sense at the time, but they were accompanied by theological and metaphysical reasoning which supported and interpreted the scientific work. Newton didn't see the clear blue water that we do between science and religion, and neither, it appears, did he see conflict between them as inevitable. Instead, Newton made explicitly *religious* arguments in order to justify his ground breaking views of space, time and the laws of nature. These views are now foundational in modern physics, even if we've forgotten Newton's religious arguments. Whatever we might think *now* of the rightness or wrongness of religious arguments like those of Newton and Galileo, it's impossible to deny that those arguments made an important positive contribution to the shape of physics as we know it.

Hence, it's not difficult to demonstrate a degree of mutual support between the science of the early modern period and the religious faith of its scientific practitioners. It becomes rather harder to demonstrate this for more recent physicists, especially those working since roughly the mid nineteenth-century, when science became 'professionalised' as an expertise in its own right. Nevertheless, several figures stand out, such as Arthur Eddington, Albert Einstein and John Polkinghorne: physicists who were convinced of the compatibility of their science with their religious faith, and who have taken the conversation between the two into new constructive areas. Eddington's work in the early years of quantum theory, examining its potential impact on human consciousness and spirituality, is notable in presaging some of the important currents of discussion today, while Polkinghorne's much more recent proposal that God's action in the world may be compared with (or made possible through) the physics of chaos theory stands as one of the prime examples of modern attempts to integrate common concerns in physics and theology.

Einstein's is probably the most oft-quoted voice in the whole modern science-and-religion dialogue, especially in his famous aphorism, 'Science without religion is lame, religion without science is blind'. Clearly, Einstein rejected the idea that science and religion could only exist in conflict, but his religious views are notoriously difficult to pigeonhole into any conventional religious orthodoxy: while he didn't espouse the personal God of **monotheism**, neither did he embrace **atheism**. In fact, his many recorded invocations of God seemed to function largely as a means for Einstein to voice his metaphysical instincts about nature. For instance, when asked how he'd feel if his theory of **general relativity** had failed experimental verification, Einstein is reported to have responded, 'Then I would feel sorry for the good Lord. The theory is correct'. Here, Einstein's confidence appears to have stemmed from what can only be a gut instinct, an *aesthetic* intuition that the rightness of his work extended beyond the empirical. Einstein is by no means alone here: many physicists speak of their experiences of awe at uncovering new insights into the secrets of nature, and they often do so in language that's more at home in religious and artistic circles. It can be difficult to separate talk of standing on holy ground from talk of the supremely beautiful in this context, and such experiences point to a widely felt hunch that physics points towards deeper levels of reality than the strictly scientific. I hardly need say that this hunch is shared by those in the creative arts, too, and also, significantly, by religious believers. For that reason, I turn now to consider the aesthetic dimensions of physics.

Beauty, wonder and design

Religious believers have often called upon the beauty of nature as evidence for the existence of God. In this, they've made similar claims to the venerable 'argument from design', which for centuries provided a close link between theology and the developing natural sciences in suggesting that examples of 'design' in nature point to the work of a supremely intelligent Creator. But the case for design suffered such a severe blow from Darwin's theory of evolution (see Chapter 4) that it fell out of favour in the mainstream sciences from the mid-nineteenth century onwards. The Intelligent Design (ID) movement in conservative Christianity has in recent decades attempted to revive the argument from design as a bona fide scientific principle, but this has been met with widespread opposition by the mainstream natural sciences. Nevertheless, the wider issues surrounding 'design' have resurfaced in the intriguing debate surrounding 'fine tuning', the realisation that many details of our universe, especially fundamental physical constants like the speed of light and the charge of the electron, are balanced so precisely that if they had been even minutely different, then stars and planets could never have appeared, still less life on earth. For many theists (including ID advocates), fine tuning is direct evidence that there must be a Fine Tuner (i.e. a Creator) who carefully balanced the physical laws and constants at the creation of the universe so that intelligent life would one day evolve. But many others (including some theists such as myself) are unconvinced by this line of reasoning, on the grounds that there exist alternative naturalistic explanations for fine tuning. The primary such explanation is that our universe is one of many universes, and ours is simply the one where the conditions have fallen out to be just right for life. And although this '**multiverse hypothesis**' is widely held in modern cosmology, it's impossible to test it empirically (at least at present), so we find that two divergent metaphysical explanations of the same empirical 'fine tuning' science emerge, one which argues from the science straight to God (i.e. where God is the explanatory Fine Tuner), and the other which goes from the science to a naturalistic but untestable explanation (i.e. the multiverse). Choosing between them largely comes down to worldview again, and since it's possible to find religious believers on both sides of this divide, we can't even conclude that a person's attitude towards fine tuning is simply a matter of whether or not they already believe in God. There's more at play here, and we can see this in the way that physicists respond subjectively to the aesthetic dimensions of their work, where the argument from design re-appears subtly.

The argument from design never disappeared from modern physics, but went underground, surfacing incognito at those points when scientists wax lyrically about the wonders of their discoveries. For, despite the fact that there's no obvious empirical content to such talk, physicists are often tempted to see their work in grand metaphysical or even theological terms. Stephen Hawking's final words in *A Brief History of Time* are a well-known example, where he speculates that discovery of a final theory of everything will allow us to 'know the mind of God'.

In light of Hawking's well-known atheism, this line is presumably a rhetorical flourish, but for many religiously minded physicists the fundamental rationality of nature inspires an aesthetic and religious sense of wonder at the awesome divine 'mind' behind it. A theological move related to the argument from design is possible here: the fact that we humans have been gifted with minds that are able to discern the rationality implanted into nature confirms that we are made in God's image, or, in other words, that God is a personal and rational being not unlike us. Of course, there are many other physicists who are unimpressed with this line of reasoning, but who are nevertheless convinced that deep and fundamental rationality underpins the universe, even if we can't say where this rationality comes from. It might be more accurate to identify this belief in deep rationality with that of Platonism (and especially with its conviction that there exist eternal transcendent 'forms' which provide the patterns for everything in the material universe), rather than with the argument for design itself. But the point is that both positions (Platonism and the argument from design) are closely related to each other in sourcing the order of nature beyond empirical research, in the realms of the metaphysical or even supernatural. It's inevitable, then, that the search for the secret of physics' success takes us to reality at its deepest and most ultimate level.

Physics, mathematics and reality

Physics can't reveal directly the ultimate source of its explanatory power, although its heavy reliance on mathematics as a tool to represent reality (and to manipulate it theoretically) suggests that the answer lies somewhere in the metaphysics of mathematics. We have no idea why mathematics should be such a powerful tool in physics, unless the deep reality we seek is fundamentally mathematical (i.e. a Platonist solution). The great theoretical physicist, Eugene Wigner, commenting in 1960 on the strange ability of mathematical physics to capture deep physical truths, said it all with the title of his famous paper, 'The Unreasonable Effectiveness of Mathematics in the Physical Sciences'. As an example, Wigner pointed to the strange fact that complex numbers (numbers based on the idea that -1 might have a square root) appear to be fundamental to nature:

> It is difficult to avoid the impression that a miracle confronts us here . . . The observation which comes closest to an explanation . . . is Einstein's statement that the only physical theories which we are willing to accept are the beautiful ones.

Two things are worth highlighting. First, that Wigner here, and repeatedly in this paper, calls upon the miraculous – a religious concept – in order to capture the mystery of why mathematics and physics work; there's no law of nature or logic telling us why they should work – it's literally a miracle, transcending nature. We should continually be delighted by it; it's a gift, he tells us at the end of the paper. Wigner might speak of miracle, but he says nothing about faith or a deity. However, a Christian such as myself easily makes the leap from Wigner's 'miracle' to the divine rationality that underpins the cosmos: Christ the divine Logos by whom and in whom all was made (John 1:3; Colossians 1:16), laws of nature and mathematics included, which are the rational and creative outworkings of Christ's divine nature. We poor humans can glimpse them because we – equally miraculously – tap into the divine rationality. Science may not have an explanation for its unreasonable effectiveness, but faith does, and a perfectly rational explanation at that, based on coherent and systematic reflection within the Christian worldview.

The second point I want to draw from Wigner is his conviction that our physical theories touch upon a deeper truth than simple rightness. Another theorist, Paul

Dirac, famously took this fascination with elegance to extremes, saying, 'It is more important to have beauty in one's equations than to have them fit experiment'. This claim has been the source of much debate in physics, but Dirac's basic point that scientific discoveries are evaluated on grounds that are aesthetic as well as explanatory is inescapable. In addition to the simple wonderment that physicists often express at the mysteries of nature – a wonderment that bears similarities with the argument from design – physicists also use their aesthetic sensibilities in evaluating theories and models, their deeply held convictions that new discoveries about nature will be beautiful as well as intelligible. The chemist-philosopher Michael Polanyi points out that the successful scientist is driven by a kind of 'scientific passion', even though this passion is supremely un-empirical itself. There's a vast number of potential facts and features of the natural world that crowd in on any scientific study, and unless the scientist is guided by her own subjective and intangible interests and passions, then she'll be lost in a morass of impossibilities, unable to see the wood for the trees. Likewise, Polanyi advocates creativity – not unlike the creativity of the artist – as an essential skill for a scientist to acquire, because (especially in the case of a major discovery) it enables the scientist to fashion a new vision of the world, a vision which, once it has been apprehended by her colleagues, changes the scientific framework (i.e. intellectual 'worldview') irreversibly. But it's impossible to construct this new framework logically from the perspective of the old: the world must be seen entirely differently, re-created.

Scientific progress is as haphazard, creative and intuitive as it is logical and systematic. A caveat is in order, though: it's possible to go too far with this way of thinking, and to conclude incorrectly that science is relative and subjective. That would be entirely wrong, but it needs to be emphasised that, in their search for the secrets of nature, physicists find that imagination, painstakingly learned skills, creativity and intuition are invaluable. In other words, if we're to make a truly critical comparison between physics and faith, we need to look at the human dimensions of both. When we do so, we find a number of stunning points of contact in the metaphysical assumptions that underpin physics, and the ways in which believers come to faith, similarities which go beyond what is empirically testable into the domain of worldview. I therefore conclude that, in this way, faith and physics are reconcilable, while being entirely distinguishable from each other.

Chapter summary

- The popular conception that physics and religious faith cannot be reconciled, like the more general assumption that science and religion inevitably conflict with each other, is a massive over-simplification of a highly complex issue.
- A common strategy for exploring the relationship between physics and religion is to focus on areas of physics that challenge our views of reality. Notwithstanding these challenges, I've suggested that we can get more directly at the relationship by examining worldview.

- Because it captures many of our untestable assumptions, worldview includes our personal attitude to faith claims, as well as our understanding of the relationship between humans and the natural world. Scientific methodology has an important bearing here, and physics makes a number of metaphysical assumptions which must also be incorporated into worldview, including the uniformity of nature and the relationship between scientific models and reality.

- The history of physics indicates that many of its early practitioners were committed religious believers who saw no essential conflict between their science and their faith, and who were often ready to justify their science with theological arguments. Ironically, since modern physics profits from these advances it effectively accepts these theological arguments tacitly.

- The argument from design has been an important feature of **natural theology** for millennia and was often invoked by scientists up until around the mid-nineteenth century. The ways that physicists today call upon beauty and elegance in nature bear similarities with the argument from design, insofar as deep-level subjective insights are being made that are not empirically testable: the science is leading the scientists beyond the science, as it were.

- In fact, such deep-level analyses are essential to the doing of science: to be effective in scientific work, a scientist needs to develop skills such as intuition, creativity and an eye for the aesthetic.

- All of the above demonstrates that, although physics is popularly perceived as being systematic and relentlessly rigorous, in practice it also uses untestable assumptions and intuitions which are not unlike the worldview hunches that inform the faith of religious believers. I therefore conclude that physics is no more irreconcilable with religious faith than is any other branch of considered human thought.

Study questions

1. Which areas of physics present the sharpest challenges to religious faith? Which present the biggest opportunities?
2. Are there areas of faith that should be rejected or revised on the grounds of physics? And are there areas of physics that can't be accepted by faith?
3. Is faith helpful in interpreting counter-intuitive areas of physics?
4. What is the relationship between physics and other natural sciences? How might we go about demonstrating or testing it?
5. Does physics teach us anything about the nature of God?
6. How would you relate mathematics to reality?
7. Does physics unveil beauty written in the fabric of nature, or does the beauty reside in our perception?

Introductory readings

Barr, Stephen M. (2003) *Modern Physics and Ancient Faith* (Notre Dame: University of Notre Dame Press). [A comprehensive account of how religious faith may come to terms with key areas of modern physics.]

Brooke, John Hedley (1991) *Science and Religion: Some Historical Perspectives* (Cambridge: Cambridge University Press). [An influential account of the history of the science-and-religion debate, arguing for complexity over conflict.]

Bussey, Peter (2016) *Signposts to God: How Modern Physics & Astronomy Point the Way to Belief* (Downers Grove: IVP Academic). [An accessible treatment of the interaction between physics and Christianity, arguing for compatibility.]

Advanced readings

Koperski, Jeffrey (2015) *The Physics of Theism: God, Physics, and the Philosophy of Science* (Chichester: Wiley Blackwell). [A sophisticated exploration of the big philosophical and theological questions raised by modern physics.]

Polanyi, Michael (1958, 1962) *Personal Knowledge: Towards a Post-Critical Philosophy* (London, New York: Routledge). [A classic in the philosophy of science, exposing the many human dimensions of the ways in which science is done and understood.]

Wigner, Eugene (1960) 'The Unreasonable Effectiveness of Mathematics in the Natural Sciences' *Communications in Pure and Applied Mathematics* 13: 1–14. [The title says it all.]

Internet resources

De Cruz, Helen (2017) 'Religion and Science', *The Stanford Encyclopedia of Philosophy*, E. Zalta (ed.), https://plato.stanford.edu/archives/spr2017/entries/religion-science. [A wide-ranging introduction to the subtleties of the relationship between science and religion.]

The Institute of Physics online resources, www.iop.org/resources/index.html. [A useful repository of up-to-date news and educational resources on the world of physics.]

3   Creationism and evolutionary biology – science or pseudo-science?

David de Pomerai and Mark Harris

Introduction

When speaking of creationism, it's important not to be too sweeping. There's a wide variety of creationist beliefs, and it might be more accurate to speak of creationism*s*, as Ronald Numbers demonstrates in his magisterial *The Creationists*. One thing can be said for certain: creationism is a *religious* position, held by many Christians and Muslims worldwide. This chapter focuses especially on the most distinctive kind of creationism, Christian young-earth creationism (YEC), which tends to reject biological evolution wholesale, and to maintain that the earth is only a matter of several thousands of years old, perhaps 6,000. Notable organisations which promote this kind of YEC maintain a high public profile – Answers in Genesis, the Institute for Creation Research, and the Creation Research Society – catering for many millions of adherents in the USA and worldwide.

At first sight, the debate between YEC and evolutionary biology tugs at the heart of what it means to 'do science'. Both sides claim to be 'scientific' – with 'creation science', 'scientific creationism', and 'flood geology' being prominent examples on the creationist side – and both sides accuse the other of being 'un-scientific' or, in other words, of being a 'pseudo-science' at best. There's a strong argument, however, for saying that this isn't principally a debate about how science should be done, but about from where we derive our philosophical and theological authority to make claims about the world. This is exactly the stance that we shall adopt in this chapter.

While mainstream evolutionary biologists are committed to a process of observation, hypothesising, and testing strictly within the confines of the natural world, YEC introduces a transcendent source of truth (the Bible) which trumps all others. The former group, like all natural scientists, derive their authority from the epistemological assumption known as **methodological naturalism**, but YEC further insists upon two supernaturally caused events – creation and flood – that change the whole picture. The upshot for YEC is that the *revelation* of Christian Scripture takes precedence over all *empirical* research on the origin and development of life, along with the age of the earth. If that research isn't consistent with a literalistic reading of Scripture, then the research is either modified until it is, or rejected outright. There's a sense, then, that the endless controversies between creation and evolution over the interpretation of empirical evidence completely miss the point, because the issues at stake are actually **metaphysical**.

This chapter will attempt to explain the state of play here by charting the historical evolution of YEC and its strategies, before presenting an overview of evolutionary science for comparison.

The creation of creationism

Seventeenth-century science into twentieth-century literalism

One of the supreme ironies of the creation-evolution debate is that YEC is a relatively recent phenomenon, only gaining widespread momentum in the twentieth century. YEC draws inspiration for its biblical **literalism** not from long-standing Christian tradition, but from a key phase in the history of science. Two linked developments in the seventeenth century are important here. First, by combining the Protestant Reformation's insistence upon the comprehensive perspicacity of the Bible with the newly emerging empiricism of the natural sciences, a number of thinkers began to treat biblical texts at face value as a source of data about the natural world, much like data from other, non-scriptural, sources. Second, the age of the earth, and an account of its physical history, became of special interest. The most celebrated attempt to date the earth was that of Archbishop James Ussher, who in 1648 made use of biblical genealogies (e.g. Gen.5), ancient near eastern texts, and astronomical results to calculate that creation had occurred on Sunday evening, 23 October 4004 BCE, and the flood on Sunday, 7 December 2349 BCE. In the same way, early accounts of the physical history of the earth took the biblical stories of creation and flood as providing reliable descriptions of what must have happened. Thomas Burnet's *Sacred Theory of the Earth* (1684, 1690) is notable for treating the biblical flood story (Gen.6–9), not in terms of divine action, but in naturalistic terms. In this way, Burnet explained the form which the earth has today, including the shape of its continents. Not only did Burnet set a trend in geological thinking for the next century and a half (which saw the biblical flood as decisive in shaping the earth we see now), his model is essentially identical to that of contemporary YEC, as put forward in the seminal YEC text, *The Genesis Flood* (authored by John Whitcomb and Henry Morris, and published in 1961). In Burnet's model, the pre-flood earth was totally smooth, but contained great underground cavities of water ('the fountains of the great deep'; Gen.7:11). The flood was caused by these cavities being broken up, and when the waters had subsided afterwards, the present shape of the seas and continents was left. While this model flies completely in the face of mainstream geology today, thanks to Whitcomb and Morris it's adhered to by millions of creationists worldwide.

In between the seventeenth and twentieth centuries, the scientific understanding of the earth and its lifeforms advanced at a whirlwind pace. By the mid-nineteenth century, developments in geology, palaeontology, and biology were indicating that the earth was very old indeed, and that life had evolved over millions of years.

These developments were not especially troubling, however, for many conservative Christians, who had found ways of harmonising the new science with the Bible. When faced with a biblical text (Gen.1) which appears to insist that the physical universe was created in six days, many nineteenth-century Christians took refuge in the day-age theory (where each Genesis 'day' was read as figurative of a much longer scientific period of perhaps millions of years) or the gap theory (where an immense time gap was understood to have occurred between God's creation of the universe in Gen.1:1 and the six days described from v.3 onwards). These 'old-earth creationist' strategies, however, fell out of favour with many twentieth century Americans who, faced with new social pressures around what should be taught in high schools, preferred to adopt the most radical alternative to the mainstream scientific picture, that of YEC.

The infamous 'Scopes trial' of 1925 was a watershed. Here, the school teacher, John Scopes, was prosecuted by the state of Tennessee for teaching evolution in defiance of a state law prohibiting it. The trial became a showcase for the creation-evolution debate, with the culpability of Scopes himself of less importance than the question of whether the Bible or modern science should take precedence in teaching about origins. The court proceedings were wide-ranging, concerning not so much the interpretation of the science, but the authority and interpretation of Scripture, and the wider impact upon ethical and political questions. In the event, the court found Scopes guilty, which had the effect of legitimating anti-evolutionary teaching for some time. This was by no means the end of the matter though, and the debate started so publicly by the Scopes trial has ever since pitched two opposing worldviews against each other, with fundamentalist Christianity on the one side and modernity (as represented by evolutionary science) on the other.

'True science'?

As Edward Davis's article, 'Science Falsely So Called', suggests, the context of the Scopes trial was the growth of fundamentalist Christianity in American society, led by figures such as William Jennings Bryan, one of the main players in the trial. This movement was attempting to establish its conservative brand of Christianity as an intellectual position in its own right against what were seen to be liberalising tendencies based on scientific **naturalism**, especially German biblical criticism and Darwinism. The fundamentalist argument was that these tendencies were examples of a false science, which steadfastly refused to countenance miracles and supernaturalism. True science, on the other hand, would be open-minded about such things, and crucially would support a literal interpretation of the Genesis creation stories.

But this 'true science' did not reach its definitive formulation until 1961, when Whitcomb and Morris published their *The Genesis Flood*, ensuring that YEC would thereafter be a statement about the significance of Noah's flood as much as a statement about the age of the earth and the failings of evolutionary science. It's no exaggeration to say that this single book has done more to influence the shape of YEC as we know it now than any other. Effectively re-packaging the earlier ideas of Seventh-day Adventist George McReady Price (1870–1963) along with the far earlier ideas of Ussher and Burnet (but with barely a nod to any of them), this book made the case that the biblical flood provided a catastrophic and divinely caused alternative to the naturalistic para-digms provided by mainstream geology and palaeontology. As with the earlier fundamentalists, Whitcomb and Morris see this as a matter of true science (their own) against false science (i.e. the mainstream, especially evolution), and for similar reasons. The Bible must be held as completely trustworthy in describing the two divinely caused events of creation and flood – the biblical flood is a witness and a warning, they believe, and to doubt this is to doubt God's power to save human souls – which means that true science must begin with the revela-tion of Scripture and must not moderate it through human philosophies such as evolution. Therefore, human beings, like all other life, were created by God in the (literal) six days of the initial creation, before the flood swept them away (except for what was preserved on the Ark). This much was a literal re-assertion of the biblical text, like the earlier fundamentalists. But unlike the earlier fun-damentalists, Whitcomb and Morris engage extensively with geology and pal-aeontology, and much of *The Genesis Flood* gives a re-interpretation of geological evidence in order to support their view that the flood was a universal cataclysm, and the earth is very young.

It's not our purpose to assess Whitcomb and Morris's arguments in detail here: many others, such as Montgomery, have done this to great effect, illustrating that Whitcomb and Morris treat the relevant science in a highly selective way, the better for them to twist it into their version of Burnet's seventeenth-century model of the earth (and such is the force of their rhetoric that it comes over as highly plausible to those Christians who have little knowledge of mainstream geology and evolu-tionary biology). What we do want to highlight, however, is the calls which cre-ationists such as Whitcomb and Morris make on the philosophy of science. Invoking Francis Bacon's (1561–1626) idea that science is principally inductive – making generalised inferences from many direct observations – creationists fre-quently claim that historical sciences such as palaeontology and evolutionary biology can't be scientific because they can't make direct observations of what actually happened in the past. Instead, the best that such subjects can do is to make untestable and hypothetical speculations, goes the argument. It's interesting to note that Darwin himself faced this accusation over *Origin of Species*. The fact that Darwin and his successors were not deterred, however, but slowly built up the enormous edifice of evolutionary science we know today, indicates two things: first, that empirical science is more sophisticated than Baconian **induction** might suggest, and second, that if the creationists' 'true science' is strictly Baconian, then it can bear only a passing resemblance to the natural sciences of today. In short, there are good reasons for judging YEC to be stuck in a pre-nineteenth century view of science, both in method and content.

In order to take this point further, we now present a brief overview of evolutionary biology as it currently stands.

Evolutionary science

The concept of evolution

Dobzhansky famously wrote that 'nothing in biology makes sense except in the light of evolution'. Evolution is the underlying process that gave rise to the prodigious variety of living organisms on earth (biodiversity), including ourselves. It has generated countless new species during the history of life, of which more than 99% are now extinct. Each species is adapted to its local environment (ecological niche), but changes in climate, geography, or biotic factors (other organisms) alter that environment over varying time-scales, causing extinction or providing opportunities to diversify into new, better adapted species (speciation). Five mass extinction events have punctuated earth's history – the most recent wiping out dinosaurs ca.66 million years ago (Ma); there's little doubt that a sixth has been set in motion by human-induced climate change.

Current evolutionary ideas stem principally from Darwin, notably his *Origin of Species*. Evolution can be summarised as 'descent with modification', but this phrase requires unpacking. Animals or plants normally give rise to similar offspring, despite minor variations. The so-called neo-Darwinian synthesis combines Darwin's insights with those of genetics stemming from Mendel's contemporaneous work on the inheritance of traits. 'Descent' in multicellular organisms usually involves two sets of genetic information (DNA), derived respectively from the father and mother. This diploid genome comprises long sequences of DNA (chromosomes) which include the genes – each specifying one or more proteins that contribute to characteristics of the offspring. Variant versions of the same gene (alleles) often differ in function to a greater or lesser extent. However, protein-coding genes comprise only a small fraction of the total DNA genome; much of the rest has regulatory functions that aren't yet fully understood. Some genes are duplicated, and extra copies may become redundant (pseudogenes) or specialised for new functions. Darwin envisaged a 'tree of life' whose branches diverge into new species 'twigs': the fact that all living things use DNA as their genetic material, with similar mechanisms for translating that information via RNA into proteins, implies that they have diversified from a common ancestor.

Genetic variation

Importantly, however, the genes transmitted to offspring aren't invariant. Beyond the mixing of parental genes that occurs during gamete development (animal sperm or eggs; plant pollen or ova), there are also random changes in the DNA sequence resulting from genetic mutation, caused by radiation or chemical damage. Usually such damage is accurately restored by DNA repair to the original sequence, but sometimes this fails, resulting in a point mutation. Such changes can occur within a gene or in its neighbouring regulatory regions, though sometimes larger genetic changes arise. DNA sequence changes within a protein-coding gene commonly alter the encoded protein. Again, the outcomes vary considerably, ranging from deleterious effects on function (human genetic diseases such as sickle-cell anaemia), through marginal or zero ('neutral') effects, to functional improvements – enabling that individual to reproduce more successfully in a changing environment or different ecological niche. Such beneficial mutations are admittedly rare, but can spread rapidly within a population provided there is sufficient selection pressure.

Selection

If space and food are abundant, populations of organisms will expand geometrically, as first noted by Malthus. When resources become limiting, this is no longer possible. Darwin's key driver for evolution is **natural selection**; essentially, a given set of environmental conditions (mainly biotic factors such as food supply, predation, or disease) promotes the reproductive success of individuals carrying certain favourable mutations, but also selects against other (less favourable) mutations. Selection can be applied artificially by humans, as in selective breeding of crop plants, livestock animals, or pets, generating the huge variety of modern breeds within the short time-scale of human history. Inadvertent artificial selection is also well documented, notably the ability of pests to evolve pesticide resistance. The distinction between favourable and unfavourable mutations is context-dependent rather than absolute. The sickle-cell mutation is common in West African populations, even though full-blown sickle-cell disease (individuals with two mutated genes) is usually fatal. However, carriers of the sickle-cell trait (one normal and one mutated gene) aren't only healthy but have increased resistance to malaria. The combined effect of all genes on an individual's reproductive success (reflected in progeny numbers) is described by the aggregate term *fitness*; this is what is implied by 'survival of the fittest'.

Artificial selection has produced significant changes within very short time-scales compared to the age of the earth (4.5 billion years) and of life on its surface (3.7 billion years). These timings are in turn based on the geological record, using best estimates for the ages of different rock strata derived from invariant rates of isotope decay. It's therefore plausible that geological time-spans are sufficient to allow the diversification of life on earth through evolution by natural selection.

Species

The taxonomic system used today originated with the Swedish naturalist Linnaeus, who employed morphological criteria to classify animals and plants. Each distinct type of organism has a Latin binomial classification – the first name denoting the genus or group and the second the species. Thus the genus *Homo* includes the only extant member, *Homo sapiens*, plus extinct species such as *H. erectus*, *H. neanderthalensis* and *H. floresiensis*. Genera are grouped into families (e.g. orchids – Orchidaceae; grasses – Poaceae), and families into orders (beetles – Coleoptera; bees, etc. – Hymenoptera). Orders are further grouped together into classes (Hexapoda in this case), and these in turn into phyla sharing a common body-plan.

The phylum Arthropoda includes insects, arachnids (spiders, etc.), crustaceans, and myriapods. DNA sequencing provides independent insights into the underlying genetic relationships between organisms, largely confirming an evolutionary basis for Linnaean classification, but also providing examples of deep genetic differences between superficially similar organisms and unexpectedly close links between dissimilar-looking species. Since DNA mutation occurs at a relatively constant rate, one can infer the timing of branchpoints when species diverged by constructing phylogenetic trees based on DNA sequence data.

New species often arise through reproductive isolation, e.g. when organisms colonise an island. In the Canary Isles, for instance, certain plant genera contain numerous species that are far more diverse than their continental relatives; examples include buglosses (*Echium*) and spurges (*Euphorbia*). This results from adaptive radiation, whereby the progeny of founder individuals adapt to a variety of available ecological niches. Several Canarian *Euphorbia* species have evolved cactus-like forms adapted to drought, even though true cacti belong to an unrelated family. Both arose by convergent evolution, whereby similar adaptations (affording an optimal design solution) have arisen independently in different groups that don't share a common ancestor with the same trait. Box-camera eyes in vertebrates and cephalopods provide another classic example of convergence. Related species are usually unable to interbreed, though in some families (e.g. orchids) hybridisation is common, suggesting that reproductive barriers aren't always erected during speciation.

Gradualism versus punctuated equilibrium

There's a long-standing debate over the rate of evolutionary change. One of the main difficulties in discerning this regards the incompleteness of the fossil record, with soft-bodied organisms especially poorly represented. Even for species whose hard parts are readily preserved (molluscan shells, vertebrate bones), there are gaps and anomalies in the fossil sequence, though occasionally a near-complete series of intermediates links early with modern forms (e.g. elephants). These exemplify 'gradualism', denoting slow progressive evolution over time.

In apparent contrast to gradualism stands the theory of punctuated equilibria, which postulates long periods of stasis punctuated by periods of very rapid evolutionary change. This may be something of an optical illusion: beyond the acknowledged incompleteness of the fossil record, periods of rapid evolution often follow mass extinction events, when surviving species diversify to fill environmental niches occupied previously by now-extinct organisms. Long periods of gradual evolutionary change are thus punctuated by bursts of rapid adaptive radiation that are brief in geological terms, but still span millions of years.

Moreover, many genes operate in tightly controlled networks, such that mutations in a regulatory 'upstream' gene can have multiple pleiotropic effects on the 'downstream' genes whose expression it controls. This is particularly true of the so-called master genes that direct animal and plant development – such as the homeotic *Hox* genes governing regional identity in many animals, or heterochronic genes specifying developmental timing. Mutations in these genes could lead to radical changes in body plan or life history, potentially contributing to rapid evolutionary change.

The origin of life

Descent by modification implies a common ancestor, an organism that must have emerged during the first billion years of earth's existence. Presumably this organism already used DNA as its genetic material, and probably resembled the *Archaebacteria* that survive today in extreme environments such as hydrothermal vents and hotsprings. Inferred conditions on the young earth's surface were probably conducive to spontaneous formation of organic molecules providing vital building blocks for life. However, it's a huge leap from puddles of primeval soup containing the requisite ingredients to a living cell capable of reproducing itself and passing on its DNA. Possibly the earliest life-forms were based on RNA, which can act both as genetic material (RNA genome in retroviruses) and also carry out many protein-like catalytic functions (ribozymes). But RNA-based life forms have left no descendants today, and other possibilities remain open. Recent discoveries of planets orbiting other stars raise the possibility of life evolving elsewhere in the universe. But maybe ours is a rare type of planet, unusually favourable for the evolution of life based on the unique chemical properties of carbon in a watery environment.

For much of earth's history, life was microbial, leaving fossilised mats and three-dimensional stromatolites generated by unicellular bacteria (prokaryotes). Higher organisms – fungi, plants, or animals – are mostly multicellular, allowing different cells to specialise for particular functions (differentiation), such as animal nerves or muscles. This became possible thanks to the emergence of novel eukaryotic cells, which are essentially combinations of two or more prokaryotic cells, one living symbiotically within another – Margulis' endosymbiont hypothesis. At least two intracellular organelles within plant cells originated in this way: the energy-producing mitochondria and photosynthetic chloroplasts, each derived from a different prokaryotic ancestor. Animal cells possess mitochondria only, but the high efficiency of their energy production (using oxygen) is essential for active lifestyles. Thus, evolution can involve elements of cooperation and networking; it's not all 'red in tooth and claw'.

The origin of animals

During the Ediacaran era (635–542 Ma), the oceans were inhabited by strange organisms that lack obvious affinities with familiar animals or plants. Within a relatively brief period, termed the 'Cambrian explosion' (starting ca.542 Ma), these biota virtually disappeared, and were replaced by animals belonging to modern phyla – including arthropods, sponges, comb jellies, marine worms, and chordates. These assignments are supported by exceptionally well-preserved Cambrian fossils, including traces of soft body parts. However, many of these fossils remain enigmatic, to say the least, because their anatomies seem unlike modern animal groups.

For Gould, these anomalies represent novel body plans that did not survive the ravages of natural selection and hence became extinct. Provocatively, he claims that if the 'tape of evolution' were rerun from the Cambrian, we might find ourselves today in a world dominated by a very different selection of organisms. Gould emphasises the randomness of survival in the evolutionary lottery, scotching any notion of progress from 'lower' to 'higher' forms, culminating in humans.

However, Conway Morris interprets these fossils very differently, as intermediates or ancestors in the appearance of new animal groups. He focuses particularly on convergent evolution, adducing numerous examples of this process and arguing that only certain design 'solutions' actually work to enhance fitness – hence these adaptations recur repeatedly in independent lineages. The example of box-camera eyes was cited earlier: likewise the convergent adaptations against drought adopted by American cacti and some Canarian *Euphorbia*s. Extrapolating speculatively from this, intelligent bipedal life may be a predictable outcome from prolonged evolution in a benign planetary environment.

One suggested compromise is that these now-extinct Cambrian animals belonged to major class-level groups (as distinct from modern groups as insects are from crustaceans), but did not represent completely different body-plans corresponding to vanished phyla.

Evolution of behaviour

Evolution moulds not only physical attributes but also patterns of animal behaviour. Because 'fitness' is measured by success in transmitting one's genes to offspring, reproductive traits have been subjected to intense sexual selection in one or both sexes, affecting structures and behaviours involved in courtship and mating. The elaborate tail feathers of male peacocks afford one obvious example, as do the heavy antlers of many male deer. Since exaggerated physical or behavioural attributes are interpreted as indicators of a sexual partner's fitness, these can become runaway evolutionary trends.

Plant pollination by specific insects creates selection pressures for both species, leading e.g. to deeper flowers and longer mouthparts – a trend which may be carried to astonishing extremes. The 30 cm-long spur of the Madagascan Comet Orchid requires a hawkmoth pollinator whose similarly long proboscis allows it to feed on nectar at the base of the spur. There is, however, a cost: this plant cannot be fertilised by other insects, and both organisms are mutually dependent on one another. They have co-evolved, and if either became extinct, the other would be doomed. Innumerable other examples of mutual dependency between organisms are known; often (though not always), there is clear benefit to both in such associations.

In parasitism, the benefits seem entirely one-sided. Parasites gain nutrients and a sheltered environment (though host immune responses attempt to combat the invader), while hosts suffer mild to debilitating disease. Levels of parasitism affect patterns of behaviour such as host dominance hierarchies and reproductive success. Here, an arms-race is in progress: as the host evolves new immune strategies to control the parasite, natural selection encourages the latter to evolve better ways of countering or evading them.

Evolution of human culture

Humans share more than 98% of their DNA with chimpanzees, and rather less with other great apes. Patterns of animal behaviour are often instinctive rather than learned, suggesting they're 'hard-wired' in the nervous system by that animal's genes. That said, most behaviours can be modified by learning through experience. Other behaviours are learned from parents or group members, resulting in 'cultural variants' particular to local groupings. Humans take this to extremes: diverse cultures have evolved rapidly over time, as documented in both written and archaeological records.

Creation, evolution, and science

We're now in a position to answer the question in our title. The precise definition of 'science' is notoriously difficult to pin down, but the overview in the previous section has hopefully demonstrated that evolutionary science qualifies on many counts, not least for its amazing explanatory scope across a huge range of biological questions, for its incorporation of many diverse kinds of scientific enquiry within itself (including branches of physics and chemistry which no one disputes as 'science'), and for its ability to spawn fertile new research programmes. The accusation of YEC, that evolutionary theory isn't scientific, seems churlish (to put it mildly) in light of this phenomenal success. It's true that evolutionary history is not accessible by means of direct experimentation in the laboratory, but this doesn't preclude a basic empiricism in historical sciences like evolutionary biology, geology, and astronomy: they proceed, just like the other natural sciences, by means of a cyclical process of observation, hypothesising, searching for more evidence, and revision/rejection of the initial hypothesis.

In comparison, YEC fails dismally as an empirical science. Indeed, there's a strong case for suggesting that YEC doesn't even qualify as a 'pseudo-science' on this score. YEC makes claims (hypotheses) that are open to empirical testing – principally the young age of the earth, and the worldwide extent and cataclysmic character of Noah's flood – but these have been shown to be entirely false by the mainstream empirical sciences countless times, *and yet YEC persists in making these claims*. In other words, YEC is such a failure as a science (and even a pseudo-science) that it can't reasonably be claimed to be one. YEC takes its certainty not from any body of knowledge about the natural world but from a transcendent source (the Bible), upon which it will not budge a single inch.

It's therefore our argument that evolution is certainly scientific, but creationism (in the form of YEC) is neither scientific nor pseudo-scientific; it's metaphysical.

Chapter summary

- There are various creationisms, but young-earth creationism (YEC) in particular has persistently challenged the scientific claims and status of evolutionary biology.
- YEC arose in the twentieth century, arguably as a conservative religious backlash against progressive modernism. YEC offers its own distinctive 'science', which posits a young earth and a worldwide flood which shaped the earth's present geology and fossil record mere thousands of years ago.
- Both sides of the creation-evolution debate accuse the other of not being scientific, although their definitions of science seem to be widely divergent. While the claims of evolutionary biology are based on painstaking observation and experimentation of the natural world by thousands of individuals working across a wide spectrum of life sciences, those of YEC must conform above all to a literalistic reading of the Bible, as the primary source of evidence concerning origins.
- One particular bone of contention concerns the question of whether study of the past can be truly scientific, since it can't be observed in the laboratory. YEC argues that the evolutionary history of life is an un-scientific hypothesis which rejects the pre-eminent status of the Bible as a source of both scientific and religious truth.
- But mainstream evolutionary science is committed to methodological naturalism and does not rely on transcendent sources of truth. Instead, sophisticated methods of study have been developed to investigate the history of life in empirical terms. The starting assumptions of evolutionary biology are quite different to YEC, and while the former's fall squarely within those of mainstream science, YEC represents a totally different worldview which cannot be described as 'scientific' in any conventional sense.

Study questions

1. How would you distinguish science from 'pseudo-science'?
2. The ancient scriptures of Christianity, Judaism, and Islam show evidence of ancient cosmologies and ancient scientific ideas. Should religious believers take account of modern scientific views when reading these texts?
3. How would you characterise the hermeneutical approach of YEC to the biblical text? What are its strengths and weaknesses?
4. Describe the essential character of those sciences that deal with the natural world of the past, in relation to the sciences that proceed by direct,

laboratory-based work (e.g. chemistry). Are the differences important enough to mean that the former sciences should always be qualified in some way (e.g. as 'historical sciences')?
5. How do the so-called 'historical sciences' relate to the study of human history (i.e. 'history')?
6. How important is Baconian induction in the natural sciences today?
7. How important is Darwin's natural selection as an evolutionary mechanism in modern evolutionary biology?

Introductory readings

Conway Morris, Simon (2003) *Life's Solution: Inevitable Humans in a Lonely Universe* (Cambridge: Cambridge University Press).
Darwin, C. (1859). *The Origin of Species*, ed. J. Burrow, Harmondsworth, Penguin, reprinting of first edition of 1859. [Where it all began: Darwin's generous, comprehensively argued exposition and defence of the evidence for natural selection.]
Gould, Stephen Jay (1989) *Wonderful Life: The Burgess Shale and the Nature of History* (Harmondsworth: Penguin Books). [This and the Conway Morris title should be read alongside each other as charting one of the most active debates in science today.]
Montgomery, David R. (2012) *The Rocks Don't Lie: A Geologist Investigates Noah's Flood* (New York: W.W. Norton & Co). [An accessible discussion of the way that the biblical flood story shaped the development of the modern science of geology and of YEC.]

Advanced readings

Davis, Edward B. (2012) 'Science Falsely So Called: Fundamentalism and Science.' In *The Blackwell Companion to Science and Christianity*, ed. J. Stump and A. Padgett (Chichester: Blackwell), 48–60. [A useful account of the early years of fundamentalist Christianity in America.]
Eldredge, Niles and Stephen Jay Gould (1972) 'Punctuated Equilibria: An Alternative to Phyletic Gradualism.' In *Models in Paleobiology*, ed. T.J.M. Schopf (San Francisco: Freeman Cooper), 82–115. [The landmark paper which introduced the idea of punctuated equilibrium into evolution.]
McCalla, Arthur (2013) *The Creationist Debate: The Encounter between the Bible and the Historical Mind* (New York, London: Bloomsbury). [A highly-penetrating overview of the origins and significance of creationisms.]
Numbers, Ronald L. (2006) *The Creationists: From Scientific Creationism to Intelligent Design* (Cambridge, MA: Harvard University Press). [A seminal classic, taking a critical but sympathetic view of YEC.]
Whitcomb, John C. and Henry M. Morris (1961) *The Genesis Flood: The Biblical Record and Its Scientific Implications* (Phillipsburg, NJ: Presbyterian & Reformed). [The founding text of YEC.]

Internet resources

Answers in Genesis, answersingenesis.org [Perhaps the most active of all YEC organisations in the Christian world currently.]

BioLogos, www.biologos.org [An evangelical Christian organisation which challenges YEC and is dedicated to introducing believers to mainstream scientific accounts of origins.]

Harun Yahya, www.harunyahya.com [The highly-influential Muslim creationist.]

Reasons to Believe, www.reasons.org [The prominent old-earth creationist organisation, led by astronomer Dr Hugh Ross.]

4   Is evolution compatible with design?

Alasdair Richmond

Introduction

The interplay between Darwin and Design is perhaps *the* most important topic
uniting philosophy, science and religion. Several vital questions concern the
impact of Charles Darwin's **evolution** via **natural selection** on our ideas about
human origins and the possibility of inferences from the organised complexity
of the biological world to the existence of a Divine Creator/Designer. Darwinism aims to explain the existence of ordered complexity by showing how it can
arise in increments from simple beginnings. Darwinism does not postulate a
directing complexity overseeing our development or argue complexity out of
existence.

In his classic exposition of Darwinism, *The Blind Watchmaker*, Richard
Dawkins argues that the only live options there are for explaining biological
complexity are Design (i.e. by a Divine agent) or evolution by natural selection.
(Not that these two views are necessarily *logically* incompatible, of course . . .)
Dawkins also says that before Darwin, there was no rationally credible option
but to believe in Design. One might disagree with one or other side of this
dilemma and yet agree with Dawkins that, between them, Darwinism and Design
exhaust the possible ways to explain the origin of species. Whatever other differences they may exhibit, Design inferences and Darwinism share at least a
commitment to viewing biological complexity as extraordinary and in need of
special explanation. The key difference is that when it comes to explaining biological complexity, Darwinism need make no reference to directing intelligence,
whereas Design arguments see accepting such an intelligence as rationally compelling or otherwise indispensable.

Biologists and geologists had speculated that species might have developed, i.e.
that each species did not necessarily represent a separate creation, before Darwin.
Indeed, ideas about the mutability of species were seriously entertained by (e.g.)
St. Thomas Aquinas (1224–1274) amongst others. Likewise, the *logical* possibility
of alternatives to Design inferences was well-articulated at least as far back as
David Hume and arguably far further still – e.g. back to **Epicurus**. Epicurus
speculated that the world contained an infinite amount of matter (in the form of
minute, indivisible particles or atoms) which constantly circulated throughout

otherwise empty infinite space. Given enough time (i.e. eternity), such random motion of matter would, suggested Epicurus, be bound to result in any degree of relatively stable, organised complexity – without any external direction, oversight or Designer. (Compare the old thought-experiment whereby an infinite number of monkeys left long enough before an infinite number of type-writers are bound to generate *Hamlet* eventually . . .) With these premises, eternity will leave no possible state unactualised, and highly ordered pockets in otherwise unremitting chaos are not remarkable. With no independent limit on the age of the universe, Epicurus could postulate as much time as he could need.

This 'Epicurean' view is one of *pure*, unchannelled randomness: there is no mechanism favouring either the generation of complex parts or their preservation once generated. Amongst other problems, 'Epicurean' evolution may remove the surprising character of order in our world, but only by removing the surprising character of *every physically possible occurrence*. In addition, modern cosmology strongly suggests our spacetime has existed for only a finite amount of time and holds only finite amounts of matter – both far short of the literal infinities needed to make our existence necessary under Epicurus' hypothesis.

David Hume's posthumously published *Dialogues Concerning Natural Religion* offers extended critiques of Design inferences via the character Philo. Philo raises a number of Design-relevant points, e.g. about inferring an infinite cause from (apparently) finite effects. However, in Hume's Eighth Dialogue, Philo revisits "the old Epicurean hypothesis" of infinite moving matter evenly distributed throughout an infinite universe. However, Philo makes some significant changes to Epicurus. First, Philo imagines that matter is finite in extent, so "every possible order or position must be tried an infinite number of times. This world, therefore, with all its events, even the most minute, has been produced and destroyed, and will again be produced and destroyed" (1776, Gaskin ed. 1993: 84). Philo's second alteration to Epicurus comes closer to evolution proper, viz. duration is endless but matter only capable of finite distributions, so "every possible order or position must be tried an infinite number of times" (*ibid.*). Furthermore, Philo postulates an "œconomy of things, by which matter can preserve that perpetual agitation, which seems essential to it, yet maintain a constancy in its forms" (1776, Gaskin ed. 1993: 85). This move reflects the need for a genuinely evolutionary theory to have at least two components: it must explain both the *generation* of variants and their *differential survival*, i.e. where variants come from and why only some survive. (Remember this bipartite structure of evolutionary theories when we come to Popper's claim that natural selection rests on a tautology.) Philo furthers points out that any animal which arose with parts externally ill-adapted either to carry out a specific function, or with parts internally ill-adapted to one another, could not survive. Its constituent parts would quickly be dispersed and thrown back into the melting-pot until such time as they underwent incorporation in a more stable animal. The world is not filled with hybrid forms composed of ill-matched halves, but rather with animals whose parts are fitted not merely to their environment but also to each other. Hume grasped the important need for internal adaptation of parts within organisms as well as external adaptation of organisms to their environment. Hume prefigures Darwin's recognition that generation, survival and propagation are not miraculous if the right conditions obtain.

As Darwin himself graciously conceded (e.g. in the 'Historical Sketch' pre-fixed to the *Origin of Species*), others had suggested before him firstly, that species were not immutable but showed clear evidence of change over time, and secondly, that many now-diverse forms of life might well have had a common ancestor. (Among the forerunners of evolutionary theory was philosopher Immanuel Kant, 1724–1804.) Amongst Darwin's direct influences, Charles's grandfather **Erasmus Darwin** (1731–1802) published a work called *Zoönomia* (1794–1796), whose views on 'generation' Charles Darwin held to have antici-pated **Jean-Baptiste Lamarck**'s views, and which in turn foreshadowed natural selection. Lamarck's *Philosophie Zoologique* (1809) postulated that the envi-ronment drove changes in animal organisation and physiology. Lamarck further postulated that acquired characteristics were transmitted directly and that Nature possesses an innate drive towards improvement so beneficial character-istics were more likely to be generated than harmful ones. This supposed "Le pouvoir de la vie" ('life force' or, more accurately, 'complexifying force') should generate order and drive animal species towards greater complexity. In Lamarckian evolution, organisms acquire advantageous new traits, said traits being handed on to succeeding generations once acquired. However, how this force worked, by what mechanism new traits arose and (especially) how acquired traits were transmitted from parents to offspring were all matters left unexplained by Lamarck.

Despite important forerunners like Erasmus Darwin and Lamarck, Charles Dar-win was the first person to advance an empirically driven, testable explanation for biological complexity. Natural selection is of enduring relevance to questions touching on the intersection of science, philosophy and religion because it marks a major achievement in explaining the origins of biological complexity and maybe even life itself in terms that fit with **naturalism**. Darwin laid a new emphasis on inheritance as the factor explaining how new features arose and relative adapta-tions as explaining how some features come to survive and predominate. What makes Darwin's contribution both so powerful and so controversial is his offering an explanation of the origins of species (and biological complexity generally) that needs no appeal to external oversight or Design. Note Darwinism is not a doctrine of pure chance or pure randomness: evolution by natural selection is not a random process, even if it proceeds without external direction.

Genotype and phenotype

Despite some similarities with Lamarck's theory, Darwin's *Origin of Species* emphasised that inherited characteristics (i.e. not acquired ones) were key to understanding evolution. However, the problem that no known mechanism could explain Lamarck's transmission of acquired characteristics could perhaps have been urged against Darwinism too *until* modern genetics. DNA provides a durable vehicle for the genetic information (not all of which gets actualised in any one organism) which composes the **genotype**. The DNA molecule is sufficiently durable to transmit this information accurately, although occasionally experiencing errors in the copying process, the all-important *mutations*.

Two crucial concepts in genetics are the genotype and the **phenotype**. The former is (roughly) the genetic information which issues in the overall shape of the organism, while the latter is the macroscopic structure of the animal itself. The (Darwinian) order of causation runs from genotype to phenotype, not *vice-versa*. The genotype undergoes changes, expressed in organisms' structure from generation of generation. Darwinism requires no mechanism by which phenotypic traits (advantageous or not) can be handed on to offspring once acquired. Rather than exhibiting pure or unchannelled randomness, natural selection is not entirely a matter of unpredictable chance. Instead, Darwinism is a theory of channelled chance: random at the level of mutation but non-random at the level of selection – albeit that Darwinism attributes the channelling to unconscious nature and not to any Designer or overseeing intelligence.

Assuming genotypic changes ('mutations') will be random, some will produce changes in the phenotype which increase the survival prospects of an animal. However, the majority of changes will not be beneficial – being at best survival-neutral or (more probably) harming survival prospects. Natural selection is the process whereby advantageous changes tend to accumulate in a population. Here's the non-random bit: those (randomly generated) traits which tend to promote the survival of their recipients will tend to survive and thus get transmitted – the (again randomly generated) traits that don't help their recipients tend to die out. Animals with advantageous changes tend to survive longer and breed more than their less-favoured rivals, and so, advantageous changes tend to accumulate. Successful phenotypes preserve the genotypes which shaped them and thus such genotypes come to predominate.

Teleology and Aristotle's four causes

One key philosophical problem centred on evolution concerns the status of **teleology**: explanations that appeal to goals in explaining (e.g.) structure, function or behaviour. (It is not coincidental that arguments to Divine Design that appeal to the order of the world are also called *Teleological Arguments*.) For example, one might say that an organism with eyes possess organs of sight *in order to* form images of its surroundings. (Or that a bat has wings *so that* it can fly.) Here, the explaining feature is the purpose for which the eyes or wings) exist. But how can a goal help to explain why an organism shows the features it does? Before Darwin, philosophical views of explanation by goal-seeking were essentially those of **Aristotle**. Aristotle divided explanation by causes into four categories, according to the kind of cause involved. The two categories that concern us are the **efficient cause** (the initiating event or what Aristotle called 'what started it') and the **final cause** (the purpose or goal). The efficient cause is more a cause as we ordinarily conceive it – whatever initiates the object's existence or a change in its existence. Darwinian natural selection offered to explain goal-seeking behaviour (and hence structures like eyes) solely via efficient causation. A handy summary:

> How can the purpose or end of a piece of behaviour serve as its cause? Here is the answer: Organisms that were able to serve that purpose were selected for; serving that purpose is that part of the chain of events that causes organisms that do behave in that way to survive and develop.
>
> (Cartwright, 1986: 208)

Paley's 'Watchmaker' analogy

Darwinism and Design agree that the manifest arrangement of parts in living things requires explanation. Classic Design arguments include William Paley's (1802) "Watchmaker" argument. Imagine finding a functioning watch on a hillside. Where we might be inclined to believe a *stone* rested on the hillside forever without feeling any need for special explanation for its existence, the watch's intricate parts and their obvious ordering to an end invite special explanation. Paley argued that not the watch's mere existence or even its complexity *per se* invite special explanation but what needs explanation is the watch's manifest ordered complexity towards a clearly identifiable goal or end-state. Such goal-oriented order invites a functional explanation like those we apply in other cases. Paley thought only intentional action by a Designer can explain ordering of parts to an end. (The need for intentional explanation of the watch's goal-directed aspects would only increase if we discovered the watch contains mechanisms that allow it to make other watches, just as living things replicate themselves.) Darwinism agrees with Paley that cases of organised biological complexity (and self-replicating living forms in particular) invite explanation. Where Darwinism departs from Paley is in introducing the notion of gradual change through the conferring of selectional advantage and not by direct external oversight.

Darwinism and theism: two pitfalls

Discussions of Darwin and **theism** might need to steer clear of two (popular) pitfalls: one is claiming that Darwinism has left the status of traditional Design Arguments completely unaffected and the other is to claiming that Darwinism has settled the matter of God's existence (in the negative) once and for all. These two extremities are not the only sustainable views. One might instead hold that Darwinism has transformed the Design debate in ways that Darwin's critics have not always absorbed or responded to constructively, but think that Darwinism has not rendered debates over God obsolete or otherwise proved belief irrational or otherwise unsustainable. Darwinism may sit ill with some traditional theistic conceptions (e.g. Biblical literalism), but it does not necessarily replace or refute all theistic arguments.

One can be a thoroughgoing Darwinian and still not subscribe to the view that Darwinism has somehow refuted religion, or exposed religious belief as being irrational or absurd. While Darwinism's success is hard to reconcile with the central claims of 'Intelligent Design' theories, Darwinism has left other arguments about God's existence untouched. For example, the issue of so-called 'cosmic **fine-tuning**' – namely, why does the physical world show the exactly right set of conditions to make the evolution of life possible? Other epistemic/evidential arguments besides Design ('teleological') arguments include the Cosmological and **Ontological arguments**. Likewise, existential arguments for belief or acquiring belief include Blaise Pascal's Wager, Søren Kierkegaard's 'Leap of Faith' arguments, Ludwig Wittgenstein's 'Form of Life' arguments, etc.

Natural selection and the status of intelligent design

Determining what a scientific theory is can be an involved matter, but one suggestion might run thus: a scientific theory is an explanatory framework that tries to unite as many empirical phenomena as possible under the simplest possible laws and makes detailed, quantitative and testable empirical predictions. Consider Einstein's (Special or General) Relativity – these theories between them united a host of gravitational, electromagnetic and optical phenomena while predicting hitherto unobserved phenomena (like time dilation, space-time curvature, gravitational waves, etc.) that could be subjected to precise observational tests. Relativity has so far been completely vindicated by observation and continues to generate new, detailed predictions that form a basis for ongoing research programmes. Now, at the risk of over-compressing several interesting debates in the philosophy of science, the fact that a theory has been successful in surviving tests does not necessarily support unrestricted claims for the theory's truth – presumably it is of the essence of scientific theories that they can (at least in principle) be overturned by new data, however well-confirmed they have been hitherto – but equally it would seem perverse to reject the best-confirmed of the available theories on the basis of that success.

Some opponents of Darwinism called for equal classroom time and state funding for teaching Creationist alternatives to natural selection, notably Intelligent Design ('ID'). If conflicts with the United States constitutional strictures on classroom promulgation of religious doctrine are to be avoided, ID has to be a scientifically motivated movement, i.e. one driven by the (presumably disinterested) scientific appraisal of the data; it is not supposed to be an exercise in **apologetics** for any given faith or religious position. Key arguments for ID include the claim that Darwinism cannot explain the origins of life or that some biological structures show evidence of 'irreducible complexity', i.e. complexity that is inexplicable in terms of graduated, step-by-step accumulation of naturally evolved changes.

There are numerous grounds for reservations about ID *as a currently viable legitimate scientific theory*. While not all versions of ID exhibit all these traits, ID often seems to exhibit versions of the following:

1) Vagueness of concepts. There is as yet no sign of anything like consensus or agreed definition as to what ID is, *nor what observational (quantitative or qualitative) evidence would support it*. Such consensus is not essential for science to progress in a given field, but the absence of such consensus discourages clear testing and results.

2) Lack of quantitative predictions. Darwinism, especially as applied to (e.g.) population-genetics or the differential spread of traits, makes many detailed empirical claims that can be expressed in directly testable quantitative terms, and has passed every test it has been put to thus far. (Cf. the increasing evidence of intermediate steps between modern-day species in the fossil record, ever-increasing evidence of the development of complexity through incremental change, etc.)

3) Inattention to/downplaying of apparent falsifiers. E.g. several instances of alleged "irreducible complexity" that have proved to be all-too-reducible. A popular ID claim is that the emergence of life is an exception to the second law of thermodynamics. However, that law says (roughly) only that the entropy of an isolated system will either stay the same or tend to increase over time. The accumulating biological order in all our ancestral **replicators** was more than offset by the accumulating disorder in the nutrients and other essential materials they pulled in from outside. Neither life nor proto-life nor indeed the Earth itself is an isolated system.

4) Misrepresentation of the nature, aims and testing-conditions of Darwinism. E.g. claims that Darwinism is a doctrine of "pure randomness", that "survival of the fittest" is an unscientific and unfalsifiable tautology or that Darwinism "cannot explain the origins of life", etc.

5) Bad historical grasp of science. E.g. some ID supporters still invoke Lord Kelvin's 1862 calculation that the Earth could only have existed for between 24 and 400 million years (i.e. too short a time for the complex life-forms we observe to have evolved) – neglecting to mention that Kelvin made his calculation long before anything was known of the roles of (e.g.) nuclear fission in producing geothermal heating or of nuclear fusion in heating the Sun. Kelvin's calculations were broadly correct, assuming the Earth's and Sun's heat were due solely to then-known chemical processes (like combustion) and without involving nuclear processes. Kelvin made his calculation in good faith and with all the then-known scientific facts at his disposal; to trot the same calculation out now is unsustainable.

6) Setting too much store by mere consistency with experience and not enough store by testable predictions. (E.g. some supporters of ID still cite approvingly Philip Gosse's 'Omphalos' – see below.) ID seems to traffic exclusively in either unfalsifiable hypotheses (like Philip Gosse's) or falsified hypotheses. Of course, one and the same claim cannot be both unfalsifiable and yet falsified, but as yet there seems to be no successful, unfalsified, quantitative predictions from ID.

So, the above suggest ID is either not really a scientific theory at all, or at best, a scientific theory vastly inferior in predictive and explanatory resources to Darwinism. Whether ID *might* have been scientifically viable had the data been different is another question – and one to which an affirmative answer could be given in theory without it following that ID *as the data stand* is a viable scientific theory. After all, had the data been (very) different from what they are, geocentric cosmology could have been scientifically viable – but they aren't and it isn't.

Evolution and falsifiability

Design arguments need not imply Biblical literalism. However, one historical Creationist story affords some instructive points. In 1857, Philip Gosse, naturalist and devout member of the Plymouth Brethren, published a book called *Omphalos: An Attempt to Untie the Geological Knot* (London, John Van Voorst). Gosse sought to combine Biblical accounts of Creation with geological evidence that the Earth had a long history. He concluded the Biblical account was literally true (i.e. the Earth was created in six days), but that the Earth was created with layers of sediment and fossils in place. He hoped (and apparently expected) that this attempted reconciliation would find favour with both scientific and religious parties to the disputes over the Earth's age and the history of life thereon. Alas, neither side adopted Gosse's view *en masse*: scientists dismissed the claim as arbitrary and untestable; theologians dismissed it as involving God playing what was effectively a massive prank or otherwise introducing a needless discontinuity into the physical world.

In fairness to Gosse, he held that Creation was the only alternative to accepting an eternal and essentially cyclical succession of life-forms. (As it were, chickens succeeding eggs succeeding chickens, forever.) Given Creation must be an irruption into the causal order, Gosse argued that any created Earth that contained true archetypes for subsequent life would have to bear false traces of a non-existent past. Thus, if Adam was the pattern of all subsequent people, he must have had a navel (or "*omphalos*" in Greek). However, since Adam was made from clay and not born of a mother, his navel only *resembled* the vestigial remains of an umbilical cord which in fact never existed. Likewise, Eden's new-made trees would contain growth rings, evidence of maturation they never underwent.

Gosse accepted this hypothesis was practically unfalsifiable for any nineteenth century observer, but held that unfalsifiability was inevitable for

Creationist hypotheses. For any conceivable physical observation, Gosse's hypothesis can be made proof against it. Whether it be growth rings in trees, sedimentation in rocks or the recession of galaxies, all could be false evidence of an Ur-Creation, a non-existent primordial world prior to the actual Creation. However, Gosse can't explain why fossils show the particular shapes and arrangements they do. (Why we do only find fake remains of extinct saurians and not those of centaurs?) If fossils are either a Divine test (a claim Gosse did *not* make) or an inevitably misleading by-product of Creation, no functional relationship existed between the remains. However, if the fragments once formed part of live animals, then we can relate them to other creatures by series of structural correspondences. Likewise, if the distribution of fossils in rock-strata results from gradual evolutionary change, then what we see is what we would expect: layers of creatures of similar ages embedded in rocks of similar ages. However, if we attribute mass extinctions to a single all-encompassing Flood, then we must explain why creatures from different stages of evolution died obligingly in layers.

Perhaps surprisingly, Karl Popper (1976: 168) once claimed Darwinism was "not a testable scientific theory but a metaphysical research programme". Popper thought "survival of the fittest" was tautologous, i.e. that survival defines which adaptations are successful and survival is defined in terms of adaptive success: "Adaptation or fitness is defined by modern evolutionists as survival-value, and can be measured by actual success in survival: there is hardly any point in testing a theory as feeble as this" (*op. cit.*: 171). In defending this claim, he invokes a species of the Epicurean 'evolving matter' hypothesis offered by Hume's Philo to exemplify his view of the essentially metaphysical nature of Darwinism:

> Even in a situation without life Darwinian selection can apply to some extent: atomic nuclei which are relatively stable (in the situation in question) will tend to be more abundant than unstable ones, and the same may hold for chemical compounds.
>
> (*op. cit.*: 168–69).

Relatively more stable matter will necessarily tend to predominate over less stable structures.

However, contra Popper, "survival of the fittest" describes what *tends* to happen, and is emphatically non-tautologous. The 'fittest' organisms (i.e. the best adapted) are not whoever just happens to survive. *Au contraire*: successful adaptations "confer fitness by an engineer's criterion of design, not by the empirical fact of their survival and spread" (Gould, 1991: 42). Contingency also shapes whether efficient mutations flourish. (Having a neck ten inches longer than your grazing rivals has little impact on your survival chances if a gigaton meteorite hits your environment.) An organism's *fitness* can be measured by investigating it and its environment without knowing the coming sweep of events. Assessing an animal's *survival* involves historical investigation. Again, an evolutionary theory must explain a) the generation of variants and b) their differential survival.

Popper's notion that survival and adaptive success are necessarily related blurs this distinction.

Contra Popper, Darwinism makes eminently testable and falsifiable claims, e.g. that when gaps in the fossil record are filled, those gaps will be filled (and many have been filled) with the remains of creatures that are explicable in Darwinian terms, i.e. no sudden vast leaps across genetic 'design space' in a single generation. Other Darwinian explanatory principles (e.g. that bilateral symmetry in any organism is best explained by locomotion) lead to falsifiable, quantifiable predictions which can be tested in a range of cases.

Two cautionary notes

Finally, two suggestions for ways *not* to read Darwinism.

Firstly, Darwinism does not straightforwardly equate evolutionary survival with *progress*, or still less with any moral (or other) value. The best-adapted are not therefore necessarily the *morally* best. Likewise, it does not follow from natural selection that the best-adapted survivors must be the most ruthless or self-centred organisms. Natural selection has favoured butterflies rather more than sabre-toothed tigers: the butterfly has survived and the sabre-toothed tiger hasn't. Should we conclude that whatever attributes butterflies have that sabre-toothed tigers lack are somehow more 'progressive'? So-called Social Darwinists (who may have only the slightest acquaintance with what natural selection actually involves) seem to assume too quickly that 'progress' must be towards greater fierceness, hostility and general chest-beating toughness. But is the butterfly more 'fit' than the sabre-toothed tiger? Should we conclude that evolution is more likely in the long term to select for prettiness of wings over fierceness? Notions of moral worth and value are best kept firmly decoupled from notions of evolutionary 'unfitness'.

Secondly, if Popper misconstrued the nature of "survival of the fittest", he was in good company. Sometimes philosophers try to turn an empirical research programme into a metaphysical schema by treating a well-confirmed theory as though it were a necessary truth. Some have proposed to write evolution through natural selection into the very definition of life, thereby undermining any claim that natural selection is non-tautologous. Such definitions effectively dismiss Creationism *a priori* and have deeply counter-intuitive consequences. While Creationism may or may not be right, it is not logically incoherent. Furthermore, such definitions distort the empirical status of Darwin's theory by making a mere analytic truth that life evolved. Neither consequence seems palatable. As Margaret Boden says: "To argue that 'creation biology' is false, or explanatorily inferior to scientific biology, one must treat evolution as a universal empirical characteristic of life, not as an *a priori* criterion of it" (*The Philosophy of Artificial Life*, Oxford, Oxford University Press, 1996, ed. Boden, Introduction: 24). Defining life based on evolution could oblige us to conclude that something could pass all our external criteria for life and still prove not to be alive because it proved not to have evolved.

Chapter summary

- Precursors of Darwinism include the purely random 'atomistic' theories of Epicurus and Hume, and the specifically evolutionary hypotheses of Erasmus Darwin and Jean-Baptiste Lamarck.
- Lamarck postulated that there is an innate drive towards complexity in living things, and that organisms both acquire advantageous traits and pass them to their offspring. The mechanisms behind Lamarck's transmission of advantageous traits and *pouvoir de vie* remain mysterious.
- Epicurus postulated that infinite matter circulating through eternity would eventually generate any imaginable degree of apparent order and complexity. However, cosmological history is too short for such pure 'Epicurean' randomness to be plausible and hence this theory fits ill with observation.
- Where Epicurean evolution is a theory of pure randomness, evolution by natural selection offers a theory of *channelled* randomness. Evolution is random at the level of mutations but non-random when it comes to the preservation and spread of adaptively advantageous traits.
- Where Aristotelean biology explained goal-seeking behaviour via a special 'teleological' kind of causation, Darwinism explains goal-seeking behaviour and parts via ordinary efficient causation.
- Contrary to claims by (e.g.) Karl Popper, Darwinism makes falsifiable and quantifiable conjectures. Evolutionary fitness and survival are not synonymous, and hence 'survival of the fittest' (i.e. the best-adapted) is not a tautology.
- Whatever other differences they may have, Darwinism and Design both take biological complexity seriously, i.e. as a phenomenon inviting special explanation.
- Design inferences are by no means the only arguments for believing in God.
- Darwinism does not equate survival-value with (especially moral) 'progress' or 'worth'.
- Writing evolution (by natural selection) into the very definition of life misrepresents the empirical and scientific status of Darwin's theory, and risks distorting and diminishing his achievement.

Study questions

1. How does natural selection differ from Lamarckian evolution?
2. How does natural selection differ from pure ('Epicurean') randomness?
3. What might it mean to say that natural selection is a process of *channelled* randomness?
4. Does it make sense to talk of a non-intentional teleology?
5. How do genotype and phenotype relate?

6. Is "survival of the fittest" a tautology, or are there differences between the notions of endurance through stability and survival through adaptation?
7. Why might there be a conflict between traditional Arguments from Designs (e.g. Paley's "Watchmaker") and evolution by natural selection?
8. How did Philip Gosse attempt to reconcile the fossil record with Genesis, and was this attempted reconciliation successful?
9. What resources might there be for falsifying evolution?
10. What implications might natural selection have for our ideas of teleology?

Primary sources

'About Darwin: Dedicated to the Life and Times of Charles Darwin', www.about darwin.com/ [Useful regularly updated guide to Darwin, his works and literature about him.]

Darwin, C. (1859). *The Origin of Species*, ed. J. Burrow, Harmondsworth, Penguin, reprinting of first edition of 1859. [Where it all began: Darwin's generous, comprehensively argued exposition and defence of the evidence for natural selection.]

'Darwin Online', *The Complete Works of Charles Darwin Online*, maintained by John van Wyhe, Cambridge University Library http://darwin-online.org.uk/ [Highly recommended electronic database of Darwin's works.]

Paley, W. (1802). *Natural Theology*, ed. M. Eddy and D. Knight, Oxford: Oxford University Press, 2006. [Enduringly important account of inferences to Design from observed nature; includes the famous 'Watchmaker' analogy for inferring Design from organised biological complexity.]

Introductory readings

Dawkins, R. (1985). *The Blind Watchmaker*. Harmondsworth: Penguin. [Classic introduction to/defence of Darwinism. Argues persuasively that only Darwinism or Design offers live options for addressing the biological. Offers convincing rebuttals to a host of criticisms of Darwinism.]

Dennett, D. (1995). *Darwin's Dangerous Idea*, Harmondsworth: Penguin. [Comprehensive survey of philosophical implications of Darwinism.]

Gould, S. (1976). 'Darwin's Untimely Burial', *Natural History* 85: 24–30. Reprinted in Gould's *Ever Since Darwin*, Harmondsworth: Penguin, 1991: 39–45. Online at: www.stephenjaygould.org/library/gould_tautology.html [Brilliantly written response to some perennial misreadings of Darwinism.]

Hume, D. (1776/1993). *Dialogues Concerning Natural Religion and the Natural History of Religion*, ed. J. C. A. Gaskin, Oxford: Oxford, University Press. [Wide-ranging dialogue survey of rational grounds for belief – includes a classic critique of Design inferences that foreshadows Darwin.]

Ruse, M., 1973, *The Philosophy of Biology*, London: Hutchinson. (Reprint Prometheus Books 1998.) [Thorough, clear survey for philosophy-minded readers of key issues in evolution.]

Advanced readings

Cairns-Smith, A. (1985). *Seven Clues to the Origins of Life*, Cambridge: Cambridge University Press. [Argues that the first true 'replicators' were not living things at all, but crystalline sub-assemblies in clays; suggests a Darwinian explanation of the generation of organic complexity out of inorganic systems.]

Cartwright, N. (1986). 'Two Kinds of Teleological Explanation', *Human Nature and Natural Knowledge*, ed. A. Donagan, N. Perovich (Jr.) and M. Wedin, Boston Studies in the Philosophy of Science, No. 89. Dordrecht, Holland: Reidel, 201–10. [Comprehensive account of goal-seeking explanation via efficient as well as teleological causation.].

McMullin, E. (1993). 'Evolution and Special Creation', *Zygon* 28: 299–335. Reprinted as Chapter 35 of *The Philosophy of Biology*, ed. D. Hull and M. Ruse, Oxford: Oxford University Press, 1998, 698–733. [Clear and judicious defence of the compatibility of Darwinism and theistic religion.]

Popper, K. (1976). 'Darwinism as a Metaphysical Research Programme', *Unended Quest: An Intellectual Autobiography*, London: Fontana, Ch. 37, 167–180. [Popper's oft-cited – albeit frankly wrong-headed – argument that Darwinism is not in fact a scientific theory but actually a 'metaphysical research programme'.]

Ruse, M. (1986). *Taking Darwin Seriously: A Naturalistic Approach to Philosophy*, Oxford: Blackwell. [Classic exploration of Darwinism's implications for (particularly) epistemology and other key areas of philosophy.]

Ruse, M. (1989). *The Darwinian Paradigm*, London: Routledge. [Accessible, thorough collection of essays on Darwinism's implications for philosophy, science, religion and ethics.]

Sober, E. (2004). *The Nature of Selection: Evolutionary Theory in Philosophical Focus*, Cambridge: MIT Press. [Comprehensive, more advanced survey of key philosophical debates in evolution and natural selection.]

Stamos, D. (1996). 'Popper, Falsifiability, and Evolutionary Biology', *Biology and Philosophy* 11: 161–191. [Useful critical account of Popper's reading (misreading?) of the potential for falsification of evolution by natural selection.]

Sterelny, K. and Griffiths, P. (1999). *Sex and Death: An Introduction to Philosophy of Biology*, Chicago: University of Chicago Press. [Extremely comprehensive, detailed survey of just about all the scientific/philosophical debates centred on natural selection and evolutionary theory.]

Internet resources

Brandon, R. (2014). 'Natural Selection', *Stanford Encyclopedia of Philosophy* ed. E. Zalta, https://plato.stanford.edu/archives/spr2014/entries/natural-selection/. [Very thorough overview of natural selection's development and implications].

De Cruz, H. (2017). 'Religion and Science', *Stanford Encyclopedia of Philosophy*, ed. E. Zalta, https://plato.stanford.edu/archives/spr2017/entries/religion-science/. [Judicious and thorough introduction to a wide variety of issues of shared interest between science and religion].

Lloyd, E. (2012). 'Units and Levels of Selection', *The Stanford Encyclopedia of Philosophy* ed. E. Zalta, https://plato.stanford.edu/archives/win2012/entries/selection-units/. [Thorough and readable survey of debates over the nature of replicators and the levels of selection generally].

5　Is there a fundamental tension between faith and rationality?

Duncan Pritchard

Introduction

One of the big questions about the nature of religious belief is whether such belief can ever be rational. Note that this is a separate question about whether religious beliefs are *true*, since one can have false but rational beliefs. If you claim that God exists, and I maintain that He doesn't, then only one of us can be right. Even so, we might both be rational in holding the position that we do. (For comparison, imagine two scientists arguing about a particular scientific claim. Only one of them can be right. Nonetheless, they might both be being rational in believing what they do.)

A related question we can ask about religious belief is whether it can ever amount to knowledge. Unlike mere rational belief, knowledge *does* demand truth, in that one cannot know a falsehood. So if you claim that God exists, and I maintain that He doesn't, then *at most* only one of us can know what we claim. A natural way of thinking about knowledge, which we will adopt here, is that knowledge results when one has a belief that is both rational and true.

These questions about the rationality of religious belief, and the possibility of religious knowledge, have been extensively covered within the philosophical field of **epistemology**. This is because this is an area of philosophy that is specifically concerned with the nature of knowledge and rationality. The goal of this chapter is to provide an overview of some of the main positions that have been offered within epistemology regarding religious belief.

Evidentialism

One natural way of thinking about whether religious belief is rational – and thereby potentially amounting to knowledge – is to examine the *evidence* that religious believers can offer in support of their beliefs. After all, that's usually how we assess how a belief is rational. Ordinarily, at least, if you have good evidence for believing something, then that belief counts as rational even if it turns out to be false. (Think about the scientist on the losing side from the example offered above. Although ultimately wrong, if she has good evidence in support of what she claimed, she would still count as rational.)

On the face of it, there is lots of evidence that a religious believer can offer in support of what they believe, such as their personal religious experiences, the evidence of scripture, testimony from peers in their religious community, and so on. But one might think that evidence of this kind is precisely of the wrong sort, in that it already presupposes the general truth of the subject's religious beliefs. For example, if there is no God, then why would we suppose that scripture offers any good evidence in support of religious belief?

The thought in play here is that the kind of evidence that is relevant for determining whether religious belief is rational needs to be in a certain sense *independent* of the subject's religious beliefs. What kind of evidence might work in this regard? The traditional answer to this question – offered by a position known as **evidentialism**, and historically associated with the work of John Locke (1632–1704) – is that what is required is evidence that any rational person ought to be able to recognise as good evidence. Imagine, for example, that one could prove, by reason alone, that God existed. This would be evidence that supported belief in God's existence that every rational person ought to recognise as good evidence. Moreover, unlike the kinds of evidence cited above, such as evidence from scripture, this is not evidence that requires you to already believe that God exists before you would consider it good evidence in support of a religious belief.

Can one prove that God exists (or, indeed, any other religious claim)? Historically, at least, many have attempted such proofs. Some have argued, for example, that one can reason from the very nature of God that He must exist (this is known as the *ontological argument*). Others have claimed that there must logically be a first cause to everything that exists, and that since the only thing that could potentially perform this role would be God, then that proves that He must exist (this is known as the *teleological argument*). These 'proofs' have been highly controversial, however, and few people today think that they represent a good way of supporting the rationality of religious belief.

There is, however, a slightly weaker kind of argument for God's existence which, while falling short of a proof, seems to satisfy the demands of evidentialism. This is the claim that there is overwhelming evidence in nature of the existence of a designer who brought the universe into existence, which is in turn evidence that there must be a God (this is known as the *design argument*). Notice that unlike the proofs just considered, which only appeal to reason, this argument appeals also to what we know about the world around us. Nonetheless, proponents of the design argument claim that the evidence is such that any rational person ought to accept that it is good evidence for the truth of at least the religious belief that God exists.

Fideism

Evidentialism puts very austere demands on the defence of the rationality of religious belief, demands that are hard to satisfy. A radically different way of thinking about the epistemology of religious belief is offered by *fideism*, a position that has been associated with the work of such figures as Søren Kierkegaard (1813–1855) and Ludwig Wittgenstein (1889–1951). According to fideism, it is simply mistaken to think that religious belief is the kind of thing that should be assessed epistemologically in terms of whether it is rational or ever amounts to knowledge. Note that the claim is not that all religious belief is irrational either, but rather that to apply categories like this to religious belief is to misunderstand it. Religious belief is rather essentially *arational* (i.e., neither rational nor irrational).

On this proposal, we should take seriously the idea that religious conviction is often a matter of faith, and hence very different from other kinds of belief that are formed by weighing up the evidence. Typically, after all, someone with religious conviction doesn't acquire that conviction because they think they have excellent evidence for what they believe (even if they do think that they have such evidence). Relatedly, we expect someone to persevere with their religious conviction even if that belief is challenged by counterevidence by those around them (e.g., by those who claim that religious belief is a delusion). This suggests that it might be a mistake to think that religious belief is even in the market for rationality (and hence knowledge).

Reformed epistemology

Fideism is a fairly radical way of responding to the challenge posed to the possibility of rational religious belief by evidentialism. A more moderate way of proceeding is offered by *reformed epistemology*, as most prominently defended by the American philosopher, Alvin Plantinga (b. 1832). According to this proposal, it is possible to have rational religious belief and religious knowledge so long as we hold religious belief to the same epistemic standards we apply to ordinary belief.

Consider ordinary perceptual belief, for example, such your beliefs right now about what is happening around you, formed via your senses, such as your sight. This seems like a paradigmatic way of forming rational beliefs about one's immediate environment and thereby coming to know truths about that environment. Interestingly, however, the evidence that one can cite in support of one's perceptual knowledge doesn't seem to meet the kinds of epistemic standards demanded by evidentialism with regard to religious belief. Indeed, for many of our perceptual beliefs we don't seem to have much, if any, evidence in support of what we believe at all. We rather simply believe what we see. Moreover, where we are able to offer evidence in support of our perceptual beliefs, this doesn't seem to meet the kind of requirement of independence laid down by evidentialism for religious belief. This is because the way that we often verify our perceptual beliefs is via perception itself (i.e., by doing more perceiving). In fact, many epistemologists accept that this is the only way we can offer evidential support for our perceptual beliefs, in that we simply do not have an independent basis for thinking that our senses are reliable.

And yet none of this seems to be at all a barrier to having rational perceptual beliefs or possessing perpetual knowledge. In particular, so long as our perceptual faculties are functioning appropriately in the right kinds of conditions, then this seems to suffice for both rational perceptual belief and perceptual knowledge, even in cases where we have no evidence in favour of our perceptual beliefs, or where the evidence we can offer is only itself perceptual.

The point being made by proponents of reformed epistemology is that a double standard is being employed when the rationality of religious belief is criticised on the grounds that it doesn't satisfy the epistemic standards demanded by evidentialism. For if perceptual belief also doesn't meet those standards, and yet we commonly think that this kind of belief is perfectly in order as it is, then why can't we say just the same about religious belief? In particular, why can't religious belief be generally rational, and amount to religious knowledge, simply in virtue of being formed in an appropriate way in the right kind of conditions? If that's right, then lacking evidence in support of one's religious beliefs, or in any case lacking non-independent evidence, might not be a barrier to rational religious belief and religious knowledge.

But what does it mean to say that religious beliefs, like perceptual beliefs, can be rational when formed in an appropriate way in the right kind of conditions? Here is where reformed epistemologists have a positive claim to make. They contend that just as our perceptual beliefs are formed via our innate sensory faculties, so we all of us have an innate religious faculty – what is known as the ***sensus divinitatis*** – that enables us to form religious beliefs. If this faculty is functioning appropriately in the right conditions, then just as our perceptual faculty can deliver us rational perceptual beliefs, so too can our religious faculty deliver us rational religious beliefs.

Now, one might object that there are relevant disanalogies between perceptual belief and religious belief. For one thing, our perceptual faculties are common to all of us, but only some of us have religious beliefs. Isn't that itself a reason to be sceptical of the *sensus divinitatis*? Why should someone who lacks religious belief be at all persuaded by the fact that religious believers can offer evidence in support of their claim that already presuppose the broad truth of what they believe? Relatedly, why should a non-believer be persuaded by an account of the rationality of religious belief that appeals to a divine faculty, a faulty that the non-believer will think is non-existent?

But notice that we have here subtly changed the question that we are asking. We want to know whether religious belief is rational, and that is not the same as whether there are reasons to hold it that even someone who is not religious would accept. The latter is a much more demanding epistemic standard, and one that reformed epistemologists explicitly resist. For example, suppose that you are in a shop and you see a local pillar of the community – someone widely accepted by all – steal something from the store. You may well grant that no-one is going to believe you that you did indeed see this, given how well-regarded this woman is by her peers. Nonetheless, since you did indeed see this for yourself, wouldn't you be rational to believe what you do (i.e., that she stole the item in question)? The point is that having a belief that is rational is not the same thing as having a belief that has evidential support that everyone will accept.

The question is thus not whether the defence of the rationality of religious belief offered by reformed epistemology would persuade a non-believer. According to reformed epistemology, once we set this question to one side, then we ought to recognise that it is offering an account of the rationality of religious belief that is at least as good as the account we generally offer of the rationality of perceptual belief. Thus, by parity of reasoning, they claim that if we wish to treat perceptual belief as rational, and amounting to perceptual knowledge when true, then we should do the same with regard to religious belief.

Quasi-fideism

We saw that reformed epistemology defends the rationality of religious belief by arguing that it is on an epistemic par with a form of belief that we tend to grant is rational (i.e., perceptual belief). **Quasi-fideism** makes a similar claim, though draws a rather different conclusion. Recall that reformed epistemologists argue that many of our perceptual beliefs lack evidential support, but are no less rational as a result, and proceed on this basis to claim that our religious beliefs can lack evidential support and yet still be rational and in the market for knowledge.

According to quasi-fideism, in contrast, many of our most basic convictions – whether regarding religious matters, or regarding everyday life – are not only lacking in evidential support, but are essentially arational in the sense we saw outlined by fideism above. That is, at the core our beliefs we do not find basic commitments that have a special kind of evidential status (as evidentialism would demand) or which are lacking in evidence but rational nonetheless (as reformed epistemology maintains). Rather, what we find is a kind of *faith* instead. The common thread between reformed epistemology and quasi-fideism is thus a kind of appeal to parity. But whereas reformed epistemologists hold that our basic non-religious beliefs – e.g., our perceptual beliefs – are rational even though lacking in evidence, and hence make a parallel claim for our basic religious beliefs, quasi-fideists make a very different kind of parity claim. They maintain that although our basic religious convictions are essentially arational, this is not a mark against the rationality of our non-basic religious beliefs because *all* belief, religious or otherwise, has arational commitments at its heart. So unless one is to argue that belief in general is not rational, then one is obliged, via parity of reasoning, to allow that non-basic religious belief can be rational even though it has arational basic religious commitments at its core.

Notice that quasi-fideism is very different to fideism. The fideist says that *all* religious belief is essentially arational, whereas the quasi-fideist only claims that our most basic religious convictions are essentially arational. Moreover, she maintains that this feature of our most basic religious convictions is shared with our most basic convictions more generally. This means that religious belief is not being held to a different kind of epistemic standard to ordinary belief, as is the case with fideism (which holds that religious belief, unlike ordinary belief, should not be held to any epistemic standard at all).

Religious exemplars

The final account of the rationality of religious belief that we will look at, like the last two accounts just discussed, also draws parallels between religious belief and other forms of belief that we generally hold are rational. Unlike reformed epistemology and quasi-fideism, however, the proponent of this account thinks that the kind of ordinary non-religious belief that we should examine in this regard is precisely *not* perceptual, but rather domains of belief like ethics or **aesthetics**. For want of a better name (as far as I know this view hasn't yet been given a name, though one can find plenty of presentations of it in the literature), we will call this proposal the ***exemplar account***, for reasons that will become apparent.

Let's focus on our ethical beliefs (even though a lot of what we will be saying also applies to our aesthetical beliefs, too, and perhaps other domains of belief as well). There are some interesting features of the ethical realm, at least as it is ordinarily understood, that deserve emphasis. One is the role of a distinctive kind of *ethical expertise* that one can acquire over time, such that one has a special ***sensitivity*** to what is ethically demanded of one. Another is the importance of certain kinds of *ethical experiences*. This second feature is closely related to the first, in that often these experiences are required in order to hone one's ethical expertise. A third feature is the role of *ethical exemplars* in this domain, people who are held to have a special kind of ethical expertise – *ethical wisdom*, if you will – and who are people that one should aim to emulate if one is to enhance one's own ethical sensibilities. Ethical exemplars are people with very refined ethical skills, acquired in part through having appropriate ethical experiences.

Let us grant for the sake of argument that the ethical domain has these features. The important point for our purposes is that on this supposition, it is a domain very unlike the perceptual domain of belief, in that in the latter case there is no corresponding role for special kinds of experience or sophisticated expertise (at least not in the sense that the expertise is related to wisdom anyway). Defenders of the exemplar account claim that the right model of everyday belief to focus on with regard to drawing parallels between the rationality of religious belief and of everyday belief is precisely a domain like ethical belief, for all the features just noted. In particular, they maintain that we acquire rational religious belief and religious knowledge not merely passively, as we do in the perceptual case, but rather through having distinctive kinds of experiences, developing distinctive kinds of expertise and **sensitivity** to the relevant facts, and, most importantly, by learning from, and emulating, religious exemplars. It is these exemplars who pass on their wisdom within this domain, and who can help us to develop our religious sensibilities.

One problem with this approach is that whereas the perceptual domain is generally regarded as delivering us with knowledge and rational belief, there is no corresponding consensus when it comes to the ethical domain (much less other domains in the vicinity, such as the aesthetical domain). Most will agree that there are facts of the matter regarding the world around us that perception is tracking, for example. Are there ethical facts that our ethical sensibilities are tracking? But, if not, then how can there be rational ethical belief, much less ethical knowledge? One might thus be similarly worried about the epistemic standing of our religious beliefs, if this is the right way to think about their epistemology.

Chapter summary

- Our focus is on whether there can be rational religious beliefs and, relatedly, religious knowledge. These are questions that are asked within a field of philosophy known as *epistemology*.
- According to *evidentialism*, rational religious belief demands appropriate evidential support. The kind of evidential support that evidentialism claims is appropriate, however, is independent of religious belief itself, which is why it tends to focus on the plausibility of purely rational proofs of God's existence.
- In stark contrast to evidentialism, *fideism* maintains that we are not to rationally evaluate religious belief in the same way that we rationality evaluate other kinds of belief, such as perceptual belief. Instead, we should recognise that religious belief is essentially *arational*, in that, in virtue of being immune to rational evaluation, it is neither rational nor irrational.
- *Reformed epistemology* offers an intermediate position between evidentialism and fideism. According to this proposal, religious belief is no less rational than perceptual belief, a variety of belief that is widely held to be rational. In particular, perceptual belief is often formed without any supporting evidence, and certainly without any independent (i.e., non-perceptual) supporting evidence, and yet it is nonetheless regarded as rational. What makes it rational is that it is formed via a reliable perceptual faculty functioning appropriately in the right kind of conditions. Accordingly, proponents of reformed epistemology argue that religious belief can also be rational, and hence can amount to religious knowledge, so long as, like perceptual belief, it is formed appropriately via a religious faculty (known as the *sensus divinitatis*), even when it is lacking in supporting evidence.
- *Quasi-fideism* also presents us with an intermediate position between evidentialism and fideism. Like reformed epistemology, it claims that we should be careful to epistemically evaluate religious belief in the same way as we evaluate ordinary belief. But whereas reformed epistemology thinks that basic religious belief, like basic perceptual belief, can be rational even though it lacks evidential support, quasi-fideism claims that both are essentially arational. Unlike fideism, however, quasi-fideism maintains that non-basic religious belief is no less rational as a result. Moreover, this claim is defended by appealing to the fact that most everyday beliefs are regarded as rational, and yet quasi-fideists maintain that even these beliefs have arational commitments at their core. Thus, by parity of reasoning, if everyday non-basic belief is rational, then so too is non-basic religious belief.
- According to the *exemplar account*, it is a mistake to compare religious belief to perceptual belief (as, for example, reformed epistemologists do).

We should instead look for similarities with other domains, such as ethics. What is distinctive about ethical practice is that it incorporates a special role for expertise, wisdom, and a distinctive kind of experience. One consequence of the exemplar account is thus that there is an important role for religious exemplars to play in one's religious epistemology (just as ethical exemplars play an important role in our ethical epistemology). But one problem that arises when appealing to an analogy with realms like the ethical is that one might be sceptical about the possibility of rational belief and knowledge in precisely these domains.

Study questions

1. Why might one be sceptical about the rationality of religious belief? Should we be? Defend your answer.
2. What kind of evidential demands are made on rational religious belief by evidentialism? Are they legitimate?
3. What is fideism, and why might one claim that this is the right way to think about the epistemology of religious belief?
4. What is reformed epistemology, and how does it go about defending the rationality of religious belief?
5. What is the *sensus divinitatis*, and what role does it play in reformed epistemology?
6. What is quasi-fideism, and how is it different from fideism? Is it plausible, do you think?
7. What role, if any, should religious exemplars play in our account of the epistemology of religious belief?
8. Does it matter that an account of the rationality of religious belief appeals to considerations that a non-believer will reject? Defend your answer.
9. Is religious belief essentially similar to belief in other kinds of domain, like perception or ethics? If so, which ones, and what (if anything) does this show us? If not, why not, and what (if anything) does this show us?

Introductory readings

Nielsen, K. (1967). 'Wittgensteinian Fideism', *Philosophy* 42, 237–54. [A famous discussion of fideism, and the fact that such a view is often attributed to Ludwig Wittgenstein.]

Pritchard, D. H. (2017). 'Faith and Reason', *Philosophy*. (forthcoming) [Presents an accessible account of some core issues with regard to the epistemology of religious belief, and in the process defends a version of quasi-fideism that he attributes to John Henry Newman and Ludwig Wittgenstein.]

Zagzebski, L. (2010). 'Religious Knowledge', *Routledge Companion to Epistemology*, S. Bernecker and D. H. Pritchard (eds.), chapter 36, London: Routledge. [Offers a nice overview of the epistemology of religious belief, while also presenting a helpful summary of what we are here calling the exemplar account.]

Advanced readings

Phillips, D. Z. (1976). *Religion without Explanation*, Oxford: Oxford University Press. [An important presentation of a form of fideism.]

Plantinga, A. (1983). 'Reason and Belief in God', *Faith and Rationality*, A. Plantinga and N. Wolterstorff (eds.), 16–93, Notre Dame, Indiana: University of Notre Dame Press. [An influential defence of reformed epistemology.]

Swinburne, R. (1979). *The Existence of God*, Oxford: Oxford University Press. [A significant defence of the rationality of religious belief, along broadly the lines demanded by evidentialism.]

Internet resources

Amesbury, R. (2016). 'Fideism', *Stanford Enclyopedia of Philosophy*, E. Zalta (ed.), http://plato.stanford.edu/entries/fideism/. [An excellent overview of the nature and history of fideism.]

Clark, K. J. (2016). 'Religious Epistemology', *Internet Encyclopedia of Philosophy*, J. Fieser and B. Dowden (eds.), www.iep.utm.edu/relig-ep/. [A helpful introduction to some of the core issues in religious epistemology.]

Forrest, P. (2013). 'The Epistemology of Religion', *Stanford Enclyopedia of Philosophy*, E. Zalta (ed.), http://plato.stanford.edu/entries/religion-epistemology/. [A first-rate presentation of the main topics related to religious epistemology.]

Swindal, J. (2016). 'Faith and Reason', *Internet Encyclopedia of Philosophy*, J. Fieser and B. Dowden (eds.), www.iep.utm.edu/faith-re/. [A useful introduction to the some of the central issues regarding faith and rationality.]

6   Is God hidden, or does God simply not exist?

Ian M. Church

"Why, O Lord, do you stand far away? Why do you hide yourself in times of trouble?"

Psalm 10:1, ESV

Introduction

The Black Death reached its climax in Europe from around 1346–1353. One of its salient features is that the Black Death did not seem to care just how pious or good its victim was – it afflicted the wicked and the virtuous all the same. The Black Death seemed to have little regard for social status or moral or religious character. People cried out to God for help and mercy, but God often seemed silent and hidden.

And many of us have experienced something like this in our own lives. To many of us, in times of suffering, God can seem completely hidden. God can seem silent.

Of course, one of the things we see in these situations is the problem of evil. If God is all-good, all-powerful, and all-knowing, how can needless evil – including the suffering of ostensibly innocent (if not good) people – happen? And given that such evil *does* occur, doesn't that at least cast serious doubt on the existence of such a God (here and throughout this essay, understood broadly within the Jewish and Christian traditions)? But there is another, related worry lurking in the neighborhood. When God seems so silent and hidden – especially in times of tremendous need – this can create what we might call the **existential problem of divine hiddenness**. As Daniel Howard-Snyder and Paul Moser note, "The existential problem often takes the form of a crises of faith, sometimes leading to a collapse of trust in God" (2002, 1). To be sure, the experience of evil is not strictly necessary for the existential problem of divine hiddenness – God can seem hidden in benign times or even good times – but the experience of evil makes the apparent hiddenness of God all the more apparent and distressing. For many faiths, a personal relationship with God is incredibly important, and not just for any soteriological role such a relationship might play but *for general human flourishing*. As such, when God seems hidden – particularly in times of acute suffering and pain – this can create a serious existential problem indeed. As Howard-Snyder and Moser explain, if God seems hidden to the people in these faith communities, "the world appears as an uncaring, inhospitable place. Despair over life itself then, is a natural result of divine hiddenness" (2002, 2).

While the existential problem of divine hiddenness is serious and broadly experienced, the philosophical literature has focused less on the *existential* angst posed by divine hiddenness and more on how the hiddenness of God poses a serious, *evidential* obstacle for theistic belief. In his seminal work, *Divine Hiddenness and Human Reason* (1993), **John Schellenberg** powerfully argued, in sum, that if God is perfectly loving, he would make it so that anyone capable of having a personal relationship with him would be able to reasonably believe that God exists. Given that some people do *not* believe in the existence of God – and after careful, sincere investigation and due to no fault of their own – then such a perfectly loving God does not exist.

In this essay, along with most of the contemporary philosophical literature, we will focus on the problem of divine hiddenness *as an argument against theistic belief*, and not as an existential problem. (As such, hereafter whenever I refer to the problem of divine hiddenness, I'm referring to the **evidential problem of divine hiddenness**, the argument against theistic belief, and not the *existential* problem.)

§1 A summary of the argument

As I mentioned above, John Schellenberg's landmark book, *Divine Hiddenness and Human Reason* (1993), is the seminal work on the problem of divine hiddenness. As Daniel Howard-Snyder and Adam Green nicely summarize Schellenberg's argument:

(1) There are people who are capable of relating personally to God but who, through no fault of their own, fail to believe.
(2) If there is a personal God who is unsurpassably great, then there are no such people.
(3) So, there is no such God (from 1 and 2).

(2016, sec. 2)

Obviously, if a theist wants to maintain their theism – and reject the conclusion of that argument – they need to be able to viably reject one of the two premises. At first blush, the first premise seems entirely incontrovertible and innocuous. It seems perfectly clear that if someone was from a society or culture that was relatively untouched by something like a traditional brand of theism, that they might live their entire lives without believing in God, due to no fault of their own. What is more, many atheists and agnostics seem to honestly and carefully consider the case for theism and don't become theists; and it might seem like a rare case indeed to discover an atheist or agnostic who rejects theism out of an explicit hatred for God or religion in general. Indeed, it seems like it would be tantamount to intellectual arrogance if a theist concluded that an atheist or an agnostic was somehow epistemically or intellectually derelict simply because they aren't theists. On what grounds could a theist challenge the intellectual integrity of every atheist and agnostic on this issue? As incontrovertible as this assumption seems to be, it is nevertheless an assumption. Let's call it the ***no-fault assumption***.

The second premise might seem a bit more suspect – or at least it doesn't seem as overtly plausible as the first premise – and so this might be what a theist looking to maintain their theism might first consider rejecting. After all, why think that a personal God who is unsurpassingly great would preclude the possibility of some-one both (i) being capable of having a personal relationship to God and (ii) never-theless failing to believe in the existence of God due to no fault of their own? Daniel Howard-Snyder and Adam Green helpfully summarize Schellenberg's argument for premise two (as it is found in his 1993 work):

(2a)   If there is a personal God who is unsurpassably great, then there is a personal God who is unsurpassably loving.

(2b)   If there is a personal God who is unsurpassably loving, then for any human person H and any time t, if H is at t capable of relating personally to God, H has it within H's power at t to do so (i.e., will do so, just by choosing), unless H is culpably in a contrary position at t.

(2c)   For any human person H and any time t, H has it within H's power at t to relate personally to God only if H at t believes that God exists.

(2d)   So, if there is a personal God who is unsurpassably great, then for any human person H and any time t, if H is at t capable of relating personally to God, H at t believes that God exists, unless H is culpably in a contrary position at t (from 2a through 2c).

(2016, sec. 2)

And insofar as this conclusion (2d) is meant to be, as Howard-Snyder and Green put it, "tantamount to [the second premise] of the main argument," this argument gives us a proof for the premise under consideration (2016, sec. 2). So if a theist wants to reject the second premise of the main argument (2) so as to maintain their theism, they will need to reject one of these premises that lead us to the conclusion of 2d.

Few traditional theists (or at least theists from the Judeo-Christian tradition) would want to deny that God is unsurpassingly great or that he is unsurpassingly loving. While there might be some question about what it means for God to be unsurpassingly loving, few theists would want to deny outright that God has this characteristic. Premise 2a seems fairly incontrovertible.

Likewise, it would be difficult for a theist to reject premise 2c. It might seem pretty clear that someone can't have a personal relationship with an agent or thing if they don't think that agent or thing exists. (Though this can be a point of conten-tion within the philosophical literature.) Even in cases of non-existent imaginary friends, insofar as we're willing to grant that someone could have a personal rela-tionship with a non-existent imaginary friend, we would presumably require that at least that person believe that their imaginary friend exists.

So that leaves the theist with premise 2b. Thankfully for the theist, there seems to be more room for disagreement here. That said, 2b certainly seems to enjoy some intuitive plausibility. While there is certainly a lot to say here, the basic idea is that if God is personal and unsurpassably loving – as we granted with premise 2a – then such a God would make it so that people who are capable of having a relationship with him would be able to do so. Of course, that won't guarantee that everyone has a personal relationship with God – maybe due to rebellion or sin, some people culpably resist. Given that being in a relationship with God is extremely desirable – indeed, according to many theists, such a relationship is essential to human flourishing – we would reasonably expect a perfectly loving God to make it so that such a relationship is within everyone's grasp. If God was perfectly loving, then, **non-culpable non-belief** would not exist. But once we grant this, then it is going to seem difficult to reject the conclusion at 2d and subsequently the conclusion at 3. Let's call this the ***perfectly loving assumption***. Of course, a theist may respond – indeed many theists *do* respond – by asking what exactly it means for God to be perfectly loving. If the case could be made that God could be perfectly loving without leading to the conclusion that non-culpable non-belief wouldn't exist – without entailing the idea that God would make his existence sufficiently manifest to everyone (or at least everyone capable of having a relationship with him) – then perhaps the conclusion of the problem of divine hiddenness can be avoided.

§2 Some objections

Perhaps the most prevalent strategy for rejecting the problem of divine hiddenness focuses on rejecting *the perfectly loving assumption* – the assumption that because God is perfectly loving, he would make his existence sufficiently manifest to everyone (or at least everyone capable of having a relationship with him). In other words, many responses to the problem of divine hiddenness have tried to find a reason why a perfectly loving God would (either via commission or omission) allow for situations where someone who is capable of a personal relationship with God nevertheless non-culpably fails to believe that God exists. Maybe sometimes God would allow for non-culpable non-belief of this sort because to make his existence manifestly clear (at least in some situations) would objectionably infringe upon a person's moral autonomy. Or maybe sometimes God would allow for non-culpable non-belief of that sort because beholding God's perfection and glory would make certain people (at certain times) jealous and resentful. Or maybe *the perfectly loving assumption* is misguided because God is transcendent and somehow beyond our understanding of love. Or maybe sometimes God allows for non-culpable non-belief of that sort in someone because they're interested in having a relationship with God for the wrong reasons. Or maybe we could make the case that there *could be* reasons for God to hide himself from some people, but we simply don't know them. If we could find reasons like these (or at least make logical room for them) that a perfectly loving God might have for being hidden from people who would otherwise be capable of a relationship with God, then we might be able to find ways to reject *the perfectly loving assumption* and resist the problem of divine hiddenness's conclusion.

And it's worth noting that such philosophical responses potentially have theological support – though such arguments don't rest on this support. For example, in Romans 9, the Apostle Paul controversially seems to give a picture of God where God chooses to have a salvific relationship with some while also choosing to withhold that relationship with others. For many, this is a troubling passage, and a tremendous amount of theological energy has been spent trying to unpack and exegete it. And while such exegesis is beyond the scope of this chapter, such passages could arguably serve as grounds for rejecting the second premise of problem of divine hiddenness we saw in the previous section. They can be used to motivate rejecting the idea that God must be perfectly loving in such a way that would entail that he would make it so that anyone capable of having a personal relationship with him would be able to reasonably believe that God exists. Perhaps God has good reasons – or perhaps it is a part of his sovereign plan – for hiding himself from some people while revealing himself to others.

Other Biblical passages arguably lend credence to such a possibility. There are places in the book of Exodus where God explicitly seems to "harden the heart" of Pharaoh (see Exodus 4:21; 7:3; 9:12; 10:1; 10:20; 10:27; 11:10; 14:4; 14:8). Similarly, in 1 Kings 22:19–23, God explicitly sends a "lying spirit" to deceive Ahab, the King of Israel, which eventually leads to his destruction. And given that having a "hardened heart" or a "lying spirit" seems to preclude having a healthy, personal relationship with God, then God doesn't seem to necessarily want to have a relationship with everyone, contra *the perfectly loving assumption*. And if God doesn't want a relationship with everyone, then either he's not truly perfectly loving or being perfectly loving somehow doesn't entail wanting a relationship with everyone. In either case, there's arguably scriptural precedent for rejecting the second premise of the evidential problem of divine hiddenness.

Another strategy for responding to the problem of divine hiddenness is rejecting what seems like the far more incontrovertible and innocuous assumption, *the no-fault assumption*. While this particular response has not enjoyed as much focused attention in the philosophical literature, it's worth mentioning at least briefly because certain religious communities might have theological or scriptural reasons for rejecting *the no-fault assumption*.

Paul's letter to the Romans again could arguably give someone material for rejecting what initially seems like a plausible assumption: that someone could be epistemically non-culpable in non-belief, be it atheism or **agnosticism**. In Romans 1:18–21, Paul seems to reject that assumption, implying that the existence of God has "been clearly perceived, ever since the creation of the world, in the things that have been made. So [people who have suppressed the truth] are without excuse." And again, this isn't an isolated passage; other Biblical passages seem to point to similar conclusions. The writers of the Psalms seem to routinely find clear evidence for God in creation (see, for example, Psalm 19 and Psalm 148), and we see similar sentiment repeated elsewhere in the Old Testament (see, for example, Job

12 and Isaiah 55). Within the Jewish and Christian traditions, there seems to be an assumption that the presence of God is sufficiently manifest in the world. And as such, a theist from such a tradition could plausibly reject the first premise of the argument from divine hiddenness noted above.

Both of these responses to divine hiddenness – the rejection of the assumption that God, being perfectly loving, wants a relationship with everyone and the rejection of the idea that non-belief can be non-culpable – face their own rejoinders. First of all, if we reject the idea that God is perfectly loving or the idea that being perfectly loving somehow entails wanting a relationship with everyone, then there is a real worry that we'll be left with a God who purposefully hides himself from some people – making a personal relationship with God extremely difficult, if not impossible, for those people. And if we think that having such a relationship with God is critically important for human flourishing – and depending on one's theological bent, singularly essential for one's eternal salvation – a God who willingly hides himself from some people seems, at least to many people, morally repugnant.

Alternatively, if we reject the plausible assumption that someone can non-culpably reject theism (in the form of atheism or agnosticism) – the assumption that someone can carefully and honestly consider the evidence for theism and nevertheless remain agnostic or atheistic – then other worries need to be addressed. If two intellectual peers – interlocutors who are equally intelligent, informed, and educated – disagree about a particular issue, it would seem intellectually *arrogant* for one of them to simply dismiss out of hand the other's disagreement as disingenuous or the product of faulty (or sinful) cognitive faculties. That's not how productive, honest disagreements are supposed to work. As such, if a theist were to reject the problem of divine hiddenness on the grounds that atheism or agnosticism are the result of the noetic effects of sin or some cognitive malfunction, then the debate seems to grind to a halt. The theist, when employing such a strategy, seems antagonistic, unfriendly, and belligerent – leaving little common ground between theists and non-theists.

Conclusion

In summary, then, according to the evidential problem of divine hiddenness, *if God is perfectly loving, he would make it so that anyone capable of having a personal relationship with him would be able to reasonably believe that God exists. Given that some people do not believe in the existence of God – and after careful, sincere investigation and due to no fault of their own – then such a perfectly loving God does not exist.* As we saw, however, such an argument rests on two key assumptions: *the perfectly loving assumption*, the assumption that because God is perfectly loving he would make his existence sufficiently manifest to everyone (or at least everyone capable of having a relationship with him); and *the no-fault assumption*, the assumption that someone can sincerely and honestly consider the question as to whether or not God exists and non-culpably maintain non-theistic belief (agnosticism or atheism).

Both assumptions can be rejected so as to avoid the problem of divine hiddenness's conclusion; however, doing so comes with challenges. If we are going to try to reject to the conclusion of the problem of divine hiddenness by denying the *perfectly loving assumption*, then special care needs to be taken to describe how God might be perfectly loving and yet purposefully hide himself from some people in certain circumstances or contexts. Alternatively, if we are going to try to reject the conclusion of the problem of divine hiddenness by denying the *no-fault assumption*, then it seems like special care needs to be taken to explain away nonbelief in a friendlier way – in a way that doesn't hide a blind arrogance or dogmatism.

Happily, the philosophical debate continues to develop. John Schellenberg, among many others, continues to refine and strengthen the problem – making it all the more problematic for theists! And research continues to develop that might help explain what it means for God to be perfectly loving and why God might sometimes be hidden for good reasons. Other theorists are developing new (and perhaps more *friendly*) ways to explain non-belief (i.e., agnosticism and atheism), and others are exploring how *unfriendly* approaches might yet be correct.

Chapter summary

- We distinguished the *existential* problem of divine hiddenness from the *evidential* problem of divine hiddenness. The former is primarily concerned with the apparent hiddenness of a personal God in the lives of believers amidst terrible suffering. The latter is primarily concerned with the apparent hiddenness of God being evidence against God's existence.
- In "A summary of the argument," we highlighted the basic contours of the evidential problem of divine hiddenness, and suggested that the argument rests on two important assumptions: *the perfectly loving assumption* and *the no-fault assumption*.
- In "Some objections," a few possible responses to the evidential problem of divine hiddenness were considered, which center on rejecting either *the perfectly loving assumption* or *the no-fault assumption*.

Study questions

1. If God is supposed to be perfectly loving, then should we expect him to sufficiently reveal himself to all rational agents capable of having a relationship with him? Why or why not?
2. What role can religious texts (e.g., the Bible) play in generating a philosophical response to the problem of divine hiddenness?
3. What relationship do you think the existential problem of divine hiddenness bears to the evidential problem of divine hiddenness?

4. How might the rejection of *the no-fault assumption* be perceived as intellectual arrogance? Does a commitment to intellectual *humility* commit us to the no-fault assumption?
5. Is there a viable, friendly way to reject the no-fault assumption?
6. Contemporary research in **cognitive science of religion** is making great strides in helping us empirically understand why some people have religious beliefs and others don't. How might this research be brought to bear to the problem of divine hiddenness?
7. Our religious beliefs (or lack thereof) are often shaped by our families, communities, and cultures. How might a better understanding of such influences be brought to bear on the problem of divine hiddenness?

Introductory readings

Barrett, Justin L. 2004. *Why Would Anyone Believe in God?* Walnut Creek, CA: AltaMira Press. [While not directly about the problem of divine hiddenness, this book brings together a lot of relevant empirical research into religious belief and non-belief.].

Garcia, Laura L. 2002. "St. John of the Cross and the Necessity of Divine Hiddenness." In *Divine Hiddenness: New Essays*, edited by Daniel Howard-Snyder and Paul K. Moser, 83–97. Cambridge: Cambridge University Press. [An excellent introduction to the *existential* problem of divine hiddenness; although not the main focus of this chapter, this is an incredibly important variant of the problem of divine hiddenness.]

Howard-Snyder, Daniel, and Paul K. Moser. 2002. "Introduction: The Hiddenness of God." In *Divine Hiddenness: New Essays*, edited by Daniel Howard-Snyder; Paul K. Moser. Cambridge: Cambridge University Press. [This is the introduction to the Howard-Snyer and Moser's edited collection on divine hiddenness, and it does an excellent job summarizing the relevant issues and debates.]

Schellenberg, J. L. 1993. *Divine Hiddenness and Human Reason*. Ithaca: Cornell University Press. [This is arguably *the* seminal work that established the problem of divine hiddenness in the philosophical literature.]

Advanced readings

Audi, Robert. 2011. *Rationality and Religious Commitment*. Oxford: Oxford University Press. [In this chapter, I have assumed a very simple view of religious belief and commitment. That said, however, how we view religious faith and belief can have a substantial impact on how we perceive the problem of divine hiddenness. This book allows the reader to explore the rationality of religious belief and the nature of religious commitments in much greater detail.]

Green, Adam, and Eleonore Stump, eds. 2016. *Hidden Divinity and Religious Belief: New Perspectives*. Cambridge, United Kingdom: Cambridge University Press. [This book contains an excellent collection of leading contemporary research on the problem of divine hiddenness and proposed solutions.]

Schellenberg, J. L. 2015. *The Hiddenness Argument: Philosophy's New Challenge to Belief in God*. 1 edition. Oxford: Oxford University Press. [Schellenberg is the seminal figure within the divine hiddenness literature. This book showcases some of his most developed work on the issue.]

Internet resources

Anon. 2017. "Argument from Nonbelief." *Wikipedia*. https://en.wikipedia.org/w/index.php?title=Argument_from_nonbelief&oldid=763750944. [The Wikipedia page for the problem of divine hiddenness, which gives an excellent, basic overview of the argument and some possible objections to it.]

Howard-Snyder, Daniel, and Adam Green. 2016. "Hiddenness of God." *The Stanford Encyclopedia of Philosophy*. https://plato.stanford.edu/entries/divine-hiddenness/. [An excellent online introduction the problem of divine hiddenness – especially the evidential problem – and the relevant philosophical literature.]

Kraay, Klaas J. 2017. "The Problem of Divine Hiddenness – Philosophy – Oxford Bibliographies." *Oxford Bibliographies*. www.oxfordbibliographies.com/view/document/obo-9780195396577/obo-9780195396577-0178.xml. [An excellent annotated bibliography on the problem of divine hiddenness; it summarizes the problem and the contours of the literature and points readers to other great resources.]

7 Does contemporary neuroscience debunk religious belief?

Sarah Lane Ritchie

Introduction

Billions of people throughout history have claimed to have religious beliefs. Many discuss this belief not in terms of conceptual content or doctrine, but as an actual experience and ongoing relationship they have with God or other forms of divinity. Vast numbers of individuals have experienced religion as a transformative, structural component in their lives – shaping not only their cognitive theological commitments, but the way they see the world in the first place. In short: they experience God as real.

At the same time, however, the various brain-related sciences have built up a remarkable body of research about brain functions and cognitive experiences – including those involving religious belief. Contemporary neuroscience has identified **neural correlates** of religious experiences, and the **cognitive science of religion** provides theoretical frameworks for understanding the evolutionary basis of religious belief. In fact, researchers using brain imaging technologies are able to reliably predict and even initiate religious experiences. When the many strands of contemporary neuroscientific research are taken as a whole, it seems increasingly likely that religious belief is a wholly natural phenomenon. But does this naturalization of religious belief mean that belief in (and experience of) God has been explained away? The goal of this chapter is to address this question, ultimately suggesting that neuroscience isn't the sort of thing that could debunk religious belief in the first place.

Religious belief as holistic and embodied

In asking whether neuroscience disproves the legitimacy of religious belief, it's helpful to first examine what we mean by "religious belief." It's common to think of belief in God as being basically about the cognitive content of that belief. For example, you might think that the word "God" refers to an all-knowing, all-powerful creator of the universe, while I might think that the word refers to a subjective perception of the ultimate source of all life – the ground of all being that I experience in moments of spiritual transcendence. If we were to debate our differing religious beliefs, we might argue about the internal logic of our respective belief systems, or perhaps the historical foundations of specific doctrines. In other words, it might feel quite natural to discuss our religious beliefs as ideas – conceptual abstractions that exist somewhere "out there" and are subject to argumentation about their relative merits. However, contemporary science paints a very different picture of religious belief. According to evolutionary biology, psychology, and the various cognitive sciences, religious belief is fundamentally embodied and holistic – it involves whole-body experiences with our environments, religious rituals that are performed by our physical bodies, and sensory experiences. In other words, religious belief is not just a product of physical processes in the brain. While propositional content is certainly one aspect of religious belief systems, the experience of religious belief itself is just that – a physically embodied phenomenon resulting at least in part from physical interactions with our environments. Belief isn't just "in our heads," but can only be understood in the context of brains, bodies, communities, and wider culture.

When discussing the embodiment of religious belief, it is helpful to recognize that belief formation is a very natural, normal element of human experience. While specifically religious beliefs might be experienced as particularly important, their formation happens via the same biological, neural, and cultural mechanisms as beliefs about (for example) which football team will win the next World Cup. Neurobiologists and cognitive scientists are describing with increasing detail the various elements of belief formation – religious or otherwise. For example, it is now widely accepted that human cognition cannot be separated from emotion (largely due to the work of neurobiologist Antonio Damasio). It turns out that feelings are not peripheral to belief formation, but integral to it. Not only do emotionally impactful experiences shape our beliefs about people, events, or religious content, but they actually change the structure and functioning of our brain. This ability of the brain to alter its structure and function in response to repetitive experience is called **neuroplasticity**. Researchers studying neuroplasticity demonstrate how habits, emotional experiences, and social contexts combine to form and strengthen various beliefs, and weaken others. Religious beliefs are formed and strengthened as people habitually engage in religious practices, participate in emotionally charged communal worship experiences, and consistently absorb the doctrinal content of a particular religious system – among many other factors. The more one engages with the various elements of belief formation, the more likely one is to develop a felt sense of religious belief. We can thus see how religious belief is socially contextualized and involves habits, sensory experiences, and cultural frameworks. Religious belief does not exist in its own unique category, divorced from a biopsychosocial context – rather, it is one type of belief that is formed through the same mechanisms as are other beliefs.

Neural correlates of religious experience

Religious belief might be a product of the overall brain-body-environment-culture system, but what do the brain-related sciences tell us about the specific relationship between religious belief and the brain itself? One way of examining this relationship is to identify the **neural correlates** of religious belief, or the specific neural activation patterns correlating with religious beliefs and experiences. Of course, beliefs and experiences are two separate phenomena, and it's important to distinguish between them when discussing the relevant research. But there's also a strong link between religious experiences of God and a felt sense of religious belief; these experiences need not be dramatic, but can be as mild as a sense of peace while reciting prayers or an experience of God's presence in worship. Religious experiences exist on a very wide spectrum. In any case, religious experiences have received substantial academic attention in recent years, perhaps because their discrete, sometimes dramatic nature makes them particularly amenable to the available brain imaging technologies. Neuroscientist Andrew Newberg has been responsible for a significant body of research on religious experiences and practices, often focusing on meditation and contemplative prayer. Brain imaging technologies (such as **fMRI [functional magnetic resonance imaging]** or SPECT [single-photon emission computed tomography]) allow researchers to measure blood flow and neural activity during specific religious practices – like prayer and meditation. By observing religious practitioners as they engage in prayer, recitation of religious texts, or meditation (for example), researchers are able to compare the brain states of religious believers with baseline brain states – in the same individual during non-religious activity, and in control groups.

Many studies suggest that religious experiences involve integrated activity between various brain structures, including the thalamus, parietal lobes, frontal lobes, and limbic system. In other words, the brain does not have a single "God spot" that is responsible for an individual's religious belief. It seems likely that more intense or mystical experiences are a product of varying levels of coordinated activation and de-activation in multiple areas of the brain. For example, both meditating Buddhist monks and praying Catholic nuns demonstrate increased activity in their frontal lobes (a brain region responsible for concentration) and decreased activity in the parietal lobes (a brain region responsible for spatial orientation). Thus, spiritual experiences not only involve coordinated patterns of brain activity, but these patterns also seem to cross religious and cultural boundaries: the content of one's religious beliefs seems not to alter appreciably the way one's brain manifests religious experiences in the first place. The upshot of this sort of research seems to be that similar sorts of religious activities and experiences (i.e. prayer, meditation, singing) involve similar sorts of brain activity, regardless of the specific religious content involved. It seems clear that religious experiences are at least accompanied (if not caused) by predictable and testable neural activation patterns in the brain. In other words, religious experiences are not free-floating phenomena with no basis in the brain.

This brings us to an important question: does neuroscientific research disprove a subject's perceived interaction with God (or spiritual realities more broadly), or does it merely suggest a correlation between religious experiences and brain activity? Put differently, we must enquire into the causal relationship between the brain and the felt experience of God: does the brain cause one's sense of (and belief in) God, or are altered brain states merely associated responses to God?

Some argue that neuroscience does prove that the felt experience of God is an illusion. Atheist thinkers such as Daniel Dennett and Richard Dawkins point to the neurobiological basis of religious experience as evidence that the brain creates a felt sense of belief – and that spiritual realities have nothing to do with it. Religious believers might feel that they are experiencing God as real, but there is no scientific reason to think that such experiences are caused by a supernatural being. One important principle here is **methodological naturalism**, or the assumption in contemporary science that only natural causes will be allowed in scientific explanations for observed phenomena. According to methodological naturalism, scientists shouldn't invoke God in their explanations of religious experiences – especially given the myriad studies linking religious experiences to specific patterns of brain activity. Another way of thinking about this involves Occam's Razor, the philosophical principle that when there exist two competing explanations for a given phenomenon, the simplest one is to be preferred. For many scientists and philosophers, the predictable correlation of specific neural activation patterns with specific religious practices and experiences disqualifies God as an explanation. Because we know that certain types of practices and brain stimulation will be reliably accompanied by a felt sense of God (or other spiritual realities), the simplest explanation is that the entire religious experience is best analysed in neurobiological terms.

This deflationary account of neuroscientific research and religious experience is bolstered by another observation: religious experiences can actually be induced in laboratory settings. For example, taking certain hallucinogenic drugs can initiate experiences that are reported as being remarkably spiritual and accompanied by long-term positive effects in one's life. Additional research has suggested that temporal lobe stimulation (via electromagnetism) can create a felt sense of spiritual presence. Less dramatically, one could argue that religious systems have long utilized ritual, music, rhythm, repetition, and emotionality to induce a felt sense of connection to God. Such practices have certainly been institutionalized and normalized as valid religious practices, but this doesn't mean that they're not neurobiologically powerful. Indeed, sceptics argue, it's no surprise that those growing up within religious structures are likely themselves to express a sense of religious belief: their brains have been conditioned, over time, to experience the doctrinal content of their religious system as real.

Others, however, will argue that experimental research on the neural correlates of religious experience proves nothing about the reality of God. They point out that the causal connection between the brain and religious belief has not been established. They argue that if God exists and interacts with human beings, then surely the brain would respond accordingly. In other words, if God does indeed interact with humans, it would be more surprising if the brain did not exhibit altered activation patterns. After all, whatever the relationship between the mind and brain, it seems evident that all mental activity is at least mediated by the brain. From this perspective, one would actually expect the brain to mirror and respond to God; brain scans could never disprove God's causal role in this situation. Paradoxically, this argument also utilizes Occam's Razor in a similar way to the deflationary argument above. Remember that Occam's Razor insists on including in our explanations only those things which are necessary to account adequately for the phenomenon in question. But how do we know what's truly necessary for an adequate account of religious experience? One might say that if God exists and interacts with people, then the simplest explanation must necessarily include God. For religious believers, the existence of God is a brute fact about reality; any scientific account of religious experience would be insufficient if it didn't factor God into the equation. Simplifying God out of the scientific explanation would, it's argued, not be a simplification so much as an erroneous omission. We can see, then, that there are various ways to interpret brain research on religious experience. While researchers may be able to predict, identify, and even induce religious experiences in religious believers, the empirical data themselves are insufficient for making judgments about the reality of God's existence. At the very least, there's a strong association between felt religious experiences and specific neural activation patterns in the brain. But how this correlation is to be interpreted isn't an explicitly scientific question. Neuroscience is limited to explanations about brain function and can't answer the question of whether God is real or not. After all, the scientific commitment to methodological naturalism prohibits religious explanations for physical phenomena in the first place. Neuroscience can explain what's happening in the brain when individuals experience God, but we must look beyond neuroscience to answer our questions about the relationship between physical instantiations of belief and their correlation with possible supernatural entities.

Religious belief and the cognitive science of religion

Neuroscientific research on religious experience is only part of the story, however. As many researchers involved with science-and-religion are quick to point out, religious belief is not an isolated phenomenon that can be exhaustively analysed by the neural imaging of isolated religious experiences. These researchers are wary of research programmes devoted only to the neuroscientific study of relatively dramatic or intense religious experiences – even while these experiences are indeed impactful for the belief of those who experience them. Instead, researchers in the **cognitive science of religion** (CSR) emphasize the naturalness of religion, studying the neurobiological, cognitive, and evolutionary bases of religious belief. Put simply, these scientists are keen to understand religious belief as a normal human phenomenon. By analysing only specific neural patterns in the brains, they argue, we fail to appreciate the multi-layered reality of religious belief – this belief involves not only neural activation patterns, but evolutionary adaptations, social structures, linguistic frameworks, and meaning-making cognitive abilities. In short, there's more to religious belief than physical brain behaviour; religious belief is a multi-faceted phenomenon that can be understood only in an evolutionary, holistic, and cognitive context.

CSR is an interdisciplinary field that draws upon neurobiology, evolutionary psychology, and the various cognitive sciences. Cognitive science in general doesn't focus predominantly on fMRI scans of religious believers so much as the mental tools that brains have evolved over long periods of time, and the way that those mental tools have enabled species to survive and thrive. For example, cognitive science might examine the mind's ability to identify and discriminate between objects, or to categorize certain beings as "agents." Among other topics, CSR researchers use knowledge of these mental tools to examine the cognitive and evolutionary underpinnings of religious belief. Justin Barrett is one such CSR scholar whose recent work has shaped the contemporary CSR field. He and others emphasize the "naturalness-of-religion" thesis, which views religious belief as a product of normal cognitive processes. In other words, religious belief isn't an abnormal phenomenon, but an expected product of the same cognitive tools that facilitate the formation of all beliefs – say, our beliefs about other people's intentions, or my bus's expected arrival time. These researchers argue that our minds are structured in such a way that religious belief is natural, expected, and a subtype of belief more generally. Religious belief doesn't require dramatic mystical experiences, but develops naturally from the rather mundane cognitive tools used for ordinary mental tasks – particularly when these mental processes are placed in a sociocultural context that reinforces religious belief.

CSR is rooted firmly in evolutionary theory. Indeed, naturalistic explanations of religious belief depend on the evolutionary concepts of natural selection and adaptation. Over long periods of time, mental tools and cognitive abilities were effectively tried, discarded, and tweaked in evolutionary terms to produce ever-increasing adaptive abilities. In other words, our pre-human ancestors were surviving at least partially on the basis of their ability to use their minds effectively in navigating their physical and social environments. For example, it was biologically useful for our ancestors to be able to discriminate between hostile body language and a welcoming posture; over time, this discriminatory ability became increasingly honed and nuanced. More relevant to the evolution of religious belief, CSR researchers emphasize the mind's tendency to engage in **agent detection**. Agent detection is the cognitive response that attributes events to the work of an intentional being; this can occur whether or not the event is actually caused by such an agent. For example, if I'm alone in the forest at night and hear movement behind me, I'm likely to (unconsciously) conclude that I'm being hunted by a bear – even if the movement is due only to the wind in the trees. While erroneous, my cognitive response in the woods is a helpful evolutionary adaptation. That is, my ancestors would be much more likely to survive in the forest if they treated all sudden movements as evidence of hungry predators; on the other hand, nothing is lost by falsely attributing **agency** to a gust of wind. In other words, our brains have evolved with a cognitive bias that "it's better to be safe than sorry."

This attribution of agency to non-sentient entities is considered a hypersensitive variety of a normal cognitive ability. How does this apply to religious belief? CSR researchers such as Barrett suggest that our hypersensitive agency detection abilities have led humans to attribute causal agency to supernatural beings (such as gods or angels). Say, for example, that an early human community was experiencing a drought. They might assume the sun, or some other celestial body, was in charge of bringing rain (as it too originated in the sky), and so ask the sun to bring rain. If it then rained the next day, this might appear as confirmation that the sun was indeed a supernatural agent responsive to human prayers and able to bring change in desperate circumstances. The community might then develop a sort of "god concept" around the sun, speaking of this god as though it had thoughts, emotions, and the ability to cause change in the natural world. This is just one oversimplified example of one aspect of the evolution of religious belief, but it demonstrates how religious belief may have developed quite naturally.

Indeed, there are many other cognitive abilities and tendencies that may have contributed to the evolution of religious belief. For example, many researchers studying religious belief have suggested that religious belief contributes to pro-social behaviour – behaviour that contributes to the overall wellbeing of one's community. In other words, religious belief may motivate and even pressure individuals to act in ways that greatly enhance the health of a specific community – thereby increasing the chances of species, communal, and individual survival. It's notable that cultures worldwide share common taboos about many "sins": murder, theft, and adultery are prohibited similarly in a great many societies. Researchers not only suggest that such antisocial behaviours are universally condemned for reasons of evolutionary survival, but also that our minds have developed cognitive abilities to discern what's "right" or "wrong." The idea here is that the moral codes developed by religious systems over time actually reinforce our cognitive dispositions toward prosocial behaviours. Not only does religious belief deter harmful behaviours, but it may also help to signal positive intentions and trust – this is called "costly signalling." People might sacrifice time, money, or even their lives because of their religious belief; these sorts of actions could help build social cohesion and cooperation. In other words, religious beliefs might be an adaptive evolutionary function, products (or by-products) of cognitive functioning that enhance our ability to survive as individuals and communities.

In any case, what we can say from a CSR perspective is that religious belief seems to be natural. That is, various strands of research suggest that our brains are predisposed to religious belief in one form or another. This is particularly striking in the growing body of research about children and religious belief. It seems that children are intuitive theists, easily forming beliefs in supernatural beings. Research in this area suggests that even very young children can conceptualize supernatural beings like God, and even distinguish between human abilities and God-like abilities. In other words, it's not that children first conceptualize about human existence and abilities and then extrapolate to the idea of God – rather, children cognitively engage very differently with the concepts of people and God, respectively. Rather than children being indoctrinated from the top-down by institutions and cultural frameworks, it seems that we are all predisposed (though not predetermined) to religious belief. As we have seen, there may well be good evolutionary reasons for this.

Religious belief disproved?

Of course, all of this brings us back to our original question: do the various brain sciences disprove the reality of religious belief? Given that, at the very least, the experience of religious belief is neurobiologically real, the question can be rephrased: do the various brain sciences explain away the religious belief experienced by so many people, proving that it denotes nothing but neural activation patterns and cognitive functioning? Not necessarily. Some may say yes – the simplest, most obvious explanation for many people is that religious belief is an evolutionary, cognitive by-product that has (perhaps) outlived its usefulness. Others may suggest that religious belief is even now a powerful cognitive tool that enhances prosocial behaviour and is thus worth encouraging – even while concluding that religious belief lacks grounding in reality. Either way, both positions conclude that religious belief is wholly caused by the brain/body interacting with its environment over long periods of time.

Yet others, however, may argue against these deflationary views: we must remember that there are limits to science. The scientific enterprise has been enormously successful in producing explanations about all manner of phenomena, but it is self-admittedly constrained to naturalistic explanations. As mentioned, the modern scientific commitment to methodological naturalism is what makes science "science." Even if the human capacity for religious belief were to be initiated by God, neuroscience could never – in principle – detect it. Indeed, even if a religious believer were experiencing the presence of God, an fMRI brain scan could only ever detect the neural correlates of that experience. The question of God's existence and interaction with humans is probably not a question that science could ever prove or disprove.

Similarly, while CSR might demonstrate that religious belief is something of a natural default position for humans, or even that belief is an evolutionary by-product of ordinary cognitive functions – one could still argue that this natural predisposition toward religion was somehow intended by God in the first place. Perhaps, after all, our innate receptivity towards God and our propensity to believe in supernatural agents is actually intended by God; one could even conclude that if God exists, we'd automatically expect our brains to have the capacity and inclination to believe in and experience that God. While some wish to exclude the possibility of any religious reality (given the scientific evidence that religious belief is a natural cognitive feature), others might well conclude that the naturalness of religious belief demonstrates creative forethought and action on God's part.

In fact, it's even possible to suggest that the naturalness of religious belief allows humans to play an active role in their own belief formation. As discussed above, belief is an embodied phenomenon, and is much more than mere propositional content about theological doctrines. Rather, belief is formed, strengthened, or weakened as the brain is used in certain ways – this is neuroplasticity. Again, rituals, prayer, communal experiences, and other religious practices serve to strengthen the felt sense of religious belief. Rather than seeing neuroscientific research on religious belief as disproving God, one might well conclude that this research offers tools for strengthening a sense of religious belief (if that is so desired). In fact, this is exactly what religious traditions have been doing for millennia: encouraging specific religious practices that serve to reinforce belief in God.

In one sense, then, the scientific evidence itself is neutral – neuroscience (or any other science) could never disprove religious belief. The scientific method seems not to be the sort of practice that could address questions outside of the natural world (although one might say that we don't have warrant to seek supernatural answers in the first place). Science might tell us how our brains naturally manifest religious experiences and belief – but we must look elsewhere for our knowledge of God's existence or non-existence.

Chapter summary

- Religious belief is fundamentally embodied, the result of a complex interplay of brain states, emotions, physical environment, bodily actions, and socio-cultural contexts.

- One important part of religious belief is religious experience, which occurs on a wide spectrum ranging from (for example) a mild sense of peace or God's presence during prayer, to more dramatic mystical experiences. Religious experiences have been analysed using brain imaging technologies, which demonstrate that such experiences are reliably and predictably associated with specific neural activation patterns. This raises questions: does the strong correlation between religious experience and neural activation prove that the brain itself is causing those religious experiences? Or, is the brain merely responding to religious realities, as it would respond to another person?

- The cognitive science of religion (CSR) is a research field analysing the evolutionary and cognitive substrates of religious belief. Cognitively speaking, religious belief is not a uniquely spiritual phenomenon, but a natural feature of the types of mental activity our brains have evolved to produce. In other words, religious belief is wholly natural.

- Many researchers argue that religious belief is an evolutionary adaptation that contributes to prosocial behaviour. The idea here is that religious systems develop moral codes that contribute to the overall wellbeing of communities and, indirectly, individuals. If religious belief provided an evolutionary edge by providing the motivational framework for moral behaviour, the cognitive mechanisms of religious belief would likely be passed on to subsequent generations.

- Contemporary science limits itself to methodological naturalism, allowing only explanations utilizing natural processes. If God does exist, and elicits belief in individuals, it's unlikely that this would be demonstrable using scientific methodologies. Strictly speaking, science is neutral on the question of God's existence or non-existence.

Study questions

1. Why might one be wary of naturalistic explanations for religious belief? What's at stake in this discussion?
2. Research suggests religious belief is embodied. If religious belief isn't merely an issue of cerebral content or doctrinal proposition, how might this change the way you think about the "spiritual" nature of belief?
3. The cognitive sciences suggest that religious belief is an evolved cognitive capacity that utilizes the same cognitive mechanisms involved in normal, ordinary mental activity. What's at stake if religious belief can be explained as an evolutionary (by-)product?
4. Given that neuroscience can identify the neural correlates of religious experience, how might (or might not) Occam's Razor guide our thinking on whether religious belief and experience correspond to God's existence?
5. If neuroplasticity means that religious belief is malleable and prone to being strengthened or weakened via religious practices, how might the naturalization of belief be a *good* thing for religious believers?
6. Could neuroscience ever disprove religious belief? If so, what would it take for this to be possible?
7. If religious belief is caused by the brain, would its evolutionary advantages (i.e. moral codes, sense of wellbeing) make it worth preserving – even if God didn't exist?

Introductory readings

Barrett, J. (2004). *Why would anyone believe in God?* (Cognitive science of religion series). Lanham, MD: AltaMira Press. [Accessible introduction to CSR and natural evolutionary explanations for religious belief; Barrett himself is a Christian but still committed to naturalistic explanations for religious belief.]

Brown, W. S., Murphy, N. C., and Malony, H. N. (2007). *Whatever happened to the soul?: Scientific and theological portraits of human nature*. Cambridge: International Society for Science and Religion. [A selection of essays tackling various aspects of the mind/body debate, with particular emphasis on theological issues arising from naturalistic explanations of the human mind/brain.]

Newberg, A., and Waldman, M. R. (2008). *Born to believe: God, science, and the origin of ordinary and extraordinary beliefs*. New York: Free Press. [An introduction to the neuroscience of religious experience and belief; helpful resource about actual neuroscientific data on specific religious practices.]

Advanced readings

Barrett, J. L. (2011). *Cognitive science, religion, and theology: From human minds to divine minds*. West Conshohocken, PA: Templeton Press. [This is a more expansive introduction to CSR and theological issues surrounding evolved human minds.]

Boyer, P. (2007). *Religion explained: The evolutionary origins of religious thought*. Cambridge: International Society for Science and Religion. [Boyer is a leader in the field; this is a more technical examination of the cognitive structures involved in religious belief and their evolutionary origins.]

McNamara, P. (2014). *The neuroscience of religious experience.* Cambridge: Cambridge University Press. [Looks at anthropological evidence for religious experience in early humans, as well as contemporary neuroscience and cognitive science. This is very technical, but remarkably comprehensive.]

Internet resources

Barrett, J., and Barrett, E. 'The Cognitive Science of Religion.' Website for the British Psychological Society. https://thepsychologist.bps.org.uk/volume-24/edition-4/cognitive-science-religion [Helpful overview of CSR and the evolutionary underpinnings of religious belief; this piece also discusses religious belief in children.]

Barsalou, L., Santos, A., Barbey, A., and Simmons, W. K. http://barsaloulab.org/Online_Articles/2005-Barsalou_et_al-JCC-embodied_religion.pdf [Emphasizes the inherent embodiment of all religious belief, and examines the role that religious practices play in fostering that belief.]

Smith, J. 'What God Does to Your Brain.' *The Telegraph.* www.telegraph.co.uk/culture/books/10914137/What-God-does-to-your-brain.html [Engages with various leading scholars focusing on the natural origins of religious belief, including Andrew Newberg.]

8 Are theism and atheism totally opposed? Can they learn from each other?

J. Adam Carter

Introduction

One very natural dividing line that – for better or worse – is often used to distinguish those who (put roughly for now) believe in God from those who do not is that between **theism** and **atheism**, where 'theism' is used to mark the believers and 'atheism' the non-believers. Such contrastive labels can serve many practical functions (e.g., signifying social identity), even when the terms in question are not clearly defined. Individuals are often, on the basis of their beliefs and values, attracted (sometimes rationally, sometimes irrationally) toward one such label more so than the other. However, once a clear statement of the substantive difference between theism and atheism is requested, things become more complicated, much more so than our casual use of these terms would suggest.

What exactly is the best way to capture the *relationship* between theism and atheism? To what extent are they opposed to one another, and relatedly, to what extent should they be regarded as *exhausting* the available theoretical options? §'Theism and atheism' will canvass a range of responses to this cluster of questions. In 'Religious disagreement', we explore the **social-epistemic** dimension of the atheism/theism divide, by focusing in particular on the issue of **religious disagreements,** including those disagreements that take very different assumptions as starting points.

Theism and atheism

The twentieth century philosopher Ludwig Wittgenstein (1888–1951) was sceptical that any sharp definition (e.g., in terms of necessary and sufficient conditions) of either theism (or by extension atheism, the denial of theism) could be fruitfully drawn. The term 'theism', which originates from the Greek term *theos* [θεός] meaning 'god', has historically been used to pick out a wide range of very different positions, all under the general description of 'belief in God' – so many, in fact, that that we might wonder whether the term 'theism' (like the term 'game') is best understood as a kind of **family resemblance** term. Just as there is plausibly no set of conditions necessary and sufficient for counting as a game despite a cluster of properties shared by many but not *all* games, so likewise we might think there are no conditions necessary and sufficient for counting as 'theism' despite character-istic similarities between the views we use this term to pick out. Or so such a line of thinking would go.

Relegating 'theism' (and by extension, atheism) to nothing sharper than a family resemblance term, however, might be premature. For one thing, even if there are various kinds of differing views that purport to accept 'belief in God' (understood minimally as a divine creator of the universe), self-described theists (unlike **deists**) typically posit further attributes. Whereas deists deny that God either interferes in the world or reveals himself in some detectable way, theists typically maintain both of these claims. Moreover, the term 'theism' can be sharpened further by associat-ing additional properties with God and, in particular, the classic properties attrib-uted to God by **monotheistic** religions (e.g., Christianity, Judaism, Islam): an all-powerful, all-knowing, and infinitely good creator.

Even if theism is used in this more specific sense, however, a further philosophi-cal issue arises when it comes to defining atheism *in terms of* the denial of theism. For no matter how much we sharpen the notion of 'God' with reference to which theism is defined, the further characterisation of atheism as a denial of theism requires some further elaboration. For there are multiple ways one might *deny* theism, not all of which comport with our ordinary usage of 'atheism'.

Atheism is typically associated with the kind of denial that is the *rejection* of the existence of God or other deities – though one might also deny the existence of God in a weaker fashion, by refraining from believing in God while not outright maintaining God's non-existence, a position typically associated with **agnosti-cism**. Let's look at each of these positions in turn.

One method of support for atheism challenges the **rationality** of religious belief. On this strategy, belief in God is, like any other kind of belief, the sort of thing that should be defensible via publicly available evidence that anyone, not just the believer herself, should be able to accept. Those who judge that the preponderance of such available evidence counts against the existence of God might then be athe-ists (i.e., they might reject the proposition that God exists) on such grounds. Inter-estingly, though, while some theists accept the evidentialist's assumption that belief in God is rationally appraisable (and then argue further that the evidence actually supports God's existence), not all do. According to **fideism** (e.g., Søren Kierkegaard (1813–1855)), belief in God is better understood as a matter of faith, not a matter of evidence. Interestingly, this means that in response to the atheist who rejects the existence of God evidential grounds, the fideist can more or less agree with such an atheist interlocutor: that is, *both* the fideist and the atheist can agree that God's existence cannot be evidentially established. Where the conflict lies in this case is the matter of whether God's existence is rational or **arational**, not the matter of where in particular the evidence points (the point of contention between evidentialist theists and atheists).

But what exactly, from the subject's point of view, is involved in *rejecting* God's existence? Must one have a certain level of confidence, or outright belief, in the non-existence of God to qualify as an atheist by rejecting God's existence, or might one simply possess some (perhaps strong) doubts? Such questions reveal that the line dividing atheism and agnosticism might not be so straightforward as a difference between on the one hand rejecting God's existence and on the other *refraining from believing* in God's existence.

Here it will be helpful to consider the definition of agnosticism offered by William Rowe (1931–2015) as 'the view that human reason is incapable of providing sufficient rational grounds to justify either the belief that God exists or the belief that God does not exist'. If one refrains from believing in God and does so because one thinks human reason is simply incapable of rationally arbitrating the matter, we might ask further: is this because human reason is *in principle* incapable of providing sufficient rational grounds one way or another, or rather, because one thinks human reason currently (i.e., situated within the current knowledge base available to us) is incapable of providing such evidence? We should note that there is scope for a further kind of agnostic: one who *grants* that there is in principle no limitation to human reason *as such* that precludes the possibility of rational belief for or against God's existence, while maintaining that *one self* is nonetheless incapable. An agnostic of this variety refrains from believing in God but not because *human reason* (a power common to all individuals) is limited, but because *she* (perhaps for reasons that apply just to her, her personal background, her own psychology, etc.) is incapable of locating sufficient reasons to warrant any sort of conviction one way or another.

We've seen already that the theism/atheism distinction invites a range of more nuanced questions. One further such question concerns – at a greater level of generality than we've considered thus far – the *psychology* of theism, atheism and agnosticism in relation to the **will,** or the capacity of human volition. According to the eighteenth century Scottish enlightenment thinker **David Hume** (1711–1776) in *A Treatise on Human Nature*, the matter of what we believe, on any given matter, depends not on the will, 'but must arise from certain determinate causes and principles, of which we are not masters' (§ 624). This psychological and descriptive position about human belief, called **doxastic involuntarism,** has been given further expression by twentieth century British ethicist Bernard Williams (1929–2003). According to Williams, if we could believe at will, and moreover if this is a power that is both common and not opaque to us, then it would be very hard to explain why we should ever be surprised when things turn out to be different than we believe. But we are invariably surprised in such cases, and so Williams thought we should reject that we possess the power to believe at will.

If Hume and Williams are on the right track, then whether one is an atheist, theist or agnostic is not something over which one has direct control. And this point, if correct, has potentially important ethical implications. Consider, for example, the **'ought implies can' principle**, often attributed to Immanuel Kant (1724–1804). As Kant wrote in his 1793 book, *Religion within the Bounds of Bare Reason*: 'For if the moral law commands that we *ought* to be better human beings now, it inescapably follows that we must be *capable* of being better human beings'. The crux of Kant's insight here is that the very suggestion that we *ought* to do something implies that we should be at least capable of doing it. With reference to Kant's principle, it looks very much as though Hume's and Williams' point about the non-voluntariness of believing would have an important implication – viz., that atheism/theism beliefs, no less than other beliefs, lie beyond the realm of *duty*, and thus that it would be a mistake to praise or for that matter blame individuals for holding such beliefs. To avoid this kind of conclusion (as will many who take belief in God to fall within the purview of praise and blame), it looks, initially at least, as though one must take issue with either Kant's principle or with the descriptive claim that belief in God is non-voluntary in a way that (paired with Kant's principle) implies this result.

In his famous essay 'The Ethics of Belief', W. K. Clifford (1845–1879) goes the latter route. He thinks that there are various things we ought to believe (namely, for Clifford, all and only that which is supported by the evidence), and further that it is within our power to conform to or to disregard this norm. The American pragmatist philosopher and psychologist William James (1842–1910) famously rejected Clifford's 'evidentialist' norm of belief, though James (like many other pragmatist thinkers) is in firm agreement with the Clifford's presumption (*contra* Hume and Williams) that we have enough control over our beliefs, including religious beliefs, that it makes sense to praise or blame us for them. If Clifford and James are (despite their differences) correct about this more basic point concerning the relationship between belief and the will, then theism and atheism can be viewed as a kind of choice, and, thus, whatever separates theists and atheists is just a matter of what each chooses.

This is precisely the assumption that underwrote the French philosopher Blaise Pascal's (1623–1662) famous 'gamble' on behalf of the theist rather than the atheist position. **Pascal's Wager** can be expressed as the following idea: if one believes in the existence of God and God *does* exist, then one gains infinite reward, but if one loses this bet (and God doesn't exist) one loses nothing. However, if one bets *against* the existence of God and is right, one wins nothing for one's non-belief, though if one loses this bet, one receives an infinite loss. Thus, Pascal concluded, you should try to bring it about that you are a theist rather than an atheist.

Whether Pascal's Wager accurately characterises a decision problem we face turns (among other things) on the more fundamental question of whether theism and atheism are positions we can choose in any meaningful sense, an issue that as we've seen is contested by philosophers more generally at the level of belief in general.

A final and important point about the theism/atheism divide concerns a separate dividing line, that between religion and science. It is not uncommon to encounter the following sort of fallacious reasoning: theism and atheism are fundamentally opposed; religion aligns with theism and atheism aligns with science; therefore, science and religion are fundamentally opposed.

One problem with this sort of dichotomous thinking – one that we've already seen – is that the dividing line between theism and atheism isn't one that can be drawn without quite a bit of terminological ground clearing and care, and even then, various open issues remain. But setting this aside, it is doubly problematic to derive conclusions about the religion/science distinction from premises about the atheism/theism distinction. Firstly, both theism and atheism have been supported on the basis of scientific considerations as well as on the basis of theological or religious considerations. Secondly, regardless of what kinds of considerations have been appealed to support theism/atheism, the relationship between religion and science is fundamentally of a different *kind* than the relationship between theism/atheism. For theism and atheism are positions that can be believed or not, whereas religion and science are not 'beliefs' as such (even if there are various specific beliefs characteristic to each), but rather ways of coming to form beliefs – viz., different epistemological methodologies. Thus, if the latter are in opposition, it will be because they are in opposition qua methodologies, not because (for instance) believing one excludes believing the other.

Nonetheless, methodologies can potentially clash for example by (i) mandating/forbidding incompatible methods; or by (ii) mandating/forbidding incompatible beliefs. As the philosopher Michael Murray (2008) has noted, there are three central views on the compatibility of religion and science: the *inevitable conflict model*, the *non-conflict model* and the *potential conflict model*. The former insists that religion and science *inevitably* conflict with one another, given that religion and science offer genuinely alternative ways of coming to understand the world and our place in it, ways that issue various kinds of contradictions. At the level of methodology, for example, science forbids while at least some religions subscribe to divine revelation as a valid method; at the level of belief, Western science holds that the Earth is billions of years old, whereas some religions deny this. The non-conflict model, by contrast, denies that religion and science can even potentially conflict because religion and science concern **nonoverlapping magisteria**, or domains of authority. As American evolutionary biologist Stephen J. Gould (1941–2002), in defence of this position puts it,

> The net of science covers the empirical universe: what is it made of (fact) and why does it work this way (theory). The net of religion extends over questions of moral meaning and value. These two magisteria do not overlap.
>
> (1997, §1)

If Gould is right, then it is a mistake to think of science and religion as even in the market for conflict.

A third position, the potential conflict model, maintains that religion and science can potentially conflict, e.g., as in the case where a religion advances verifiable empirical claims (e.g., the age of the earth). In response to potential conflicts, however, some thinkers, including the Italian polymath Galileo Galilei (1564–1642), have suggested that religion and science are at least potentially revisable with reference to the other (as opposed to mutually exclusive in light of any potential incompatibilities observed). (For related discussion, see the chapter 'Faith and Reason', this volume).

Religious disagreement

Is *rational* religious disagreement possible? Can theists and atheists expect to fruitfully engage with one another in dialogue, or are theists and atheists better off 'agreeing to disagree'? Such questions have been pursued in recent work in **social**

epistemology, and in this section, we'll consider how some of these insights might help us to think more clearly about religious disagreements and their potential significance.

Firstly, for some ground clearing: we need to distinguish between the **ethics** and epistemology of disagreement. The question of what you *should* do when you find yourself in a religious disagreement with someone might be one sort of thing (e.g., concede, compliment your interlocutor's impressive arguing skills, etc.) from a point of view where ethical considerations are given priority, and a completely different sort of thing from a purely epistemic point of view – viz., roughly, the point of view where getting to the truth is what matters. Let's hereafter restrict ourselves here to the following specifically *epistemic* gloss of the question: what is epistemically rational to do in the case of a religious disagreement? One lesson from social epistemology is that what rationality requires in the face of any sort of disagreement might vary considerably depending on what you already believe about the person with whom you are disagreeing.

Suppose we take 'G' to be the proposition 'God exists.' You assert G, you interlocutor denies G. If your opponent if a child, or someone who you think hasn't given due consideration to the question or perhaps lacks what you take to be information relevant to answering the question, you are not going to regard (prior to the disagreement) such an individual to be as likely as you are to be right on the matter. In such a case, the fact that such an individual disagrees with you might not be very rationally significant for whether you should continue to hold your belief.

Things become much more interesting, however, when we control for such differences. Suppose that, prior to finding out that your interlocutor disagrees with you on the matter of whether God exists, you regard your interlocutor to be an **epistemic peer** – viz., someone you took to be just as cognitively competent and well informed on the matter at issue as you are. What does rationality require of you now that you've found out this person disagrees with you?

There are two central positions on this matter. The **conciliatory view** says that, in a revealed peer disagreement, rationality requires that you adjust (to some degree) your confidence that the proposition at issue is true. Thus, if you discover that someone you think is as smart and as well informed as you in matters that are relevant to determining the existence of God disagrees with you about G, then according to the conciliatory view, it is rationally impermissible to remain just as confident as you were before on the matter of whether G is true. The **steadfast** view, by contrast, denies this claim and permits one to rationally 'hold one's grounds' in the face of a revealed peer disagreement.

It's a difficult and contentious matter in contemporary social epistemology which of these two positions is more plausible. And in the case of religious disagreement, things can get especially tricky. For example, the matter of determining who *counts* as an epistemic peer in the first place is relatively straightforward in the case of mundane, non-religious disagreements – say, about whether a particular store is open on a Saturday. Anyone plausibly counts as your epistemic peer here provided they've been exposed to the same kind of evidence as you have and are in OK cognitive shape (i.e., not drunk, hallucinating). But in the religious case, it's not so clear, as there often times will not already be agreement on what counts as the right kind of evidence that's relevant to settling the dispute. For example, one who takes revealed scripture to be evidence relevant to the matter of whether God exists will perhaps not regard someone not acquainted with such scripture as equally likely to be right on the matter. To the extent that mutual recognition of epistemic peerhood seems more difficult to establish in the religious case than in more mundane cases where there is antecedent agreement on the matter of what kind of evidence is the relevant kind, the problem of accounting for the rational significance of religious disagreements becomes all the more philosophically challenging.

As philosopher John Pittard (2014) has suggested, one way to gain traction here is to distinguish between the **first-order** and **higher-order epistemic significance** of religious disagreements by distinguishing more carefully between two kinds of evidence: *first-order evidence*, which directly concerns the truth of some target proposition, *p*, and **higher-order evidence** *vis-à-vis p*; higher-order evidence doesn't bear directly on whether *p* is true but rather on the matter of whether one has *rationally assessed* the relevant first-order evidence. Thus, if the proposition under discussion is *The bank is open Saturday*, then the testimony of the bank's manager constitutes first-order evidence; if the bank manager also tells me that I've ingested a mind-altering pill, then this new evidence has second-order significance. It doesn't directly concern the matter of whether the bank is open, but it concerns my capacity to rationally assess the first-order evidence I have.

With this distinction in mind, we can now briefly consider how the epistemic significance of religious disagreements might potentially differ (along the first-/second- order dimension) across cases. For example, proponents of the conciliatory view will be inclined to suggest that when we discover that someone we regard as an epistemic peer disagrees with us regarding the matter of whether God exists, this fact of such disagreement has a kind of second-order epistemic significance for us: it is not evidence that bears directly on the issue of whether God exists, but it bears (perhaps, as a kind of *higher-order defeater*) on our own ability to assess the first-order evidence.

By contrast, as Pittard notes, religious disagreement might also have a kind of first-order significance. Here, it will be helpful to briefly consider J.L. Schellenberg's (1959–) problem of **divine hiddenness**, according to which God's hiddenness motivates an argument for atheism. As Schellenberg sees it, a loving God would not make rational non-belief possible, given that God is all-just and non-belief carries with it culpability on some Christian accounts. But the ubiquity of apparently rational religious disagreement is evidence for the possibility of rational non-belief, and thus has first-order epistemic significance vis-à-vis the question of whether God exists.

Here is, of course, not the place to attempt to adjudicate the divine hiddenness argument. Rather, the example is meant to be illustrative of how, generally speaking, there are two interestingly different ways to think about the epistemic significance of religious disagreements, and that this is so *regardless* of whether one is already inclined toward the conciliatory or steadfast view.

As a final point, it will be worth bringing together a lesson from 'Theism and atheism' with the material surveyed in this section. In 'Theism and atheism', it was shown that the matter of the distinction between religion and science is best understood as a standalone philosophical problem, one that is not helpfully thought of as mapping on to the theist/atheist divide. With this point in mind, it will be useful to now consider that disagreements concerning theism and atheism do not themselves settle, and should be regarded as independent of disagreements on the matter of whether religion or science respectively offers a better method of engaging with the world and our place in it. That said, the more general structural points concerning the significance of disagreements bear importantly on the latter kind of dispute much as they do on the former. In this respect, social epistemology offers important tools for thinking critically about both kinds of disputes.

Chapter summary

- The task of defining theism and atheism faces an initial difficulty given the variation in what people take 'belief in God' to refer to. This initial difficulty can be overcome to some extent by stipulating that God have certain properties, e.g., the properties typically assigned to God by classical monotheistic religions.

- Atheism is typically associated with the kind of denial that is the *rejection* of the existence of God or other deities, though one might also deny the existence of God in a weaker fashion, by refraining from believing in God while not outright maintaining God's non-existence, a position typically associated with *agnosticism*.

- One method of support for atheism challenges the rationality of religious belief. On this strategy, belief in God is, like any other kind of belief, the sort of thing that should be defensible via publicly available evidence that anyone, not just the believer herself, should be able to accept. This assumption that religious belief is rationally appraisable is denied by *fideists*, who regard religious belief to be arational.

- If the **ought-implies-can principle** is correct, then theism/atheism are praiseworthy or blameworthy only if the matter of whether we believe in God is in some relevant sense voluntary. The more general issue of whether belief is subject to our direct control is what separates doxastic voluntarists (e.g., Clifford and James) and doxastic involuntarists (e.g., Hume and Williams).

- It is problematic to attempt to deduce conclusions about the religion/science distinction from premises about the atheism/theism distinction. Firstly, both theism and atheism have been supported on the basis of scientific considerations as well as on the basis of theological or religious considerations. Secondly, theism and atheism are positions that can be believed or

disbelieved, whereas religion and science are not 'beliefs' as such (even if
there are various specific beliefs characteristic to each), but rather ways of
coming to form beliefs – viz., different epistemological methodologies.
- *An epistemic peer*, relative to a given topic, is someone who is as cognitively
competent and well informed on that topic as you are. According to the
conciliatory view, rationality requires that you adjust (to some degree) your
confidence about whether God exists upon finding that someone you regard
as an epistemic peer on the topic of God's existence disagrees with you.
The *steadfast view*, by contrast, denies this claim and permits one to rationally 'hold one's grounds' in the face of a revealed peer disagreement.
- *First-order evidence* directly concerns the truth of some target proposition,
p; higher-order evidence doesn't bear directly on whether *p* is true but rather
on the matter of whether one has rationally assessed the relevant first-order
evidence.
- Disagreements about theism/atheism, as well as disagreements about science
and religion, can potentially be either first-order or second-order epistemically
significant; however, it is problematic to draw conclusions about the relationship
between religion and science from facts about theism/atheism disagreements.

Study questions

1. Is the statement 'All deists are theists' true?
2. On what issue are fideists and evidentialists divided?
3. What is Rowe's account of agnosticism, and can this account be unpacked
   in different ways to get different versions of agnosticism? Discuss.
4. Does the theism/atheism distinction mark a difference in *choice*? What kind
   of answer would David Hume and Bernard Williams give to this question?
   What kind of answer would W. K. Clifford and William James give? Explain.
5. What does Kant's 'ought-implies-can' principle have to do with the matter
   of whether theistic/atheistic belief is praiseworthy/blameworthy?
6. What is Pascal's Wager? What is it intended to show?
7. Which model, if any, do you think best represents the relationship between
   religion and science: the *inevitable conflict model*, the *non-conflict model*
   or the *potential conflict model*? Explain and defend your answer.
8. What is the difference between the conciliatory view and the steadfast view
   as regards the epistemology of disagreement?
9. What is it for a religious disagreement to be second-order epistemically
   significant as opposed to first-order epistemically significant?

Introductory readings

Feldman, Richard. (2007). 'Reasonable Religious Disagreements', In *Philosophers without
Gods: Meditations on Atheism and the Secular Life*, Louise M. Antony (ed.), pp. 194–214.
New York: Oxford University Press. [Seminal paper in the epistemology of disagreement
defending a conciliatory approach to revealed peer disagreements.]

Gould, Stephen Jay. (1997). 'Nonoverlapping Magisteria', *Natural History*, 106, pp. 16–22. [Argues that religion and science are in principle non-conflicting given that they concern different areas of inquiry.]

Greco, John. (2017). 'Knowledge of God', In *The Oxford Handbook of the Epistemology of Theology*, W. Abraham and F. Aquino (eds.). Oxford: Oxford University Press. [Defends a particular approach to issues in religious epistemology.]

Hawthorne, John. (2007). 'Religious Knowledge', *Philosophic Exchange*, 37 (1), Article 1. [Paper written for undergraduates which covers some key issues in religious epistemology.]

Murray, Michael. (2008). 'Religion and Science', In *A Critical Introduction to the Philosophy of Religion*, pp. 193–226. Cambridge: Cambridge University Press. [Defends a potential-conflict model against alternatives of the relationship between religion and science.]

Russell, Bertrand. (1949). 'Am I an Atheist or an Agnostic', *The Literary Guide and Rationalist Review*, 64 (July), pp. 115–116. [Short discussion of the relationship between atheism and agnosticism.]

Advanced readings

Flew, A. (1984). 'The Presumption of Atheism', In *Canadian Journal of Philosophy*, J. Houstion (ed.), pp. 29–46. Haddington, Scotland: Handsel Press. [Influential contribution to the dialectical position between theists and atheists.]

Greco, John. (2015). 'No-Fault Atheism', In *Divine Hiddenness*, Adam Green and Eleonore Stump (eds.). Cambridge: Cambridge University Press. [Criticises atheist diagnoses of the divine hiddenness argument from a social-epistemic perspective.]

Martin, Michael. (1990). *Atheism: A Philosophical Justification*. Philadelphia: Temple University Press. [A sustained and sophisticated defence of atheism.]

Pittard, John. (2014). 'Conciliationism and Religious Disagreement', In *Challenges to Moral and Religious Belief: Disagreement and Evolution*, Michael Bergmann and Patrick Kain (eds.), pp. 80–97. New York: Oxford University Press. [Engages with the issue of what the rational response should be in the face of revealed peer disagreements.]

Rowe, William. (1979). 'The Problem of Evil and Some Varieties of Atheism', *American Philosophical Quarterly*, 16, pp. 335–341. [Seminal paper defending an atheistic response to the problem of evil.]

Schellenberg, J. L. (2015). *The Hiddenness Argument: Philosophy's New Challenge to Belief in God*. 1 edition. Oxford: Oxford University Press. [Schellenberg is the seminal figure within the divine hiddenness literature. This book showcases some of his most developed work on the issue.]

Internet resources

Basinger, David. (2016). 'Religious Diversity (Pluralism)', *The Stanford Encyclopedia of Philosophy* (Winter 2016 Edition), Edward N. Zalta (ed.), https://plato.stanford.edu/archives/win2016/entries/religious-pluralism.

De Cruz, Helen. (2017). 'Religion and Science', *The Stanford Encyclopedia of Philosophy*, E. Zalta (ed.), https://plato.stanford.edu/archives/spr2017/entries/religion-science. [A wide-ranging introduction to the subtleties of the relationship between science and religion.]

Howard-Snyder, Daniel and Green, Adam. 'Hiddenness of God', *The Stanford Encyclopedia of Philosophy* (Winter 2016 Edition), Edward N. Zalta (ed.), https://plato.stanford.edu/archives/win2016/entries/divine-hiddenness.

Pittard, John. (2016). 'Religious Disagreement', *Internet Encyclopedia of Philosophy*. www.iep.utm.edu/rel-disa/.

Smart, J. J. C. (2011). 'Atheism and Agnosticism', *The Stanford Encyclopedia of Philosophy* (Summer 2016 Edition), Edward N. Zalta (ed.), https://plato.stanford.edu/archives/sum2016/entries/atheism-agnosticism.

Vitz, Rico. (2016). 'Doxastic Voluntarism', *Internet Encyclopedia of Philosophy*, www.iep.utm.edu/doxa-vol/.

9 Is fundamentalism just a problem for religious people?

Emma Gordon

Introduction

The word **fundamentalism** typically conjures up images of impassioned religious commitments – ones that are especially rigid in nature and advocate a literal, unquestioning and inflexible adherence to scripture. However, if we consider the traits, attitudes and behaviours we associated with religious fundamentalism – an approach that, of course, does not encapsulate all religious viewpoints – it becomes apparent that it is possible to be a fundamentalist about non-religious positions, so long as we strictly and dogmatically hold to a particular discipline or worldview. This is the rough characterization of fundamentalism that we will use herein.

Now, one might well wonder whether it's possible to be a fundamentalist about *true* claims; if your religion or worldview happens to accurately reflect everything about the reality it purports to represent, are you a fundamentalist simply because you adhere to it strictly and dogmatically? And, if you are a fundamentalist of such a stripe (e.g., one with all or mostly true beliefs), is this type of fundamentalism necessarily *problematic*? For the purposes of this chapter, we will assume that fundamentalism need not require a view to be false – you can be a fundamentalist regardless of whether your position gets things right, as fundamentalism is about certain ways of thinking and of conducting oneself in discourse. And with respect to whether there's anything wrong with being a fundamentalist about correct worldviews, there are good reasons to suppose that fundamentalism is *always* problematic, whether it's in the religious sphere or elsewhere. While this is intuitive, let's flesh it out by looking at three specific concerns: one about intellectual character, one about attaining **knowledge** and one about practical consequences.

Firstly, being a fundamentalist seems to be incompatible with a number of the character traits and dispositions that most would view as part of being **intellectually virtuous**. For example, open-mindedness and intellectual humility are typically conceived of as **intellectual virtues** – ones that involve the ability to hear and take seriously countervailing evidence. The archetypal fundamentalist, however, is dogmatic, inflexible and overly confident in their views – all ways of being that seem to preclude the manifesting of the aforementioned virtues.

Secondly, there are **epistemological** problems with any kind of fundamentalism. Insofar as one might think that knowledge requires beliefs to be **sensitive** (i.e., that knowing a proposition *p* requires that one would not have believed that *p* if *p* were false), being a fundamentalist might preclude one from having any knowledge – or, at the very least, preclude one from having knowledge in the particular area about which one is a fundamentalist. And even if you don't think that knowledge requires sensitive belief, you should nonetheless be able to see that a fundamentalist attitude has the potential to reduce access to various kinds of epistemic goods. After all, fundamentalists as such are limited in their capacity as inquirers. For instance, if you're dogmatic about your beliefs and unable to engage with the weight of evidence against them, you're likely to not only have less knowledge but also less understanding. Thirdly, and most obviously, fundamentalism has a long history of generating morally troubling practical consequences, undergirding a range of dangerous ideologies associated with persecution and terrorism.

Having sketched the rough shape of fundamentalism and considered some of the reasons why it is generally speaking intellectually and morally problematic, the goal of this chapter is to focus on one particular case study of a candidate for *non-religious* fundamentalism – specifically, the position of **scientism**, which (in its strongest forms) claims we can only acquire knowledge through the natural sciences. It is here that the potential for non-religious fundamentalism is perhaps seen most clearly, and, dialectically speaking, it is most convenient. For, typically at any rate, critiques of religious fundamentalism have been levelled from the perspective according to which religious fundamentalism violates certain principles of reason often associated with science. It will thus be interesting to explore in some detail whether and to what extent science could itself be taken to its own extreme – viz., specifically by being held and embraced in ways that mirror arguably problematic aspects of religious fundamentalism.

In what follows, we will begin by looking at what scientism involves and by considering the nuances of the position in order to see which type(s) of scientism are candidates for fundamentalism. Next, we will turn to arguments in favour of scientism, which we may want to balance against the idea that scientism is problematically fundamentalist. We will then move on to look at arguments *against* scientism, some of which help to bring out ways in which a fundamentalist scientism might be detrimental to intellectual progress. Finally, we will revisit and reconsider the criteria a position might have to meet in order to count as fundamentalist, and evaluate whether (or to what extent) scientism appears to meet this criteria.

What is scientism?

Susan Haack (b. 1945) – a vocal critic of scientism – says that it is "an exaggerated kind of deference towards science, an excessive readiness to accept as authoritative any claim made by the sciences and to dismiss every kind of criticism of science or its practitioners as anti-scientific prejudice." Similarly, when Raymond Tallis

(b. 1946) identifies "neuromania" and "Darwinitis" as two particularly common strands of modern scientism, he says that the former gives excessive significance to the explanatory power of neuroscience and the latter gives the same to evolutionary theory. However, describing scientism (or variants thereof) in this particular way makes the position immediately uninteresting, as its exaggerated nature – and hence its higher likelihood of being fundamentalist position – is on these conceptions built into the very definition. Rather, in order to have a meaningful debate about scientism we would be better to view it as a value-neutral description of inquiry. From this vantage point, we can better assess its accuracy and more fairly consider whether it is a form of fundamentalism.

For a more neutral characterization of scientism we can look to prominent defender of scientism Alexander Rosenberg (b. 1946), a **philosopher of science** who defines the view as "the conviction that the methods of science are the only reliable ways to secure knowledge of anything" and adds that "being scientistic just means treating science as our exclusive guide to reality, to nature – both our own nature and everything else's." Often, this scientistic thesis is combined with the related claim that there are no principled epistemological limits to science (i.e., that it is possible for science to give us knowledge of everything). However, before we go any further, we should note that scientism comes in a variety of strengths. We might call the two broad categories here *restricted* and *unrestricted*. Restricted scientism applies the theory to some specific topic – for example, you might see restricted forms of scientism about **metaphysics** or free will. For the purposes of considering whether scientism might be a form of fundamentalism, it makes more sense to focus on *unrestricted* scientism, which claims that only science is capable of providing us with knowledge about *any* part of reality. For example, in a broadly similar fashion to Rosenberg, biologist and historian of science William Provine (1942–2015) seemingly discounts anything that science doesn't directly tell us exists, from moral laws to free will and gods.

In addition to telling us how we *can* get rational belief or knowledge, scientism is also characterized as telling us how we *can't* get these epistemic goods (whether generally or in specific domain). In particular, Rik Peels (b. 1983) characterizes a scientistic worldview as ruling out the possibility of gaining knowledge through common sense beliefs, no matter how widely shared. As he describes it, this class of beliefs includes beliefs based on memory (e.g., where I was on my last summer holiday), religious beliefs (e.g., that God exists), basic logical beliefs (e.g., that the law of excluded middle holds), beliefs about free action (e.g., that I could have freely chosen to go cycling this afternoon), beliefs about one's reasons (e.g., that I stayed at home *because* I have work to do), moral beliefs (e.g., that the subjugation of women is wrong) and introspective beliefs (e.g., that my shoulder hurts). The distinction between common sense and scientific beliefs that Peels offers relies on paradigmatic instances of each type – this sort of "cluster model" is one very natural way to carve out the distinction. That being said, some theorists might also aspire to generate necessary and sufficient conditions for scientific and non-scientific beliefs respectively.

Now that we better (i) understand the different types of scientism on the table, (ii) have isolated a particular type that is relevant to the question of non-religious fundamentalism – i.e., unrestricted scientism (which is about reality as a whole) – and (iii) have considered what sources of knowledge scientism might deny, we can turn to explore the question of whether scientism is a *plausible* position to adopt.

Why endorse scientism?

Are there strong arguments to suggest that we should endorse strong (i.e., unrestricted) scientism? Evaluating this question will help us assess what fundamentalism about science might involve, and in doing so give us a deeper sense of the problems that scientism embraced in such a manner could potentially give rise to.

The first and simplest argument in favour of scientism might just be this: science has an impressive track record (and perhaps the most solid track record) for expanding our base of human knowledge, and so therefore, it's at least prima facie plausible that science affords us the ultimate source of knowledge about reality. On this way of thinking, it is stressed that science has undeniably led us to develop sophisticated medical interventions, complex computers, enormous planes and so on. As well as facilitating invention, science has been successful in uncovering not just many, but also important truths – many of which have revolutionized our perspectives and approaches (e.g., the discovery that the earth revolves around the sun). As Peels discusses, this sort of pro-scientism argument is often combined with the observation that science reveals "grand and unifying truths." As Rosenberg puts it "[the] phenomenal accuracy of its prediction [and the] breath-taking extent and detail of its explanations are powerful reasons to believe that physics is the *whole truth* about reality" (my italics).

We can grant unrestricted scientism the success aspect of the claim. However, this is perhaps not enough to actually secure the position. After all, although the success of science suggests scientific exploration is valuable, worthwhile and important, the mere fact of the success of science doesn't go very far toward establishing the other half of unrestricted scientism's claim – namely, that there's something amiss with *non-scientific*, "common sense" sources of potential knowledge (e.g., memory). This means the "science is successful" argument for scientism isn't sufficient – at the very least, we also need a complementary argument that cleaves a more obvious wedge between scientific and non-scientific sources of belief.

To that end, consider the following: scientific beliefs are testable, and they're the product of processes with built-in safety mechanisms (e.g., controlled trials, double-blind peer review and so on). Common sense beliefs don't obviously have such built-in safety mechanisms, so the thought is that our scientific beliefs come with a level of reliability that non-scientific beliefs simply cannot offer. However, is it really so apparent that we can't test our common sense beliefs in relevantly analogous ways, or at least, in ways that are epistemically respectable enough to give us knowledge? For example, we might ask about things we see, or check things we remember against the memories held by other people in attendance at the same event. A critic might respond that these cases of 'asking' or 'checking' are the exception rather than the rule. But here we have two replies waiting. First, even if these cases are the exception (e.g., even if our common sense beliefs are not often checked against our other beliefs, the fact that at least *some* are is enough already to militate against unrestricted scientism's strong thesis that common sense beliefs fail to aspire to knowledge. Secondly, there's a case to be made that safety mechanisms are to some extent in place even in cases where we simply trust our basic belief forming faculties. After all, our most basic belief-forming faculties (e.g., perception, memory, introspection) are ones for which we can infer a track record of success – if (by hypothesis) perceptual were *unreliable*, then we would for example have walked into trees and be terrible at catching objects, avoiding mid-ranged obstacles, etc. But we are not. So perception of the sort we trust implicitly is probably reliable.

It is worth noting that the pro-scientism argument canvassed also carries with it a commitment to the claim that beliefs are only rational if they are *testable*. While this assumption has some intuitive appeal, it breaks down under closer scrutiny. As Peels observes, science assumes an external material world, and that belief is not really testable *without* the assumption of an external world – but do we really want to say it's not rational to believe that there is an external world? If that sounds implausibly sceptical, then perhaps we should back off the claim that beliefs are irrational if untestable – and thereby back off the claim that common sense beliefs are categorically not rational.

A third avenue of defence for scientism compares our *understanding* of scientific knowledge to the understanding we have of common sense beliefs. More specifically, we seem to understand how we achieve scientific knowledge – we design and conduct experiments, we carefully check the results, we repeat the process, etc. On the other hand, it is much harder to say how we might attain non-scientific knowledge, especially knowledge of God or of moral facts, so should we really claim to have religious or moral *knowledge*? There are several avenues of reply for an opponent of scientism here: firstly, **metaethicists,** moral epistemologists and philosophers of religion have plenty to say about how we might attain these latter kinds of knowledge – it is not as though we lack any potentially satisfying explanation here. Secondly, some purportedly scientific beliefs are themselves based on somewhat mysterious sources – for example, mathematicians will generally believe in objective mathematical truth, but we don't have an entirely clear grasp on *how* we would acquire such knowledge. The point here is that unrestricted scientism may be too quick in suggesting there is a marked difference between our understanding of scientific and non-scientific sources of potential knowledge, undermining their ability to keep these two sources of belief separate.

We might, however, advert the contemporary work on **cognitive biases** as a strategy for defending scientism's rejection of common sense beliefs, as this body of work shows just how problematic such beliefs can be. There are lots of fascinating instances of such biases, such as the availability heuristic and the anchoring effect. When the former is present, we assume that just because we can recall something, it must be more significant than other options – for example, if two people are talking about lead poisoning and then someone they know dies, quickly concluding that lead poisoning is a likely cause is an instance of the availability heuristic in action. Meanwhile, the anchoring effect refers to our tendency to give too much focus to the first piece of information we receive when making a judgement. This is precisely the sort of bias in play when we end up paying more than the average price for a piece of clothing when the first piece of information we receive is that the item has allegedly been marked down from an enormous price. Extrapolating from such cases, the proponent of scientism might argue that the fact that common sense is riddled through with cognitive biases gives us a reason to doubt that common sense beliefs can aspire to knowledge.

A response to this line might point out that there remain many unanswered questions about biases that may increase or decrease their power to discredit non-scientific beliefs. For example, it would be useful to know to what extent such biases really are undermining the reliability of our beliefs (after all, sometimes cognitive biases are themselves reliable!) and furthermore, to the extent that knowledge involves ability, it would be relevant to know whether the extent to which biases explain belief formation is such that it excludes ability at least playing some significant role in the default case. In sum, it seems like the jury is still out on whether cognitive bias literature provides enough evidence to support scientism's claim that common sense beliefs are not candidates for knowledge. Further, might there not also be some biases that interfere with scientific methods and beliefs based on scientific evidence?

Another, possibly more robust defence of scientism points out that science offers us debunking explanations of many of our common sense beliefs. For example, some cognitive scientists have developed views according to which religious beliefs can be explained *without* appealing to the existence of God, spirits or supernatural entities. While there are competing views on this score, if any *one* such view of any type of non-scientific belief is right, then such beliefs immediately seem to lack credibility. While this is a promising avenue for the scientism advocate to pursue, it is far from conclusive – a good debunking explanation needs to (i) explain any independent evidence for such beliefs (especially sources of religious belief that are not studied by cognitive science of religion, such as arguments for God's existence), and (ii) explain *away* such beliefs (e.g., in the case of religious beliefs, explain why they exist and why they are not sources of knowledge). Further, it's not clear that (ii) can be accomplished by scientists alone – arguably, philosophy is also needed.

The final argument we'll consider in favour of scientism is that science seemingly tells us that some of our common sense beliefs are illusory. Belief in free will is a common example here, as there are studies on readiness potential suggesting that our brain is prepared to act before we would consciously claim to have made a choice (classic experiments on readiness potential concern seemingly spontaneous bodily movements). The best response here might be to point to critical work on readiness potential – for example, some cognitive neuroscientists (e.g., Aaron Shurge) as well as philosophers (e.g., Alfred Mele, b. 1951) have appealed to follow-up experiments that they claim show that spontaneous brain activity merely *look*s like pre-conscious decision making. Further, even if readiness potential experiments discredit the notion of free will, this only really helps the advocate of *restricted* scientism about free will – to deny common sense beliefs as candidates for knowledge (and therefore better support *unrestricted* scientism), many more classes of such beliefs must be shown to be illusory.

Why reject scientism?

We have looked at some of the arguments in favour of endorsing unrestricted scientism – and to the extent that any are convincing, they may be relevant to our ongoing attempt to assess the ways in which scientific fundamentalism is problematic. We can now turn to survey this debate from the opposite side, evaluating reasons to *reject* scientism and taking these considerations into account when building a picture of what scientific fundamentalism would look like.

Arguments against scientism are less widespread than points in favour of scientism, but Peels has recently proposed a range of anti-scientism arguments that are worth considering. Firstly, there's what he calls the *fundamental argument* – the thought here is that scientific knowledge is seemingly based on other things that *provide* knowledge, and that science can only generate knowledge if those things also count as knowledge. For example, scientific knowledge might be based on *seeing* something in a petri dish, *remembering* that one conducted a particular experiment yesterday or *introspecting* about the fact one needs to conduct a further ten trials. The crux of this argument is that if science gives us knowledge, it can only do so because there are also *non-scientific* sources of knowledge, viz., the same kinds of sources that afford us the kind of common sense beliefs the epistemic status of which scientism impugns. What should we make of this argument? One possible criticism is that it could support e.g. memory as a non-scientific source of knowledge, but perhaps not moral or religious beliefs (because we don't appeal to those in our scientific endeavours).

Peels also presents an argument from **self-referential incoherence**. Recall that unrestricted scientism holds that only science can provide knowledge, and then consider that this thesis is not *itself* a product of science. This means that scientism doesn't meet its own criteria for knowledge, and therefore (by the position's own lights) we should surely not endorse it. Once again, there are a few avenues for the advocate of scientism to pursue here. Among them is the unsatisfying and ad hoc response that scientism is true and we should simply make an exception for it. A more satisfying response is this: might not the success of science and the evidence for debunking explanations of non-scientific belief sources count as scientific evidence for scientism?

A third argument against scientism highlights that there seem to be non-scientific principles involved in the pursuit of natural science. For example,

Mikael Stenmark (b. 1962) points out that when we're doing science, we compare different theories using criteria like the following: explanatory power, simplicity, precision, unifying power and elegance. When we balance different criteria like these in order to choose a theory, it's far from obvious that we can do this on a scientific basis – for example, four scientists who have access to the same data might very well embrace four different theories due to prioritizing one such criteria over another. In sum, then, there are non-scientific values at the heart of scientific practice, and these can't clearly be judged using scientific research. So, once again, we have cause to doubt that scientism can so neatly divide scientific and non-scientific beliefs, isolating the latter from the former.

Is scientism a kind of fundamentalism?

Having now canvassed some of the key arguments both for and against adopting unrestricted scientism, we can see that the truth or falsity of the position is far from obvious – there are compelling objections to every potential piece of support for scientism, but so too are there potential replies, and there are also plenty of problems with anti-scientistic arguments. What, if anything, can this tell us about whether we should characterize scientism as a problematic form of fundamentalism, something akin to religious fundamentalism?

Here the answer (perhaps unsurprisingly) will be a qualified one. We do have some good reasons to think that unrestricted scientism can be a fundamentalist position. For one thing, both religious fundamentalism and unrestricted scientism are apt to claim that there is only one source of our knowledge about reality – the former claims it is holy scripture, while the latter claims it is natural science, with both views hastily downgrading other potentially legitimate sources of knowledge. In addition, common to both staunch advocates of scientism and religious fundamentalists is a kind of close-minded, highly dogmatic discounting of evidence against the view.

On the other hand, there are also some significant *dissimilarities* between scientism and religious fundamentalism. Firstly, only *some* forms of scientism are even in the market for being comparable to religious fundamentalism – the view isn't necessarily fundamentalist in nature (just as there are rigid, close-minded endorsers of just about every possible position). In addition, many advocates of scientism see that there are problems with the picture, and consider there to be a need for arguments for scientism. And further, those who endorse scientism may well be interested in refining their arguments in response to reasonable debates – this is evidenced by the fact that scientism as a view has evolved over time. This attitude towards one's commitment to scientism does not sound inherently fundamentalist in nature, as it involves taking counterevidence seriously and being willing to adapt one's beliefs to reflect the nuances of that evidence.

We have seen that fundamentalism is not just a problem for religious people – and staunch advocates of unrestricted scientism are a good example of why.

However, it *is* possible to support even unrestricted scientism *without* doing so in a fundamentalist manner. So, scientism (at least as defined here) is not inherently fundamentalist in nature, in the same way that religious commitments are not necessarily fundamentalist.

Chapter summary

- The chapter's focus is on how non-religious positions can nonetheless still be fundamentalist in nature. This issue is explored through the lens of *scientism* – a view according to which only the natural sciences can provide us with knowledge.
- As explored here, fundamentalism is characterized as a position of close-mindedness, and insensitive to countervailing evidence. It is possible to be a fundamentalist regardless of whether what one believes is true.
- According to *restricted* scientism, there are *some* domains in which we can only gain knowledge through the natural sciences. According to *unrestricted* scientism, science is the only source of knowledge about reality across the board (ruling out "common sense" beliefs as candidates for knowledge, potentially including not only religious and moral beliefs but those based on memory and introspection as well). It is *unrestricted* forms of scientism that are most likely to be candidates for a kind of fundamentalism.
- Arguments in favour of scientism may be used to suggest that embracing a fundamentalist scientism is potentially less problematic than it would be if scientism turned out to be false. Among those arguments are the following:

  (1) Science gets successful and significant results (response: this doesn't mean that common sense beliefs *don't* provide knowledge).
  (2) Scientific beliefs are testable, and have built-in safety mechanisms (response: this may commit one to the claim that only testable beliefs are rational, and it's also not clear that we *don't* test our common sense beliefs).
  (3) We understand how we achieve scientific knowledge, but not how we achieve knowledge based on common sense beliefs (response: philosophers take themselves to be answering questions about how we arrive at e.g., religious and moral knowledge. In addition, some seemingly scientific beliefs appear to be based on mysterious sources).
  (4) Our common sense beliefs are riddled with cognitive biases, so we should only consider science as a reliable source of knowledge (response: more work needs to be done to show that cognitive biases really do undermine *all* of our common sense beliefs and thereby bar them from providing knowledge).
  (5) There are debunking explanations that show why we *think* we have, for example, moral or religious knowledge (response: these explanations

must also explain away any independent evidence, such as arguments for moral facts or God's existence, and must explain *why* these beliefs are not sources of knowledge).

(6) Some common sense beliefs (e.g., beliefs in free will) appear to be illusory (response: at best, this shows we should adopt *restricted* scientism, and there are also competing experiments suggesting there are flaws in the studies that aim to disprove free will).

- Arguments against scientism can help to illuminate further reasons why it is problematic to be a fundamentalist about scientism. Among those arguments are the following:

(1) Scientific knowledge appears to be based on other, non-scientific sources of knowledge (response: this is a less useful defence of religious/moral beliefs than it is of memorial beliefs, as we don't appeal to the former in science).

(2) Scientism may be self-referentially incoherent, as the position *itself* is not a product of science (response: perhaps there is scientific evidence for scientism, e.g., the success of science and experiments that aim to debunk common sense beliefs).

(3) Natural science uses non-scientific principles (e.g., elegance and simplicity) when evaluating theories (response: but scientific theories are also supported by scientific considerations and not merely non-scientific principles like elegance and simplicity).

- In sum, the strongest forms of unrestricted scientism can be a form of fundamentalism – however, just as religious people are not necessarily fundamentalists, not all supporters of even strong forms of scientism have fundamentalist attitudes about the position.

Study questions

1. What intellectually virtuous traits are seemingly incompatible with being a fundamentalist?
2. Why might it be impossible to have knowledge about something about which one is a fundamentalist?
3. What is the difference between restricted and unrestricted scientism? What is one example of a form of *restricted* scientism?
4. Name three types of beliefs that Peels places under the heading of "common sense beliefs," and give an example of each type.
5. Should we think that beliefs are only rational (or candidates for knowledge) if they are testable? Defend your answer.
6. What work remains for an advocate of scientism who wants to offer a debunking explanation of common sense beliefs?
7. Outline how the argument from self-referential incoherence can be used to attack scientism, and evaluate the effectiveness of this argument.

8. Do scientists appeal to non-scientific principles when pursuing natural science? Explain your answer.

9. What does the strongest type of unrestricted scientism have in common with religious fundamentalism?

10. How might an advocate of scientism best tackle the task of avoiding fundamentalism in their approach?

Introductory readings

De Ridder, J. (2014). 'Science and Scientism in Popular Science Writing', *Social Epistemology Review and Reply Collective* 3(12): 23–39. [Looks at the problematic impact of scientistic epistemology on popular science writing and suggests strategies for improvement.]

Padgett, A. (2007). 'Science and Religion: Philosophical Issues', *Philosophy Compass* 3(1): 222–230. [A survey of philosophical issues related to the relationship between science and religion, including the differing epistemological perspectives that are relevant understanding scientism.]

Rosenberg, A. (2012). *The Atheist's Guide to Reality* (New York: W. W. Norton and Company). [A controversial but accessible book in which Rosenberg argues the case for scientism, claiming that science can answer all questions about reality and the meaning of life.]

Ruthven, M. (2007). *Fundamentalism: A Very Short Introduction* (Oxford: Oxford University Press). [A concise discussion of how we should define the term 'fundamentalism' and an exploration of its historical, political, social and ideological roots.]

Advanced readings

De Ridder, J., Peels, R. and van Woudenberg, R., eds. (2016). *Scientism: A Philosophical Exposition and Evaluation* (New York: Oxford University Press). [An edited collection of recent papers examining the nature and plausibility of scientism.]

Peels, R. (2016). 'The Empirical Case against Introspection', *Philosophical Studies*. [Assesses and criticizes the scientific arguments against the claim that we can reliably form beliefs through introspection, which has implications for the strong scientistic claim that common sense beliefs cannot yield knowledge.]

Williams, R. (2016). *Scientism: The New Orthodoxy* (New York: Bloomsbury Publishing). [An edited volume of papers in which a range of leading philosophers consider the role of science in religion, social science and other subjects in the humanities.]

Internet resources

De Cruz, H. (2017). 'Religion and Science', *Stanford Encyclopedia of Philosophy*, E. Zalta (ed.), https://plato.stanford.edu/archives/spr2017/entries/religion-science. [An in-depth exploration of the connections between science and religion, including a section on the scientific study of religion.]

Hughes, A. (2012). 'The Folly of Scientism', *The New Atlantis*, www.thenewatlantis.com/publications/the-folly-of-scientism. [An op-ed article exploring the attempt to supplant philosophy with science.]

Kidd, I. (2014). 'Doing Away with Scientism', *Philosophy Now Magazine*, https://philosophy now.org/issues/102/Doing_Away_With_Scientism. [A short and accessible article explaining and criticizing scientific fundamentalism.]

Taylor, J. E. (2017). 'The New Atheists', *Internet Encyclopedia of Philosophy*, J. Fieser and B. Dowden (eds.), www.iep.utm.edu/n-atheis/. [Summarizes the positions of major contemporary advocates of scientism, including Richard Dawkins and Sam Harris.]

10 Why should anyone care about the science-and-religion debate?

Michael Fuller

Introduction

Why should anyone care about the science-and-religion debate? It might reasonably be assumed that, in fact, few people with an interest in either science or religion do. After all, it's perfectly possible to be a scientific practitioner and have little interest in religion, or vice-versa; and it's perfectly possible to be interested in both, without seeing any need for there to be a 'debate' between them. Indeed, the academic study of science and religion generally assumes that the interaction between the two is rather more subtle and complex than the word 'debate' suggests. But this is an issue about which many people do care – and care very passionately.

In examining present-day attitudes, it can be helpful to explore where those attitudes have come from. We might expect today's science-and-religion debate to be shaped significantly by the history of that debate. This chapter will look at that history and consider in the light of it the issues which may lie behind people taking an interest in the science-and-religion debate today. It will then look tentatively towards the future – for one significant reason for engaging with a debate today is surely for the benefits which that engagement might bring tomorrow.

Background: conflict and dialogue

For there to be a debate at all, of course, two sides need to be seen as being opposed to one another regarding some issue. For over a century, the view has been widely proclaimed that 'science' and 'religion' (however these are understood) are two ways of thinking which are thus opposed. This has been dubbed the 'conflict thesis', and it has become an assumption which frequently lies behind the very expression 'science-and-religion debate'.

Although the word 'debate' might suggest an open discussion, with the possibility of people being persuaded to change views they have previously adopted on some subject, it might also be argued that debates often serve principally to entrench, rather than to modify or change, the views of those who taking part in them. They tend to be a means by which divisions are intensified, rather than rapprochements attained. For this reason, those engaged in the academic study of the interactions of science and religion have generally preferred the term 'dialogue'. In doing so, they're often making reference to a celebrated fourfold typology developed by Ian Barbour to characterise the possible relationships between science and religion: conflict, independence, dialogue, and integration.

In using these terms, Barbour suggests that science and religion may be seen as in conflict with one another, competing over the same territory – a struggle in which only one can emerge triumphant. Or they may be seen as entirely independent of one another, exploring different issues by different means – each of great importance in the human quest for understanding of ourselves and our environment, but at the risk of generating situations of conflict when one trespasses into territory properly belonging to the other. Or they may be seen as capable of mutually-beneficial dialogue; or they may be seen as capable of ultimately being integrated, to form what Barbour calls an '**inclusive metaphysics**'.

Barbour's system has been much commented upon, and other (usually more complex) ways of relating science and religion have been proposed to capture in more detail the rich range of possible interactions between them. However, Barbour's typology immediately alerts us to the possibility of a variety of relationships between 'science' and 'religion', and warns us to beware of over-simplistic accounts of the science-and-religion debate. In fact, as we shall see, there's a lot more going on in this debate than might at first sight be apparent.

Where, then, does this notion of conflict between science and religion originate? What are its historical roots? In understanding these, can we cast light on those passionate views which some people bring to the science-and-religion debate today?

The science-and-religion debate: some historical perspectives

A great deal of work has been done in recent decades concerning the history of those things which we today refer to as 'science' and 'religion'. To start with the former: the term 'science' is a voracious one, which has gathered to itself a wide variety of approaches to a wide variety of phenomena in the natural world (including phenomena associated with human beings, as a part of that world). Various ideas have been expressed concerning a 'scientific method' which these approaches might have in common, and various critiques have been offered of that method as a means of arriving at truth about the natural world. For example, it's sometimes said that the practice of science is associated with the construction of theories about how the world works, the conduct of experiments to test those theories, and the amendment (when necessary) of our theories in response to the data generated by those experiments. Such an approach may indeed typify the approach of some sciences, such as physics and chemistry. But some sciences, such as psychology and anthropology, may rely on data which is generated and gathered in rather different contexts to the clinical environment of a laboratory, and which may require more careful collection, nuanced analysis, and tentative interpretation than is required in the case of (say) atomic and molecular spectra. Other sciences, such as archaeology and palaeontology, may not be so amenable to systematic investigation through experimentation because they are reliant on chance finds which must then be fitted into postulated historical narratives, either confirming those narratives or requiring their amendment. In these cases, the theory which lies behind the practice of the science, shaping both the way in which it's developed and the way in which its findings are interpreted, explicitly takes a narrative form.

The historian Peter Harrison has suggested that the modern understanding of 'science' stems from around the time of the Enlightenment movement of the eighteenth century and derives from the merging of two earlier approaches to the natural world: the approaches known as natural philosophy and natural history. Natural philosophy sought to explain the causes of things and to predict future happenings on the basis of an understanding of their behaviour. (It's worth remembering that Sir Isaac Newton's *Principia* (1687), which in many respects laid the foundations of modern physical science, has as its full title *Philosophiae Naturalis Principia Mathematica* – 'The Mathematical Principles of Natural Philosophy'.) Natural history was concerned with categorising and explaining the relationships between entities such as plants and animals.

There's no obvious reason why the investigation of natural phenomena in these ways need lead to any conflict with religious beliefs. Indeed, it's been suggested that in the Western Christian context such investigations might have been carried out in the expectation that they'd fully support such beliefs. The natural world, after all, was seen as the creation of God and, in investigating it, people were 'thinking God's thoughts after him'. This view gave rise to the enterprise of **natural theology**, which reached its zenith in a book of that title by William Paley, published in 1802. Paley famously likened the remarkable orderliness and smooth functioning of the natural world to a watch: such a contrivance couldn't have come about by chance, but bore witness to the divine hand which had ordered it. The nascent sciences, in other words, were seen as being useful in supporting and justifying Christian belief (an exercise known as **apologetics**): they certainly weren't seen as undermining it.

This approach soon brought problems with it, however, as the historian John Hedley Brooke has pointed out:

> The problem for Christian apologists was this: In seeking to capitalize on the most accessible proof of God's existence, and one having the authority of the sciences behind it, they came close to saying that what they meant by God was the craftsman, the mechanic, the architect, the supreme contriver behind nature's contrivances. From this to atheism *could* be one short step. It only required an alternative metaphysics in which the appearance of design could be dismissed as illusory.

> (p. 195 of Brooke's *Science and Religion*)

This goes some way towards explaining the shock felt in some (though by no means all) religious quarters by the arrival of such an 'alternative metaphysics' in the shape of Darwin's theory of evolution by natural selection. In turn, it's doubtless the reverberation of this sense of shock which accounts, at least in part, for the hostility towards Darwinism which is still expressed by some religious believers today. It may even in part explain why that theory is associated in some people's minds with an atheistic outlook.

However, there are other ways of thinking about God than simply as a 'supreme contriver', and ever since Darwin's own day there have been religious thinkers who have quite happily accommodated his ideas to their faith. As long ago as 1889, an Oxford theologian named Aubrey Moore wrote of Darwinism as a friend of religious belief rather than a foe, since it provided grounds for theologians to take seriously the idea of a God who's active within nature rather than absent from it. Despite the expression of such conciliatory sentiments, however, it's to the debates which ensued upon the publication of Darwin's *Origin of Species* in 1859 that we must look for the main shape of the science-and-religion debate as it has come down to us today.

One of the principal instigators of what came to be called the conflict thesis was the naturalist Thomas Henry Huxley (1825–1895) – 'Darwin's bulldog', as he was known. In lectures and publications popularising Darwin's ideas, Huxley was at pains to point out the incompatibility of science and established religion; and he was a gifted rhetorician, with a memorable, inflammatory turn of phrase. Huxley was a principal player in an event that was long held to be a turning-point in the relationship between science and religion: a debate which took place in Oxford in 1860 between (amongst others) Huxley and the Bishop of Oxford at the time, Samuel Wilberforce. Although the view became widespread that this was an occasion on which science (in the person of Huxley) triumphed over religion (in the person of Wilberforce), closer scrutiny of what actually happened at the time doesn't provide much support. It would appear, rather, that this was an early instance of what would now be termed spin-doctoring by Huxley and his supporters: Huxley's agenda was not to pit science against religion *per se*, but rather to use science to attack the privileged position of the Church of England of the day, enjoying as it did considerable influence within the ancient Universities and learned societies at the time, and to establish science as a profession in its own right (rather than being, as had hitherto been the case, the preserve of gentleman amateurs – many of these, of course, themselves being clergymen). In this campaign, Huxley was undoubtedly successful, as can be seen (for example) by the plummeting numbers of clergy involved with the Royal Society in the latter part of the nineteenth century. Although Huxley clearly had issues with the Church of his day, towards religious matters such as the existence (or otherwise) of God he was less confrontational: it was he who coined the word 'agnostic' to describe his position, rather than declare himself an atheist. (Darwin, too, came to embrace the term 'agnostic' as the best description of his position concerning God.)

Evolutionary theory offered Huxley a convenient tool with which to wage his campaign. Others had no need of specific issues. The titles of two highly influential books of the late nineteenth century, each of which went through many editions, speak for themselves: John William Draper's *History of the Conflict between*

Religion and Science (1874) and Andrew Dickson White's *A History of the Warfare of Science with Theology in Christendom* (1896). (Draper, incidentally, had been another participant in that Oxford debate of 1860.) These books were at pains to assert that the conflict they presented had deep historical roots, although it has since been demonstrated that this assertion assumes a highly-selective reading of history. The motivations of Draper and White have been much discussed: it has been suggested that the former was driven by anti-Catholic sentiment, whilst the latter wrote as he did in response to being branded an infidel for using his position as President of Cornell University to foster unbelief there.

Doubtless, their motivations for promoting the conflict thesis were complex blends of public and personal factors. Suffice it to say that, in the words of a more recent writer, 'Historians of science have known for years that White's and Draper's accounts are more propaganda than history' (p. 6 in Numbers' *Galileo Goes To Jail*). It's widely recognised that what has been going on when 'science' has been seen to be at odds with 'religion' has generally been a combination of socio-political and ideological factors (on both sides of the debate) as much as it is about science and religion in themselves.

Recall Harrison's suggestion that the Enlightenment period brought with it modern understandings of 'science'. He maintains that it brought a particular understanding of 'religion', too: indeed, he goes so far as to maintain that, in the way in which it's understood today, 'religion is . . . a cultural construction of the modern West'. Religions came to be seen as sets of propositional beliefs and ritual practices, so that they could be categorised and compared with one another, almost after the fashion of biological specimens. This Enlightenment understanding may be questioned, however, not least in that religions tend to be a great deal more complicated than this assumes. To take the case of Christianity: if one were to compare denominations from within the World Council of Churches, it might be concluded that religion embraces many different beliefs on matters of detail (for example, concerning the role and status of saints) alongside others upon which Christians generally concur (such as the existence of God). Moreover, liturgical practices between denominations may vary considerably. A great many general statements along the lines of 'Christians are people who believe *x*' or 'Christians are people who do *y*' might therefore immediately be refuted by citing a particular church whose members do not necessarily believe *x* or do *y*. Moreover, the religious beliefs and practices of any individual are likely to be embedded in a rich complex of personal, familial, social, political, and other factors, so that even within a particular church there's likely to be considerable variation on such matters. Nailing down exactly what we mean by 'religion' is therefore far from straightforward.

Where do these historical considerations leave us? It would appear that both 'science' and 'religion' are complex ideas in themselves, and that the relationships between them are similarly multi-faceted. Despite the current prevalence of the idea that there must be conflict between them, perhaps the realisation will ultimately spread that this 'conflict thesis' simply fails to do justice to the realities we're dealing with. The narratives devised by particular individuals like Huxley,

Draper and White a century or more ago, in support of particular agendas which applied then, need not necessarily command our continued support today.

These, then, are some of the historical roots for the perceived conflict between science and religion. They indicate why some people in the past have cared about the science-and-religion debate. But why might people continue to care about that debate today?

The science-and-religion debate: some contemporary perspectives

The science-and-religion debate has been conducted primarily in the West, and (as we have seen) it has been shaped and driven by particular historical agendas, some of which persist today. For example, various forms of American creationism have taken the form they have because of particular ideologies and particular fears within some Christian groups there, which are deeply informed by the 'conflict' narrative. Science is seen by these groups as inherently anti-religious, not least because the narratives constructed by science (such as those concerning evolution) are seen as contradicting biblical ones (such as those concerning creation) – no matter that there is a long history of Christians reading biblical accounts of events like the creation in non-literal rather than historical ways. If science contradicts the Bible on this matter, creationists may aver, then it may also be seen as undermining it in other ways, for example by threatening ethical and other societal norms.

No doubt it's this creationist hostility towards science – in particular, towards evolutionary biology – that's at least partly to blame for the reciprocal hostility expressed in the anti-religious polemic of scientific authors such as Richard Dawkins. The inheritor of the rhetorical mantle of T. H. Huxley, Dawkins' will be a familiar name to anyone who has taken an interest in the contemporary science-and-religion debate, and his considerable literary and polemical gifts have coloured that debate to a significant extent. Responses by religious and philosophical commentators to his writings, and to others of the 'new atheist' movement, have ranged from the irenic (David Fergusson's *Faith and Its Critics*) to the pugnacious (Terry Eagleton's *Reason, Faith and Revolution*), the former attempting to take the heat out of the debate through the constructive engagement of those involved in it, the latter wittily repaying Dawkins in his own combative coin.

It's possible that some readers approach the literature of the 'new atheist' movement, and the responses it has generated, in order to be persuaded which side in the science-and-religion debate is to be believed. Dawkins' explicit proselytising at the outset of his bestseller *The God Delusion* ('If this book works as I intend, religious readers who open it will be atheists when they put it down') suggests that he is targeting such persuadable readers. However, it's hard to resist the suspicion that Dawkins's writing is likely to be less effective in converting people to his view than it is in bolstering the beliefs of those who already think as he does – and the same will undoubtedly be the case for the readership of books upholding the 'conflict thesis' from within a religious perspective.

Of course, by no means all writers on science and religion insist on the conflict model. Many scholars have preferred Barbour's model of dialogue between science and religion, not least those whose interest in the science and religion debate comes from the desire to establish a new form of Christian apologetic writing – seeking to demonstrate the continuing relevance of the Christian faith in an age which is deeply informed by the thinking of the natural sciences. Some of these scholars, such as John Polkinghorne and Arthur Peacocke, have themselves had distinguished scientific backgrounds and have held ecclesiastical offices. The desire expressed by these and other authors to broaden our understanding of how the interactions of science and religion might be mutually beneficial offers another reason for engaging with the science-and-religion debate.

In addition to all this, in recent years there has been an increasing realisation that much of the writing around science and religion has proceeded with particular models of 'science' and 'religion' in mind, seeing the former chiefly in terms of its expression in physics and the latter chiefly in terms of its expression in Christian theology. In consequence, recent years have seen a broadening-out of the dialogue to include a variety of sciences and a variety of religious traditions. Anyone engaging with the science-and-religion debate now is faced with a richly nuanced range of understandings, far removed from the monolithic caricatures of 'science' and 'religion' that have been used to support the conflict thesis in the past. The possibility of widening and deepening the ways in which 'science' and 'religion' can be understood is another admirable reason for caring about the science-and-religion debate today.

The future of the science-and-religion debate: some prospects

The argument so far suggests that there are two contradictory trends in the current state of the science-and-religion debate. On the one hand, some continue to hold fast to the conflict thesis, presumably (as we've seen) with the intention of (a) confirming those who agree with their beliefs, and (b) persuading those who disagree to forgo their superstitious folly/arrogant hubris (delete as applicable) and embrace a better way of seeing the world. On the other hand, there's the opening out of the debate to embrace the radical diversity of those things referred to in shorthand as 'science' and 'religion' and, in accepting their complexity and the complex history of the relationships between them, to seek a way forward that might combine fruitfully the insights of both. It's the present writer's view that the sterility of the former approach to the debate has little to commend it. Where might the latter lead us?

Let's suppose that, at some point in the future, the tide of intellectual fashion has finally turned against the conflict thesis, and it's generally recognised that the mutual interaction of science and religion is possible, to the benefit of both. This movement, from hostility and mistrust to mutual recognition and respect, has an interesting parallel: the **ecumenical** movement within the Christian churches. Historically, different denominations have treated each other with hostility comparable to that of present-day upholders of the conflict thesis concerning science and religion. However, over the last half-century or more, ecumenical organisations have achieved a huge amount in breaking down centuries of antagonism between Christians. An important part of the process by which they've done so has been a dialogical one. Theologians, philosophers, and historians representing different churches have produced agreed statements on matters previously considered to be divisive, thereby paving the way for warmer relationships to flourish. It might be argued that the dialogue which has been pursued by science-and-religion scholars is an analogous approach, with the similar aim of producing peaceful, harmonious, and mutually beneficial relationships.

But this is only part of the story. Ecumenists may have made significant breakthroughs at institutional levels, but at the grassroots level, historical legacies of animosity may still prevail. Science-and-religion scholarship risks running into a similar situation: as the historian Ronald Numbers has commented, 'the message [regarding the origins of the 'conflict myth'] has rarely escaped the ivory tower. The secular public, if it thinks about such issues at all, *knows* that organised religion has always opposed scientific progress' (p. 6 of *Galileo Goes To Jail*). Now, ecumenical breakthroughs at grassroots level have often come about when churches engage locally in action together, to pursue a project in the community of which all can see the benefit. Given that it might reasonably be maintained that 'science' and 'religion', however they are understood, are both endeavours which have human flourishing as their ultimate goal, might the science-and-religion debate achieve a new momentum through their similarly engaging in joint projects at the grassroots level? Might this, in fact, inspire a whole new wave of interest in the science-and-religion debate?

Such projects are in fact already being pursued. To cite a couple of examples, back in the 1960s the Church of Scotland set up its Society, Religion and Technology (SRT) Project, with the aim of engaging with and commenting upon technological change. Amongst the enterprises with which that Project has subsequently engaged was a collaboration between theologians, ethicists, and scientists within the University of Edinburgh concerning the ethics of genetic engineering in non-human species: the resulting publication enjoyed a wide readership, both within and beyond the Academy and the Church. The SRT Project continues to address bioethics, as well as economics, and energy-related issues. Another initiative linking the sciences and churches in practical action is the Eco Congregations Project. This describes itself as 'an ecumenical programme helping churches to make the link between environmental issues and Christian faith, and to respond in practical action in the Church, in the lives of individuals, and in the local and global community'. Here, scientific insights regarding ecological issues are brought to bear in practical programmes of action at the local level, drawing together scientifically and religiously informed people in projects of mutual concern.

In these examples, we can see new possibilities for practical engagement between those coming from scientific and religious perspectives. Initiatives such as these offer the possibility of fresh stimulus to the science-and-religion debate/ dialogue – and an entirely new set of responses to the question of why anyone should care about it.

Conclusion

There is a temptation, when surveying science, religion, and the debate between them, to assume that we're talking about monolithic entities locked in a one-dimensional argument. But in truth, as is increasingly being recognised, there are many sciences, many religions (indeed, many different approaches to religion within individual religious traditions), and consequently many aspects to the science-and-religion debate. The antagonisms expressed by some who have engaged in it, historically and in the present day, may be off-putting to many; but fresh ways of looking beyond such antagonisms are emerging, along with new, practical opportunities for science and religion to engage beneficially with one another. The historical roots of the alleged enmity between science and religion are now becoming better and better understood: the time has come for the science-and-religion debate to move past such enmity to new, fresh ground, allowing them to both serve and promote human flourishing in every aspect of our lives.

Chapter summary

- 'Science' and 'religion' are both complex constructions, which have evolved and changed historically in the ways in which they're understood.
- The science-and-religion debate takes the form it does because of particular historical agendas which have been pursued in the past.
- Understanding that past history is important in understanding the contours of the present-day science-and-religion debate.
- The nature of that debate is changing to reflect changing understandings of both science and religion.
- There are many reasons for engaging with that debate, not least in terms of broadening and deepening our understanding of what science and religion are.
- The science-and-religion debate is not just about abstract ideas. Already there are points at which the engagement of science and religion over practical issues may be seen. It's to be hoped, and expected, that such engagement will increase in the future over (for example) ecological and ethical issues.
- Anyone with an interest in all aspects of human flourishing has good reason to care about the science-and-religion debate.

Study questions

1. To what extent does an appreciation of the past history of what we now label 'science' and 'religion' help us to appreciate present-day attitudes towards them?

2. Is it helpful to think of 'science' and 'religion' as radical alternatives to one another? If so, how? If not, why not?
3. How might we account for the hostility expressed by some of those who see 'science' and 'religion' as locked in conflict with one another?
4. How might such hostility best be addressed?
5. Is it possible – and is it desirable – to keep social and political issues out of the science-and-religion debate?
6. What might be achieved by the science-and-religion debate as it has recently been pursued?
7. On what possible practical projects might scientific and religious practitioners usefully collaborate with one another?

Introductory readings

Brooke, J. H. (1991). *Science and Religion: Some Historical Perspectives*, Cambridge: Cambridge University Press. [A classic exploration of the roots of the contemporary relationship between science and religion in the West.]

Dawkins, R. (2006). *The God Delusion*, London: Transworld Publishers. [A bestselling re-iteration of the 'conflict thesis' from a standard-bearer of the 'new atheism'.]

Dixon, T. (2008). *Science and Religion: A Very Short Introduction*, Oxford: Oxford University Press. [An excellent, readable (and, yes, very short!) introduction to the academic study of science and religion.]

Eagleton, T. (2009). *Reason, Faith and Revolution*, New Haven, CT: Yale University Press. [A combative, intelligent, and frequently very funny response to the 'new atheists' Richard Dawkins and Christopher Hitchens.]

Fergusson, D. (2011). *Faith and Its Critics*, Oxford: Oxford University Press. [A more measured and thoughtful response to the rhetoric of the 'new atheist' movement.]

Gould, S. J. (2001). *Rocks of Ages: Science and Religion in the Fullness of Life*, London: Jonathan Cape. [A book responding to the American science-and-religion context, in which Gould argues that science and religion are 'non-overlapping magisteria'.]

McCalla, A. (2006). *The Creationist Debate*, London: T & T Clark. [An illuminating exploration of creationism in the USA, probably the most high-profile area of conflict between those professing scientific and religious perspectives today.]

Numbers, R. L. (ed.) (2009). *Galileo Goes to Jail, and Other Myths about Science and Religion*, Cambridge, MA: Harvard University Press. [A multi-authored unpacking and debunking of 25 commonly held assumptions about the history of the relations between science and religion.]

Advanced readings

Barbour, I. G. (2000). *Religion and Science: Historical and Contemporary Issues*, London: SCM Press. [A classic and wide-ranging exposition of the field of science and religion, setting out views which have shaped and stimulated many other studies in this area.]

Brooke, J. H. and R. Numbers (eds.) (2011). *Science and Religion Around the World*, Oxford: Oxford University Press. [A multi-authored introduction to the interaction of science with 'world religions': an important extension of discussions beyond the Western Christian context.]

Dixon, T., G. Cantor and S. Pumfrey (eds.) (2010). *Science and Religion: New Historical Perspectives*, Cambridge: Cambridge University Press. [A fascinating collection of papers, developing Brooke's 'complexity thesis'.]

Harrison, P. (2015). *The Territories of Science and Religion*, London: University of Chicago Press. [An exploration of how 'science' and 'religion' have come to have the meanings they possess today, and how that historical trajectory has constrained the possibilities for relationships between them in their modern understandings.]

Internet resources

Biologos: http://biologos.org/. [This American website extends an invitation 'to see the harmony between science and biblical faith as we present an evolutionary understanding of God's creation'. It stands against the 'warfare' model and advocates 'evolutionary creation' as a way of bringing together scientific and biblical accounts of origins.]

Eco Congregation: www.ecocongregation.org/. [This website is a portal, giving access to a wide variety of organisations operating in the UK, Europe, North America, and South Africa. Their common goal is to help Churches make links between environmental issues and Christian faith.]

Society, Religion and Technology Project: www.srtp.org.uk/. [The website of the Church of Scotland's Society, Religion and Technology Project. News of current activities, and an excellent archive of past ones.]

11 What provides a better explanation for the origin of the universe – science or religion?

David Fergusson and Katherine Snow

Introduction

Within contemporary western culture, many people assume that science and religion offer two directly competing explanations of the origin of our universe. According to this common perception, religion had historically provided the authoritative account of the creation of the cosmos, but has since yielded this role to science, whose big bang theory provides us with our current definitive explanation of how the universe began. In what follows, however, we'll see that the picture is far more complex.

In the first place, neither the religious nor the scientific accounts are equipped to erase the persistent mystery surrounding the questions of how and why our universe came to be. It isn't easy to describe, in either scientific *or* religious language, some state or time when our universe did not exist, since throughout human experience our universe has always surrounded us. Questions of whether the universe might have always existed, or might have arisen out of nothing, force us to confront inherent limits on what we can know with any degree of confidence as finite and limited beings. Any perception that theologians or scientists have provided a final answer to these questions may simply result from our willingness to delegate the most difficult philosophical problems to those occupying positions of cultural power and authority, presuming (or hoping) they must have access to special information or possess some unique insight.

Secondly, we must be cautious about trying to make any direct comparison between these two different ways of attempting to explain the universe's origin, or about trying to judge whether one is better than the other. A comparative judgement suggests a competition between the two, and this may prove to be misleading. As we'll see below, for much of its history the practice of science was closely linked with that of religion. Scientific, theological, and philosophical methods tended in the past to be employed in concert, and this was particularly the case when it came to the highly difficult and obscure question of the origin of our universe. However, during the late modern era into the twentieth century, and specifically in the several decades following the development of Einstein's theory of **general relativity** in 1915, scientists did eventually develop a way to treat this question naturalistically. The result was that a solely scientific account of the origin of the universe arose. At its core, this account consisted primarily of a new kind of mathematical model of the universe considered as one system evolving over time. This model isn't easy to translate out of the language of mathematical physics into a non-numerical language, and arguably loses much of its nuance and primary purpose when so translated. Religious accounts, on the other hand, do not use numerical representation, nor do they try to designate quantitative relationships between different component parts of the cosmos over time. They retain the same focus they have had for millennia by offering a metaphysical description of the dependence of everything upon a creator God. For the monotheistic religions, this typically includes not merely an account of a non-physical originating cause, but also describes the act of creating the universe in a way which incorporates notions of divine intentionality and purpose, concepts which in turn characterize the created world as possessing elements of spiritual and moral significance.

With these broad points established as our framework, we now turn to a brief overview of the two different types of account of the origin of the universe, religious and scientific. We'll suggest that over the course of western history, these have become fundamentally separate types of description, and that in both cases they remain open-ended and lead to further questions.

Religious accounts of the origin of creation

The simplest way to sum up the basic idea of a religious account of the origin of the universe is to say that it traces the source of the universe itself and everything within it to a divine being or beings. Many variations on this theme can be found in ancient cultures. In most cases, the divine beings were represented as all-powerful creators only partly accessible to human understanding, but deserving of worship for creating and continually sustaining the world. The approach that dominated the Hebrew Bible, classical Greek philosophy, and early Christian theology adopted a model of spiritual or intellectual **agency** to explain the world, as opposed to some type of first physical cause which was like other physical causes (only more powerful). These accounts exhibited several unifying features.

First, they belonged to a unified system of knowledge that included the study of nature. Physics, philosophy, metaphysics, and theology were intertwined in the way these systems addressed various questions, including the origin of the universe. The modern division of labour with its separation of disciplines, methods, skills, and guilds was not a feature of the ancient world. Until the modern era, physical and metaphysical accounts of the universe's origin were undertaken as part of a single intellectual project. Scholars, usually trained in a wide range of disciplines, moved freely, with no sense of embarrassment, between material and theological explanations for phenomena. The **cosmologies** of well-known Greek philosophers such as Plato (ca.424–348 BCE), Aristotle (384–322 BCE), and Plotinus (204–270 CE), as well as the early Christian theologians whom these Greek thinkers influenced, didn't restrict themselves to explaining how the world started physically. Although this was one feature of their work, various moral and spiritual considerations were also evident. The appeal to God as the explanation for the world was in large part intended to teach human beings about the nature of the soul, the proper aspiration of the spiritual self, and humankind's final destiny.

Second, unlike modern thinkers facing radical sceptical challenges, thinkers like Plato and Aristotle were less concerned with proving the existence of God. Their intention was to explain the way the world worked. God was a necessary part of any overall account of why, how, and to what end the universe existed. But cosmology wasn't primarily a project for demonstrating the existence of God, though it could later be used in this way to combat sceptical challenges.

And, finally, the ancient philosophers remained conscious of the mysterious and therefore provisional character of what they proposed. No single approach could claim a decisive triumph over rival cosmologies. Different possibilities remained in play. In Section 29 of his well-known cosmological work *Timaeus*, a work which was to influence later Christian theological writers, Plato concedes that we shouldn't look for more than a likely story in such difficult matters.

Plato's highly influential theories of the universe and its origin or ultimate foundation took as their starting point the need to explain all the motion and change we see around us. Motion, he argues, can be communicated to one object by another moving object, or else it can arise from a self-moving object. He concludes that the source of all motion in the physical universe must arise from self-moving objects. Without these, we'd have an infinite regress of communicating movements, but no beginning in a self-mover. For Plato, this seems absurd since it can't properly explain the motion we now observe. Consequently, he's led to the view that there is a self-mover responsible for the movements of the heavenly bodies. This must be described in terms of a soul or mind. Clearly, this appeals to a concept of God, though not the God of later Christian orthodoxy. In the *Timaeus*, Plato weaves together a mythical story of the creation of the world with references to religious, moral, or spiritual aspects of human existence. In this work, Plato presents God as a kind of sublime craftsman who created the world from a supply of indestructible matter that had always existed.

A similar set of arguments can be found in Aristotle, who was a pupil of Plato. Aristotle also ruminated on possible explanations for motion, including what were then perceived as the daily movements of the sun, moon, planets, and stars (an apparent beehive of activity in the sky we now know is partly a result of the earth's own motion). Writing in his *Metaphysics*, Aristotle claims that the motions of the heavenly bodies must have had their origin in an 'unmoved mover'. This is a God without movement who imparts motion to the heavenly bodies. But this occurs not through God giving them a physical nudge to get them started; rather, the process is described in terms of an eternal attraction. Through their desire of God, the heavenly bodies follow their orbital paths. Aristotle thinks of this not as a temporal, ordinary causal relationship, but as an eternal dependence of the universe upon the unmoved mover or 'prime mover'. Again, the prime mover doesn't act like a normal physical cause; divine 'activity' is restricted to contemplating God's own mind and thoughts. Like Plato, Aristotle assumed that the matter which made up the universe was eternal. Unlike the account Plato gave in the *Timaeus*, however, there was no creation act for Aristotle. Moreover,

Aristotle's God had no direct providential involvement in human affairs, thus reducing God's religious significance.

Following the emergence of Christianity in the Graeco-Roman world, theologians reflected on the ways in which the arguments of the classical philosophers could be integrated with what the Bible said about God. The philosophers' arguments were adapted in several ways and reconciled with claims contained in Genesis 1 about the creation of the world. Several shifts are evident. First, by around 200 CE, almost all Christian theologians asserted that God had created the world out of nothing rather than fashioned it out of pre-existing matter. This doctrine of **creatio ex nihilo** ('creation from nothing' in Latin) entailed a departure from the classical Greek notion of the eternity of matter. One feature of this shift of perspective was to stress that the material world expressed a good and wise intention on the part of God. Second, the world was said to have been created through the word or wisdom of God. This perpetuated aspects of the ancient Greek accounts which also invoked a deity to explain order and purpose in the cosmos (our word 'cosmos' comes from the ancient Greek word for 'order'). At the same time, for Christian theologians the creation act, and the created universe which resulted from it, formed part of a single 'economy of salvation' in which Jesus was identified with the creative word ('logos' in Greek) of God. This added a further dimension to the way in which God's origination of the world was linked to its moral and spiritual meaning.

Overall, the early Christian doctrine of creation continued to form one element within an integrated worldview representing a unified body of knowledge, interweaving what we would today call scientific, philosophical, and religious approaches to questions of the origin of the universe. This type of presentation continued throughout much of the Middle Ages in the work of Islamic writers such as Al-Ghazali (1058–1111) and Christian writers such as Thomas Aquinas (1225–1274). Appeals to religious principles to address issues of first principles and ultimate causes were understood as the only way to achieve a complete explanation of the causal processes observable all around us, or to reach any account of the origin of the world itself. These thinkers thus continued the tradition of fusing religious and scientific concerns into a single account.

With the Renaissance and the early modern period major changes began to take place in our ways of speaking and thinking of the universe and its origins or underpinnings. After the work of scientist-philosophers like Galileo (1564–1642), Descartes (1596–1650), Newton (1643–1727), and Leibniz (1646–1716), geometry, algebra, and calculus increasingly provided ways of defining and predicting nature's behaviour precisely, especially the motion of the planets, without relying upon God. At a time of growing religious diversity and scepticism in post-Reformation Europe, this raised sharper questions about the need for, and function of, religious explanation. The exclusion of God from equations describing motion in the heavens was famously expressed by the French mathematician Laplace (1749–1827) in his (alleged) remark to the Emperor Napoleon in 1814. When Napoleon asked Laplace where God featured in his book of cosmology, Laplace replied '*Je n'avais pas besoin de cette hypothèse-là'* – in English, 'I had no need of that hypothesis'.

Much of the theoretical ground for a clear separation of scientific and religious explanations of the world was prepared by the work of **David Hume** (1711–1776) and Immanuel Kant (1724–1810) during the Enlightenment. Both philosophers raised serious questions about the validity of appeals to God in any type of human explanation(s) of the world – to include explanations of the world's origin. The necessity of a first cause to end the indefinite chain of past causes was countered by the suggestion that the world might simply be an inexplicable brute fact, without any ultimate or transcendent explanation for the whole. Highly conscious of the inescapable limits placed on human knowledge, these thinkers also began to question whether the notion of a necessary and self-sufficient being requiring no follow-on explanation was intelligible. Even if the idea of God was not logically incoherent, the concept of **divine sufficiency** seemed to exceed full comprehension; the child's question 'Who made God?' was not one which could be answered without inducing some further puzzlement. These challenges began radically to question the longstanding designation of God as the ultimate cause of the universe.

The pressure towards greater separation between scientific and religious accounts of the world increased as the new sciences of geology and evolutionary biology arose in the nineteenth century. These sciences challenged the validity of literal, causal, historical readings of the Biblical accounts of the history of the Earth and the human species; this seemed likewise to weaken the credibility of reading the Genesis 1 account as if it belonged to the genre of a scientific textbook. These scientific advances, particularly after the time of Darwin, further reinforced the growing separation between religious and scientific explanations. Science increasingly became the domain of a professional group who proceeded to work independently of all religious bodies. Religion came to be viewed as dealing with faith-based claims about dependence, divine presence, trust, moral practice, and existential meaning. This basic division began to reshape the way in which the origin of the universe was explained, creating two contrasting types of explanation where historically there had been only one unified account. While this split is, to a great extent, rooted in scientific and cultural developments of the eighteenth and nineteenth centuries, it was cemented in the early twentieth with the arrival of the theory of general relativity. As we'll see in the next section, this theory provided scientists with a sophisticated new way to model the universe quantitatively as a single dynamic system, offering a route towards addressing the question of the origin of the universe which differed greatly from any path attempted before.

This divide did create some tension between the two approaches to the origin of the universe, as figures on both the religious and scientific sides alike have resisted the tendency to maintain them as two wholly different kinds of endeavour, and attempted instead to establish a single account capable of commanding unanimous assent. This is sometimes pursued by seeking a re-convergence between, or unification of, the two accounts, which entails the difficult task of trying to translate between religious, often metaphysical, and metaphorical narratives on the one hand, and the equations of general relativity, quantum theory, and probability calculations on the other. One example of these types of efforts comes with the **fine-tuning** debates which now include discussions of a hypothetical **multiverse.** Some theologians seek to insert God as a causal explanation for those quantifiable aspects of our universe that scientists consider to be extremely finely-balanced, offering God as the reason our universe was given the precise set of characteristics we observe, and thus meshing religious explanation with a quantitative scientific model. Yet these strategic moves to draw together types of explanation which have become so different are fraught with the potential for misunderstanding, even with the best of intentions on both sides.

Much less harmonious attempts to create a comprehensive narrative of the origin of our universe arise when one side seeks to discredit the other entirely and drive it from the field. Some theists look to challenge scientific cosmologies outright (just as young earth creationism challenges evolutionary biology), though these have gained little credence with a wider audience. Far more influential have been claims by prominent atheist scientists (such as biologist Dawkins, or cosmologists Hawking or Krauss) that scientific accounts of the origin of our universe can vanquish and replace all religious explanations of cosmic origins. Yet we'll see that our current scientific understanding is highly limited, making this strategy problematic.

Scientific accounts of the origin of the universe

As already noted, by the time Einstein developed his theory of general relativity in the early part of the twentieth century, scientific work was increasingly being conducted in intellectual isolation from religious and philosophical considerations. In 1917, Einstein presented his first efforts to apply general relativity to cosmological scales. He claimed that since the entire universe must be interconnected via the force of gravity, we could now calculate its past, present, and future behaviour by viewing it as a single dynamical system. Hence, the modern discipline of scientific cosmology was born. This discipline has generated our scientific, quantitative theory of the origin of the universe – what is commonly referred to as the standard cosmological model, or the theory of the big bang.

The standard cosmological model rose to scientific acceptance mainly on the back of three facts: 1) as noted above, Einstein's theory allowed scientists to model mathematically something they designated as the *entire observable universe*; 2) astronomers Edwin Hubble and others observed in the 1920s that our universe appeared to be expanding; and 3) in 1964 scientists discovered the Cosmic Microwave Background (CMB), which permeates all space, even between stars and galaxies. Interpreting the CMB as a relic of the immensely hot and dense early universe, when the first atoms formed, and before the universe had expanded and cooled sufficiently to form stars and galaxies, the CMB was quickly seen as decisive evidence in support of the big bang model. In addition, the ratios among various chemical elements existing in the universe today, especially the three building-block elements of hydrogen, helium, and lithium, seemed to correspond, on the whole, with what the big bang model predicts.

For several decades, the nature of the initial moment of the big bang itself was a topic scientists were unwilling to touch. Many early cosmologists found the idea of a universe somehow condensed to a point logically abhorrent. Even Hubble himself refused to take his own model of expansion as a literal, realist description of the universe. Scientists also knew that while relativity could describe conditions soon after the '$t=0$' moment, the equations of general relativity broke down very close to it, suggesting the need for a new kind of mathematical physics.

The discovery of the CMB led to increased confidence that the big bang model was right, and so scientists began to seek a theory covering the actual origin moment. This required a treatment of gravity on the quantum scale, but despite physicists' and mathematicians' best efforts for fifty years, a solution has proved elusive. Thus far, many theorists place their hope in loop quantum gravity and string theory, but these theories have yet to achieve widespread acceptance, largely because of the difficulty of testing them.

At the same time, cosmologists have found one possible way around this difficulty, namely the idea that inflation, a type of super-fast (exponentially so) version of the expansion we still observe in the universe, played a crucial early role in the universe. Currently, inflation is thought to have acted as a kind of 'bubbling up' of the infinite sheet of spacetime known as the multiverse, which is perpetually undergoing such bubbling. The hypothesis of a **multiverse**, out of which our observable 'bubble universe' popped up via a random process of inflation, partly sidesteps the $t=0$ problem. However, it does this at the cost of replacing our own big bang with a much bigger entity which is significantly more complex and less well-defined. It's unclear where the multiverse might have come from, and might have what caused it; it isn't even clear if the multiverse hypothesis will ever be open to **empirical** testing. The consensus on inflation is also precarious. While cosmologists agree that it seems likely that an inflation-like process shaped our universe, there's still disagreement over many of the details, including what kinds of forces or fields were involved in the process.

Overall, then, the scientific account of the origin of the universe currently comes in two basic forms (though there are also many other competing models with smaller followings). Those who adhere to the (still speculative) theory of the multiverse rely on inflation from an unexplained, undefined, and unobservable sheet of spacetime. Those who question the multiverse hypothesis must conclude that there's currently no comprehensive scientific model of the initial origin of the universe. In this case, perhaps the best we can say at present is that the universe originated in an almost infinitely hot, compact, and energetic initial phase.

Both choices become even thornier from here. Even if in the future we were able to establish a rigorous physics of the multiverse, we'd still run up against the same problem that the non-multiverse option already encounters, namely that it's unclear how the actual origination moment of the whole natural system (e.g. the initial sheet of spacetime) can be described by mathematical physics, which can't cover a time or scenario in which there were no forces or fields. Physics can model the creation of new physical states from others, but it can't describe their creation from nothing at all, even in principle, since it has no such principles.

Such difficulties mean it's premature to think that we have a comprehensive scientific narrative of the entire universe. Big bang theory describes a simplified and generalised account of a reality that's only partially open to our observations, and it calls upon highly-uncertain – even speculative – ideas like inflation and the multiverse. Caution is in order concerning claims that big bang theory captures everything important about the universe we inhabit, even if we're speaking only of its strictly physical aspects.

Conclusion

It's important in the context of science and religion to acknowledge that purely scientific accounts of the ultimate origin of the universe are, given the current stage of our scientific thinking, impossible. Scientific models presuppose physical reality; a scientific theory (which makes empirical predictions) can't be formulated without assuming the real existence of the empirical entities assumed in the model, even if these entities concern the most basic physical scenario imaginable (e.g. a quantum vacuum). Hence, one loses the sense of an ultimate 'origins' account.

Religious explanations of the origin of the universe are also open-ended, always changing and incomplete, though in different ways from scientific explanations. New insights and perspectives on Christian Scripture are apparent in an ecologically-conscious age. The encounter with other religions generates closer comparison of theological ideas and practices, including ways of handling the metaphysical aspects of universe origination and the ongoing relationship of the divine with the world. Discovery of intelligent extra-terrestrials would surely add further complexities to the discussion. And no religious account should claim to have provided a demonstrable proof that a divine being made the world; adopting this view remains largely a matter of personal faith and commitment.

Scientific and religious accounts of the origin of the universe have very different strengths and weaknesses. Neither can be claimed as complete, finalised, or immune to doubt. One common feature of both types of account is their amount of uncertainty in taking us to the brink of what we can know, or know how to formulate. We might view these mutual limitations and uncertainties in a positive light. They can remind us that a great deal of mystery persists around the subject of the origin of the universe, no matter which mode of approach we favour. Generating both intellectual humility and curiosity, this mystery can also move us to develop new ways of approaching these central questions in the future.

Chapter summary

- Neither religious nor scientific attempts to explain the origin of the universe are fully adequate in answering the questions of how and why our universe came to be.

- These accounts consist of very different types of explanation; as such, they can neither be fully harmonised nor regarded as competitors.
- Religious explanations focus on the act of creation or origination as the establishment of a relationship between God and a world which is viewed not materialistically but in terms of a dependence, trust, and divine purpose.
- Scientific accounts have had great success in building up a rough sketch of the history of our observable universe using general relativity. But these accounts are currently incomplete, and they are in principle incapable of capturing the ultimate origins scenario.

Study questions

1. Are there ways in which religious and scientific explanations of origins must still on occasion be seen to either directly collide or satisfactorily converge?
2. Many Christians believe that the big bang is what we'd expect to see if the *creatio ex nihilo* doctrine is correct. What are the arguments for and against this claim?
3. Why did people have problems with accepting the authority of the church on the origination of the universe?
4. Discuss ways in which the cultural influence enjoyed by big bang theory today may be similar to the cultural influence enjoyed by the church in the past. To what degree is this cultural influence of scientific cosmology warranted?
5. Assess whether the multiverse constitutes a satisfactory explanation of our universe's origin.
6. Does it matter if the multiverse remains an untestable hypothesis?

Introductory readings

Danielson, Dennis R., *The Book of the Cosmos: Imagining the Universe from Heraclitus to Hawking* (Cambridge, MA: Perseus Publishing, 2000). [An historical overview of the way in which human beings in the West have explained the origin and nature of the universe.]

Oord, Thomas Jay, ed., *Theologies of Creation: creatio ex nihilo and Its New Rivals* (New York: Routledge, Taylor & Francis Group, 2015). [A survey of religious and scientific creation or origins accounts.]

Weinberg, Steven, *The First Three Minutes: A Modern View of the Origin of the Universe* (2nd Ed.) (New York: Basic Books, 1993). [This book, now in its second edition, gives a popular-level overview of the big bang model.]

Advanced readings

Carr, Bernard, ed., *Universe or Multiverse?* (Cambridge, UK: Cambridge University Press, 2007). [A compilation of contributions from a number of prominent cosmologists on the controversial multiverse issue.]

Drozdek, Adam, *Greek Philosophers as Theologians: The Divine Arche* (Aldershot: Ashgate, 2007). [Provides an overview of the ways in which science and theology were integrated in the ancient world.]

Einstein, Albert, 'Cosmological Considerations in the General Theory of Relativity', available online via Princeton University Press: einsteinpapers.press.princeton.edu. [The paper which launched an entire discipline.]

Internet resources

Ned Wright's Cosmology Pages: www.astro.ucla.edu/~wright/cosmolog.htm. [Dr Ned Wright of UCLA offers an information-filled page with a helpful FAQ section and four-part cosmology tutorial.]

Hans Halvorson and Helga Krag, 'Cosmology and Theology': https://plato.stanford.edu/entries/cosmology-theology. [This extensive essay in the Stanford Encyclopedia of Philosophy contains an overview of the debates and discusses ways in which conversations about cosmic origins continue amongst scientists and theologians; also contains a useful bibliography on the topic.]

12 Do logic and religion mix?

James Collin

What is logic?

'Logic', said Mr Spock, 'is the beginning of wisdom'. Anyone familiar with ancient Hebrew wisdom literature would notice that Spock was both echoing and transmuting the claim of the Book of Proverbs that the 'fear of the Lord is the beginning of wisdom'. Might both of them be right? Could it be that **logic** and religion are compatible or even mutually supportive, or is it the case – as some proponents of atheism, and even some religiously committed people, claim – that logic and religion mix like oil and water? Answering this question sensibly will, of course, involve saying something about what logic is. We often hear that we need more logic in our lives, that political discourse, business, even personal relationships would be improved if they were conducted in a more logical way. Sometimes people are even criticised for being *too* relentlessly logical. All of these claims are often made though without a clear sense of what logic is, how it has developed in recent decades, and how it might be applied to the cases at hand. Things are often not much better when the topic is religion. In an eyebrow-raising passage from *The God Delusion*, biologist and New Atheist Richard Dawkins tells us:

> I've forgotten the details, but I once piqued a gathering of theologians and philosophers by adapting the ontological argument [for the existence of God] to prove that pigs can fly. They felt the need to resort to Modal Logic to prove that I was wrong.
>
> (*The God Delusion*, London: Bantam Press, 2006, p. 84)

Cuius rei demonstrationem mirabilem sane detexi hanc marginis exiguitas non caperet, as Pierre de Fermat might say. More pertinent to the question at hand, though: what exactly is supposed to be so bad about using logic to show that an argument fails? As it turns out, nothing really, for logic is the study of the **validity** of arguments. 'Arguments', in the philosophical sense, aren't merely disputes or quarrels; rather, they are sets of claims which aim to establish a conclusion, and 'validity', in the logical sense, isn't merely the correctness of a claim, but whether a claim *follows* from a set of (usually different) claims. Here are some examples:

1. Either he is for us or he is against us.
2. He is not for us.
3. Therefore, he is against us.

1. If Herzog is a great filmmaker then Kinski is a great actor.
2. Herzog is a great filmmaker.
3. Therefore, Kinski is a great actor.

1. If Herzog is a great filmmaker then Kinski is a great actor.
2. Kinski is *not* a great actor.
3. Therefore, Herzog is not a great filmmaker.

1. Some Scots wear kilts.
2. All people who wear kilts drink whisky.
3. Therefore, some Scots drink whisky.

1. If you eat five pieces of fruit and veg a day then you are healthy.
2. You are healthy.
3. Therefore, you eat five pieces of fruit and veg a day.

1. All Scots wear kilts.
2. Some people who wear kilts drink whisky.
3. Therefore, some Scots drink whisky.

The first four of the these arguments are logically valid – the conclusion logically *follows from* or is *entailed by* the premises – but the last two arguments are invalid – the conclusion does not follow from the premises. To see this, note that in the first four arguments it is impossible for the premises to all be true and the conclusion false. In the final two arguments, this is not the case. Premise 1 of the penultimate argument tells us that if you eat five pieces of fruit and veg a day then you are healthy, but it does not tell us that *only* if you eat five pieces of fruit and veg a day then you are healthy, so it leaves open the possibility that you are healthy for some other reason. (Note also that whether it is *true* that you are healthy *only* if you eat five pieces of fruit and veg a day is irrelevant when it comes to the validity of an argument. All that matters from the point of view of validity is whether the conclusion *follows* from the premises, whatever those premises happen to be. A corollary of this is that an argument can have false premises yet still be valid, or a true conclusion yet still be invalid.) The last argument is invalid because it leaves open the possibility that some non-Scots wear kilts, and that the people who wear kilts *and* drink whisky are all drawn from this group.

Something else you may have noticed is that certain bits of vocabulary are playing a special role here: the connectives *If. . . then*, *or*, and *not*, and the quantifiers *all* and *some*. These special terms are all *logical* vocabulary. Why are they special? One reason is this: arguments are valid if and only if we can swap out all the bits of *non*-logical vocabulary for any other bits of non-logical vocabulary and the conclusion still follows from the premises. For example, any arguments with the following logical forms are valid:

1.   Either P or Q.
2.   Not P.
3.   Therefore, Q.

1.   If P then Q.
2. P.
3.   Therefore, Q.

1.   If P then Q.
2.   Not Q.
3.   Therefore, not P.

1.   Some thing x has the property F.
2.   For all things y, if y has the property F then y has the property G.
3.   Therefore, some thing x has the property G.

Here, the dummy sentences P and Q stand for any sentences, the variables x and y stand in for names of things, and the dummy predicates F and G stand in for any predicates. An argument is valid then when it has the right sort of logical form, such that if the premises were true the conclusion must also be true, no matter what *specific* premises or conclusions are involved.

Whether logic and religion mix is a question which, as we will shortly see, concerns quite recent developments in logic, and logic has indeed progressed. In the second edition of his *Critique of Pure Reason*, Immanuel Kant (1724–1804) famously proclaimed that logic had not progressed since Aristotle (384–322 BCE) and therefore that there was apparently no more progress to be made. Great thinker though he was, in this case Kant was wrong on both fronts. For one thing, between the times of Aristotle and Kant, luminaries of philosophy and theology such as Boethius (c. 480–525), Ishâq al-Kindî (d. 870), Ibn Sînâ (d. 1037), Peter Aberlard (1079–1142), William of Ockham (c. 1287–1347), John Buridan (c. 1300–1361), and many others had all advanced logic in significant ways (though much of this work had been, temporarily at least, lost). For another thing, in the nineteenth century logic undertook a quite breathtaking and unprecedented transformation.

This transformation began in earnest when the brilliant British logician George Boole (1815–1864) realised that we could understand logic *algebraically*. Take a very simple bit of algebra: $x = 2y$. Depending what number we 'plug in' in place of x, we get a different result for y. If $x = 2$ then $y = 1$, if $x = 800$ then $y = 400$, and so on. What value we assign to *x* affects what value is assigned to *y*. Boole's great insight was that we can apply algebraic methods to logic; instead of plugging numbers into variables, we can plug truth-values into dummy sentences such as the *P*s and *Q*s above, thus giving us a means of calculating the truth-values of complex sentences based on the truth-values of their components. This was the *mathematisation of logic*. Boole had developed an algebra of correct reasoning. Not only was this a turning point in the history of logic, it paved the way for logic gates, the fundamental building blocks of circuits required for the development of computers. (Microprocessors today contain tens of millions of logic gates.) The transformation continued with the pragmatist philosopher Charles Peirce (1839–1914) in the USA and the mathematician Gottlob Frege (1848–1925) in Germany: two figures whose personalities were as invidious as their minds brilliant. They deepened the mathematisation of logic. Boole had applied algebraic methods to truth-values, but here the mathematical notion of a function was expanded to apply to, not just numbers, but objects of any kind. This allowed for a mathematical account of the logic of sentences which are about objects: sentences with quantifiers such as 'there are' and 'for all'.

Why get excited about this, you may ask. By giving mathematically precise accounts of more and more kinds of expressions, we learn, in the most precise way possible, how to reason with those expressions. Logic had become a fully-fledged branch of mathematics; the study of the validity of arguments had become the precise mathematical, scientific study of the validity of arguments. Today, if you take a good course in logic you will learn how to transform sentences of a natural language like English into the formal languages studied by logicians. Using these formal languages, you will be able to prove, mathematically, whether an argument is valid or not. There is a parallel here with the mathematisation of nature. Laws of motion, expressed in the form of equations, unlocked a wholly unprecedented ability to comprehend and make predictions about the natural world. As Alexander Pope wrote in his epitaph for Isaac Newton, 'Nature and Nature's laws lay hid in night: God said, Let Newton be! and all was light'. Just as the scientific revolution opened up the possibility of gaining an algebraic grasp of the laws of nature, so too the logical revolution ushered in the possibility of gaining a mathematical grasp of the laws of reason itself. The laws of reason hid in night: God said, Let Frege be! and all was light.

Logic and religion

We should now have some sense of what logic is and what it has the power to do, but how can we apply this to the question of whether logic and religion mix? Typically, when we think about whether we ought to accept or reject certain theological claims, we start with premises of a broadly empirical kind: *Consider the way the laws of nature are balanced on a razor's edge, such that if they were even the slightest bit different, complex life could not possibly exist anywhere in the universe. This provides reason to think that God created the universe.* Or, *Look at all the evil and suffering in the world. This provides reason to think that a loving God does not exist.* In making these kinds of claims, considerations of correct reasoning certainly play a role. It is a substantive question whether the characteristics of our universe provide reasons to think that it either is or is not the handiwork of God, and a substantive question whether there are successful arguments from these premises to the existence or non-existence of God. The premises, however, all involve observation, in a very broad sense, of the world and its various intriguing features, and it is from these empirical premises that arguments are built. The idea of the rules of correct reasoning *without any reference to observable features of the world* being used to support or undermine theological claims is somewhat mystifying. How could this possibly work?

Recent developments in logic have resuscitated interest in what was something of a dusty old historical curio: the **ontological argument**. Around a millennium ago the philosopher-theologian, monk, and future Archbishop of Canterbury Saint Anselm (1033–1109) thought he had struck upon an argument demonstrating that disbelief in God leads to contradiction. Hence, reason alone shows us that we must believe in God. Anselm's formulation of the argument still attracts debate today, but it won't concern us here, except to say that it involves *perfect being theology*: the idea that God is, by definition, a perfect being. What will concern us is the way in which quite recent developments in *modal logic* – the logic of possibility and necessity – precipitated an entirely new set of ontological arguments and allowed us to see, in a deeper and more perspicuous way than ever before, the logical structure of those arguments. That fresh developments in mathematical logic might reenergise this millennium-old article of theology was quite remarkable. It was as though you had ventured into your attic, brushed the cobwebs off some old Underwood typewriter you were fairly convinced did not work any more, only to find it was a shiny, state of the art laptop, with more processing power than you thought possible.

To see how this happened we need to think a bit about modal logic. Modal claims have to do with what is *possible* and *necessary*, and we all are committed to various modal claims. Perhaps you are six feet tall. Your being five feet tall, though, is possible: it *could have been the case* that you were five feet tall. The world could have turned out that way. There are less mundane examples. Newton's inverse square law $F = G \frac{m_1 m_2}{r^2}$ describing gravitational attraction is (at least approximately) true, but it could have been the case that gravitational attraction is accurately describable by an inverse *cube* law $F = G \frac{m_1 m_2}{r^3}$. The world could have turned out *that* way. Modal logic is the study of how to reason with modal claims. Like logic more generally, theorising about modal logic has a long history, but underwent a mathematical transformation in more recent times, beginning with the American philosophical pragmatist C. I. Lewis (1883–1964) and culminating in the 1960s with the work of Saul Kripke (1940–). Modal logic today is a technically sophisticated branch of mathematics, and proofs in modal logic – not to mention even more technically sophisticated meta-theorems: proofs about systems of modal logic themselves – are liable to boggle the mind of the uninitiated. But the core idea behind modal logic, its conceptual nucleus, is startlingly simple. Imagine the space of possibilities as a vast array of *possible worlds*. Every global possibility is represented as a possible world. In our world – the actual world – unicorns never evolved, but a creature like a horse but with a single horn could have evolved. So in the language of possible worlds, we would say, 'There is a possible world in which unicorns exist'.

Three things must be understood about possible worlds. The first, naturally enough, is that they are *possible*. A possible world is a way things *could* have been. The second is that they are *comprehensive*. A possible world is a *comprehensive* way things could have been. That means no detail is left out of a possible world. When philosophers talk about 'the actual world', they don't mean 'planet Earth'; what they mean is absolutely everything that is actual. That could be our entire universe, but it could also be the entire multiverse, if there is such a thing. A possible world is maximal in this sense; it includes everything, but a possible world is also comprehensive in another sense. A possible world is not vague or incomplete in any way (unless of course reality could be vague or incomplete in some way). For any beach, say, in a possible planet in a possible world it is determinate how many grains of sand are on that beach. It can't be the case that there is somewhere between 106 and 1010 grains of sand on a beach, but no specific number. It can't be the case that there is someone whose height is somewhere between 5 and 6 feet, but who has no particular height. A possible world, then, is comprehensive in the sense of being complete with respect to every detail.

The third thing is a little trickier to grasp. It is that a given possible world can be possible *relative* to some worlds but not to others. This is to capture the idea that some kinds of possibility are relative in this way. For example, the sentence 'It is biologically impossible for a person to run a two-minute mile' is true in the actual world (and other possible worlds where persons have a similar enough biology to our own), but is *not* true in possible worlds where people's biological make-up is such that they can or do run two-minute miles. In modal logic, this idea of relative possibility shows up in the form of an *accessibility relation* between worlds. Depending on the modal logic used, it may not be the case that all worlds are 'accessible' from all other worlds. With respect to biological possibility, the actual world does not 'access' the two-minute mile world, but other possible worlds will. If however we are dealing with *absolute*, ground-level possibility – metaphysical possibility – this accessibility relation becomes completely unrestricted; every possible world is accessible from every other world. That's because metaphysical possibility is not relative to any particular circumstances at any possible world; it is what is possible in an ultimate sense, what is possible *full stop*. This means that the accessibility relation is **reflexive, symmetric,** and **transitive** (more on this shortly; it will be important).

Imagine, then, the array of all possible worlds stretched out before you. Something is possible if it is true, if it obtains, in at least one possible world; something is necessary if it is true in all possible worlds; and something is impossible if it is true in no possible worlds. In some possible world, it is true that there are unicorns, and in others it is true that you are seven feet tall. In yet others, it is both true that there are unicorns and that you are seven feet tall (your being seven feet tall and there being unicorns are 'compossible'). In every possible world, it is true that bachelors are unmarried, that triangles are trilateral, and that $2 + 2 = 4$. In no possible world is it true that there are square circles, that there are objects that are both red and green (and monochromatic), or that $2 + 2 = 5,000,000$.

Ontological arguments

Recall that Anselm's ontological argument involved the idea that God is, by definition, a perfect being. A perfect being is a being who possesses all the perfections *essentially*. Were a being to possess all perfections *inessentially*, it would, in some broad sense, be a matter of *happenstance* or *luck* that the being happened to possess all the perfections. But a being like that simply isn't perfect. A truly perfect being would be one for whom perfection is part of its essential nature: one that *couldn't fail* to possess all the perfections, because it was essentially perfect. Necessary existence is a perfection, since a being which is fortunate or lucky, in some broad sense, to *exist* isn't a maximally great being. You lack the perfection of necessary existence. In fact, your existence is unnervingly contingent when you think about it. If your parents had never met, you would never have existed. Not only that, but if either of their pairs of parents had never met then you wouldn't have existed. You can keep iterating this, generation after generation, after generation. So the prior probability of you ever existing is vanishingly small. What all this goes to show is that you are not a maximally great being. A maximally great being isn't one that's merely lucky to be alive, to exist, it's one that couldn't *fail* to exist. If God exists then, God exists necessarily. Perfect being theology and modal logic mix, but it's an explosive combination. They result in this modal ontological argument:

1. Possibly a perfect being exists.
2. Necessary existence is a perfection.
3. Therefore, a perfect being exists.

That's it. That's all there is to the modal ontological argument, or at least to this particular rendering of it. What is most remarkable about the argument is not its simplicity, but that it is valid, indeed provably so. That is to say, it can be demonstrated that the conclusion that a perfect being exists follows from these two premises. At this stage, however, it probably isn't very clear exactly *why* the argument is valid. The first premise only claims that a perfect being possibly exists, and the second has to do with our concept of perfection: a perfect being is the sort of being that would be a necessary being, if real. How could these jointly entail that a perfect being in fact exists? As we noted earlier, one can represent possibilities as a vast array of possible worlds, with each individual world representing a comprehensive set of possibilities. This could be visualised in something like the following way:

$$@ \quad w_1 \quad w_2 \quad w_3 \quad w_4 \quad w_5 \quad w_6 \quad w_7 \quad \ldots$$

Here, @ represents the actual world, and w_1, w_2 ... etc., represent all the other possible worlds, stretching out into infinity. Unfortunately, it would be impossible to represent the complete, unimaginably vast array of possible worlds in this way, but, thankfully, we don't need to. Instead, we can start with the actual world, on its own, and build our way up from there, as required. Here, then, is the actual world:

$$@$$

If a perfect being is possible, then, in the language of possible worlds, there is a possible world – accessible from the actual world – in which a perfect being exists. Call this world w_1. We represent accessibility with an arrow. As w_1 is possible from the point of view of the actual world, we draw an arrow from the actual world to w_1. To note the existence of a perfect being at w_1, we write 'P'.

$$@ \longrightarrow w_1 P$$

So far, all we have supposed is that it is possible that a perfect being exists. Now recall that a perfect being is a *necessary* being. A being that is wholly perfect is not a flimsy thing in that most fundamental of senses; that is to say, the sense of being *existentially* flimsy, something that could fail to exist just as easily as exist. That means a necessary being, if it exists, exists in all accessible possible worlds. If a perfect, and hence necessary, being exists at w_1, then it must exist at all worlds accessible from w_1, for that is what it means to be necessary. The crucial question then is this: *which* worlds are accessible from w_1? When dealing with absolute, fundamental, metaphysical possibilities, as we noted, the accessibility relation is transitive, reflexive, and symmetric. Set aside the first for the moment. **Reflexivity** simply says that if something is actual, then it is possible. This much is a platitude, and we can represent it by drawing arrows showing that each world accesses itself:

$$\circlearrowright @ \longrightarrow w_1 P \circlearrowleft$$

However, reflexivity plays no role in this ontological argument, so we can safely ignore it from here. **Symmetry** is more important here. Symmetry says that accessibility goes both ways. If w_1 is a possibility for us, then we are a possibility for w_1. If w_1 represents one comprehensive set of possibilities for @, then @ represents one comprehensive set of possibilities for w_1. We can depict this by making the arrow of accessibility point both ways:

$$@ \underset{\longrightarrow}{\longleftarrow} w_1 P$$

As necessary beings exist in all accessible possible worlds, and the actual world is accessible from w_1, the perfect, necessary being at w_1 exists at the actual world. So, with the premise that the existence of a perfect being is at least *possible*, and a little bit of modal logic, we arrive at the conclusion that a perfect being actually exists:

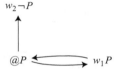

We don't have to stop there. Not only does the being exist at the actual world, it *necessarily* exists at the actual world. To see this, imagine that it didn't necessarily exist at the actual world. That would mean that there is at least one accessible possible world – call it w_2 – where the being does not exist. Here '¬P' means *there is no perfect being*:

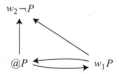

Now recall that the accessibility relation is transitive. A relation is transitive when if one thing bears that relation to a second thing, and the second thing bears that relation to a third thing, then the first thing bears that relation to the third thing. *Louder than* is a transitive relation. If noise one is louder than noise two, and noise two is louder than noise three, then noise one is louder than noise three. Absolute possibility is transitive in this way. If the actual world is accessible from w_1, and w_2 is accessible from the actual world, then w_2 is accessible from w_1:

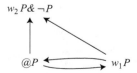

What we have just depicted, however, cannot possibly be the case, because, by definition, a necessary being at w_1 exists in *all* possible worlds accessible from w_1, including w_2:

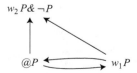

The assumption that there are any possible worlds where this perfect being does not exist leads to the absurdity that there both is and is not a perfect being at w_2, therefore we must reject the assumption. As such, the perfect being not only actually exists, but *necessarily* exists. The net result of all this is that the mere possibility of a perfect being combined with a little bit of modal logic entails the necessary existence of a perfect being. Logic and religion – at least *theistic* religion – apparently mix very nicely indeed.

At this point in the discussion, something is apt to trigger in the backs of our minds. Surely one cannot establish something as momentous as the existence of God as easily as *that*. Even if each step of the argument looks to be in good order, there must be *something* wrong with it. Now, we should not hold on *too* tightly to heuristic principles such as these. Science, and the scientific image of the world it produces, has the ability, and the right, to offend our expectations and intuitions. Quantum entanglement, the relativity of simultaneity, and many other things are all deeply counterintuitive. That, of course, is the thing about reality: we bump up against it. It is a source of friction with our beliefs, expectations, and conceptual apparatus more generally. If science can produce results that offend our intuitions, then why not mathematical logic? Advances in mathematical logic may well throw up some surprises. Moreover, and after all, what was so 'easy' about establishing the existence of God this way? It took a few millennia of developments in logic and metaphysical theorising to arrive at an argument like this, even if the argument itself is striking in its simplicity and elegance. One would not, after all, write off the Schrödinger equation as inherently suspicious just because of its simplicity and elegance. For one thing, hard labour has gone into making it simple and elegant.

Of course, in fact, logic and philosophy more generally *can* and should throw up surprises, but in this case, our intuitions may actually be tracking something; establishing the existence of God through logical arguments *may* be possible, but not quite as quickly as this. For, with one very important modification, the argument can be run in the other direction. Start with the premise that it is possible that a perfect being does not exist; that is to say, there is an accessible possible world – call it w_1 – in which a perfect being does not exist:

$$@ \longrightarrow w_1 \neg P$$

Now, assume that there is a possible world – call it w_2 – in which a perfect being exists:

$$
\begin{array}{l}
w_2\, P \\
\uparrow \\
@ \longrightarrow w_1 \neg P
\end{array}
$$

As the accessibility relation is symmetric, the actual world is also possible for w_2, which we can represent by showing the arrows pointing in both directions:

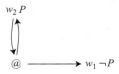

A perfect being has the perfection of necessary existence, which is to say it exists in all accessible possible worlds. At this point, the **transitivity** of the accessibility relation becomes important. The actual world is possible relative to w_2 and w_1 is possible relative to the actual world. Transitivity tells us that, therefore, w_1 is possible relative to w_2:

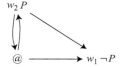

As necessary beings exist in all accessible possible worlds, this means there must both exist and not exist a perfect being at w_1:

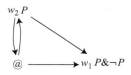

This is absurd. So we must reject the assumption that there is a possible world in which there exists a perfect being, meaning that it is impossible that a perfect being exists. This gives us a kind of reverse ontological argument:

1. Possibly a perfect being does not exist.
2. Necessary existence is a perfection.
3. Therefore, a perfect being cannot exist.

This argument too is provably valid. The conclusion that there cannot be a perfect being provably follows from the premises that possibly a perfect being does not exist, and that necessary existence is a perfection. What is most troubling about this is that you may have thought that it was both possible that a perfect being exist and possible that a perfect being not exist, but this simply cannot be the case, for if it were we could prove that a perfect being both does and does not exist. The mixture of logic and religion then is doubly explosive: to establish theism, you only need to establish the possibility that God exists, and to establish atheism, you only need to establish the possibility that God does not exist. Modal logic doesn't give us an immediate route to either theism or atheism; instead, it raises the stakes precipitously in both directions.

Conclusion

Settling which ontological argument is the right one involves delving into some of the deepest and most difficult issues in epistemology and metaphysics: how can we know what is possible, and what underpins facts about what is and is not possible? These are questions that some of the best minds in philosophy are wrestling with today. This is what is so enduringly fascinating about the ontological argument. It is an immaculate, crystalline piece of argumentation through which the deepest thinking about theology, metaphysics, epistemology, and the laws of reason itself are refracted. This is the remarkable situation we find ourselves in. The most fundamental premises behind two competing world views – world views that shape our thought and deeds in innumerable ways, that mould our deepest hopes and aspirations, our conception of what is good and valuable and noble, the purposes we give to or find in life – the truth or falsity of either of these fundamental premises could be unmasked by the work of philosophers in obscure areas of metaphysics and epistemology over the next few years. And with this work in hand, we will be able to point to mathematical logic as establishing, with dispositive force, the truth or falsity of theism, and all the hopes, values, moral codes, purposes, and deeds that are bound up with it. Or, perhaps, we'll still be debating this another millennium from now.

Chapter summary

- Logic is the study of the *validity of arguments*. An argument is logically valid when it has the right sort of logical form, such that if the premises were true the conclusion must also be true, no matter what specific premises or conclusions are involved.
- Aristotle was a pioneer of logic, but logic has been in development from his time to today, with many advances made in medieval times. In the nineteenth century, logic was mathematicised by people such as George Boole, Charles Peirce, and Gottlob Frege. The mathematisation of logic transformed the study of the validity of arguments into a precise branch of mathematics.
- An ontological argument, aiming to show that the existence of God could be established through reason alone, was first given by Saint Anselm of Canterbury.

Anselm was also an important proponent of *perfect being theology*: the idea that God is a perfect or maximally great being.

- Modal claims have to do with what is *possible* and *necessary*. *Modal logic* is the study of the validity of arguments involving claims about what is possible and necessary. The development of modal logic invigorated interest in ontological arguments and led to the creation of a number of new ontological arguments. The intuitive idea behind modal logic is that one can represent possibilities as possible worlds. If something is possible, it holds in at least one possible world. If something is necessary, it holds in all possible worlds.

- Using modal logic, it is possible to prove the existence of a perfect being from the premises (i) that a perfect being possibly exists, and (ii) that necessary existence is a perfection. However, it is also possible to prove a perfect being cannot exist from the premises (i) that a perfect being possibly does not exist, and (ii) that necessary existence is a perfection.

Study questions

1. What does it mean for an argument to be valid? How would you explain the notion of logical validity to someone unfamiliar with it? How does it differ from other uses of the word 'valid'?
2. What is gained by the transformation of logic into a branch of mathematics? Is anything lost?
3. What sorts of attributes would a perfect being have?
4. How do we come to know mundane modal facts such as *I could have been taller than I am*? How do we come to know more exotic modal facts such as *The laws of nature could have been different*?
5. Which modal ontological argument do you find more convincing: the argument for theism or the argument for atheism? Defend your answer.
6. Are there other areas of the relationship between science and religion where modal logic, or the idea of possible worlds, could aid our understanding?
7. How many different kinds of possibility are there? What are the differences between them? Do we have to reason differently about them? Is metaphysical possibility special?

Introductory readings

Oppy, Graham (2008), 'The Ontological Argument', in Paul Copan and Chad V. Meister (eds.), *Philosophy of Religion: Classic and Contemporary Issues*. Malden, MA: Blackwell. [A clear introduction to ontological arguments by an expert in the field.]

Priest, Graham (2000), *Logic: A Very Short Introduction*. Oxford: Oxford University Press. [A pithy, clear, and concise overview of logic and its philosophy.]

Yandell, Keith (2016), *Philosophy of Religion: A Contemporary Introduction*. London: Routledge. [A clear but rigorous introduction to the philosophy of religion with very good material on the concept of God, ranging over a variety of religions.]

Advanced readings

Hoffman, Joshua, and Gary S. Rosenkrantz (2002), *The Divine Attributes*. Hoboken, NJ: John Wiley and Sons. [A recent and acclaimed analysis of perfect being theology.]

Maydole, Robert E. (2009), 'The Ontological Argument', in *The Blackwell Companion to Natural Theology*. Malden, MA: Blackwell Publishing Ltd. [Defends a number of ontological arguments using modal logic. An excellent guide to recent modal ontological arguments and interpretations of older ontological arguments in modal logic terms, though only for the logically sophisticated.]

Priest, Graham (2008), *An Introduction to Nonclassical Logic: From If to Is*. Cambridge: Cambridge University Press. [An excellent introduction to non-classical logic, including various systems of modal logic. Requires some background in basic logic.]

Internet resources

Himma, Kenneth, E., 'Anselm: Ontological Argument for God's Existence', *Internet Encyclopedia of Philosophy*, J. Fieser and B. Dowden (eds.), www.iep.utm.edu/ont-arg/ [A clear account of Anselm's ontological argument(s) and contemporary modal versions of it.]

Magnus, P.D. (2014), 'forall x', www.fecundity.com/logic/download.html [An open source introduction to formal logic.]

Morley, Brian, 'Western Concepts of God', *Internet Encyclopedia of Philosophy*, J. Fieser and B. Dowden (eds.), www.iep.utm.edu/God-west/ [A very clear overview of both how great thinkers in western philosophy have understood God, and the divine attributes of classical theism.]

Oppy, Graham (2016), 'Ontological Arguments', *Stanford Enclyopedia of Philosophy*,(ed.) E. Zalta, https://plato.stanford.edu/entries/ontological-arguments/ [A detailed overview of a number of ontological arguments and objections to them.]

13   Does science show that we lack free will?

Tillman Vierkant

Choices are a fundamental part of what it is to be a human being. From the mundane question of whether to have chocolate or cheese for dessert to the life changing decision of whether or not to accept the new job in a different country, choices are everywhere. Even more dramatically, a choice can be a matter of life and death. We assume that the murderer has a choice when she pulls the trigger. We also assume that normally the choices that humans make are free and that normally they are responsible for the choices they make. In contrast to the lion that cannot help stalking and killing its prey, humans can decide not to kill. If they do it nevertheless, then we can hold them responsible for their deeds because they would have been able to do otherwise.

The capacity that allows us to make these free and responsible choices normally comes under the heading of free will. However, while it is widely accepted that free will is a central part of human life and human interaction, it is much less clear what exactly it consists in, or whether we even have it. The former question has exercised philosophers for centuries, but the latter point has become particularly urgent over the course of the last decades with the rise of the sciences of the mind.

In this chapter, we are going to look at three types of challenges from the sciences that seem to undermine free will and a scientific explanation of why we might have belief in free will even if it were an illusion. We will then turn to philosophy and see whether conceptual clarification can help us with these challenges. It will turn out that the scientists, despite their very sophisticated experimental machinery, often are remarkably unclear about the concept of free will. Finally, we will ask how much of the scientific challenge survives these conceptual clarifications.

Prediction, confabulation of motives, illusions of choice, and why the belief in free will is nevertheless important

Prediction

In the Hollywood film *Minority Report*, scientists have figured out a way to predict if and when people will commit a murder. Using this technique, they can prevent the crimes ever happening, instead imprisoning criminals who have never committed a crime, but whom they know would have done if not stopped by the police. The film plays with our intuitions in an interesting way. It is very hard for us to accept that it could be just to put somebody in jail despite the fact that they have not yet committed a crime, because they could have decided not to commit the crime at the last moment. On the other hand, if they really do not have that ability at all, then it seems that they are not free and should not be punished for a choice they did not have.

Fortunately, this film is just science fiction and, as we will see, there are good reasons to assume that it will always stay fiction, but looking at the scientific literature, one could be excused for thinking that the first steps on the way to the prediction machine have already been made.

Choon Siong Soon in the lab of John Dylan Haynes (see e.g. Haynes in Clark et al. 2013), for example, put his subjects in a **fMRI** scanner and was able to predict which choice they would make a full eight seconds before the subjects themselves were aware of their choice. These experiments themselves were inspired by the earlier work of Benjamin Libet (Sinnott-Armstrong 2010), who also found that there are traces of an impending action in the brain before the subject knows of it. Libet himself did not make predictions, because his method (**EEG**) did not allow for it, and the timescales were also much smaller (300msc) between the onset of the brain trace (the so-called readiness potential) and the conscious awareness of the intention to move now. Nonetheless, he prepared the groundwork for a whole industry of experiments that examine the relationship between brain states that would allow a scientist to predict the behaviour and the conscious awareness of the subject.

So far, all of these predictions are only about very simple decisions, like when to flick one's wrist or whether to push the left or the right button, but they are surprising and worrying because they seem to demonstrate a point of principle. It really seems possible that, like the scientists in *Minority Report*, real neuroscientists of the future might be able to know about our choices before we do – and if that is correct, then it looks as if we don't really have a choice at all. Whether someone commits a crime or not, for example, seems not up to them but is already determined by their brains before they even know about it.

Confabulation of motives

If we want to know why somebody did do something, we ask them. We assume that the agent knows why she decided to act in the way she did. Since the days of Freud, we have learned that this is not always the case. Sometimes an agent might act for a motive that they are not aware of. Somebody might e.g. have held a grudge against their mother since their childhood and act in all kinds of unpleasant ways towards her, even though at the same time they honestly assert that they do not. But we do assume that such cases are relatively rare and that most of the time we are justified in assuming that agents know what reasons they had for their actions. This also is crucially important for our sense that people are responsible for their actions, because when we criticise each other we do so because we think that the person who acted wrongly is able to understand and act on reasons and that she culpably failed to take some reasons into account.

In recent years, an ever-growing body of research, especially in social psychology, seems to undermine that certainty. The experiments seem to show that most of the time we are not aware of a whole host of elements that influence our decisions in very significant ways. What is worse, this is not only true for mundane decisions, but also for decisions that clearly have a moral dimension.

The psychologist Jonathan Haidt developed a number of experiments that he describes as moral dumbfounding. In one experiment (Murphy and Haidt unpublished) he has people read a vignette about a brother and sister who have sex. The vignette is structured in such a way that all the reasons that are usually given against incest are excluded. The sex is consensual, protected, happens only once, nobody else knows about it and neither agent suffers any psychological damage from it. Subjects are then asked to judge whether the incest was wrong. Most people judge that it was and when asked to give reasons for their judgment they cite reasons that had been explicitly ruled out in the vignette. When that is pointed out to them and they can't find any other reasons, they will nevertheless not change their judgment but insist that the act is wrong even though they can't give reasons for their judgment.

What the dumbfounding experiments seem to demonstrate is that the reasons we give to justify our actions might not always be the ones that make us act, but instead **confabulations**, invented reasons that we make up to justify our judgments. However, this finding does not demonstrate that we are not aware of the reasons that make us act at all. Once all other explanations fail, subjects are well aware that they have strong moral gut feelings about incest.

But often we might not even have that. In a striking series of experiments, psychologists could e.g. show that the mere presence of a picture of eyes will have dramatic effects on the cooperative and pro-social behaviour of people. In one example, researchers could show that the mere presence of an image of eyes reduced littering by half in comparison to an image of flowers (Ernest-Jones et al. 2011). Clearly, the picture does not constitute a moral reason at all, and yet it seems to be the picture that makes the difference between pro-social and asocial behaviour. This looks like bad news for the influence of our conscious will on our behaviour. We seem to be influenced massively by factors that we are not aware of and which also clearly are morally irrelevant.

Illusion of choice

Normally our senses give us access to the world. When we see a house, we assume that there really is one. But we are all aware that while our senses tend to be reliable, there always is the possibility of illusion: It is not surprising to us that we can be tricked into seeing a house where there is none. Intuitively, choices are different though. It seems almost nonsensical to suggest that we could be tricked into thinking that we made a choice when in fact we did not, or that we made a different choice to the one we thought we had, or that we felt that we moved of our own free will, when in fact we were forced by someone else to move. It is also good that we know our own choices in a special way, because, after all, we are responsible for these choices. Free will might seem threatened if we actually had no idea whether or not we made a choice and what choice we made, because if we do not know our choices, then how can we control them and be responsible for them?

Despite the fact that our intuitions are so strong on the matter, scientists have come up with a whole host of experiments that suggest that we can be tricked about our choices in a number of ways. Famously, researchers in Dan Wegner's lab (Wegner and Wheatly 1999) tricked subjects into rating a movement as voluntary when in fact it was forced by a confederate of the experimenter.

Peter Johannson and colleagues (Hall and Johannson in Clark et al. 2013) developed a paradigm called choice blindness, where they get subjects to justify why they made a choice, but the choice subjects then justify is in fact one they did not make. For example, subjects are asked to decide which of two photos shows the more attractive face. They are then given that photo and asked to justify their choice – but unbeknownst to them, the photo they are given is the one that they did not choose. In most such cases, subjects don't notice the change and proceed to justify a decision they did not make.

The importance of the belief in free will

Given the enormous amount of evidence from the sciences, it is quite understandable that some thinkers have been convinced that free will is nothing but an illusion. Still, the philosophical mainstream very much resists that conclusion and we will look in the next section at the reasons for the scepticism.

Before moving on to philosophy, there is one worry that can be raised without much conceptual analysis. If freedom of the will really is an illusion, then why do we all believe we have it? This is a worry that has recently been addressed by a number of social psychologists. In a nutshell, the answer to the worry is: Belief in free will is psychologically and socially useful. When people are primed to doubt the existence of free will, they are less nice to each other. Psychologists Baumeister (Baumeister et al. 2009) and colleagues have found e.g. that subjects are more likely to serve hot salsa sauce to people who dislike it if they had been read a story before that argued that free will is an illusion.

What is free will?

Does prediction really show that we are not free?

In the first section, we discussed a number of scientific results that seem to show that we do have not free will. But what does this actually mean? Think, for example, of the first worry we discussed, i.e. the worry that scientists might be able to predict our decisions. This, it was suggested, shows that we are determined by our brains and not free to make choices. But is it actually really obvious that we cannot be free if we are determined?

Perhaps surprisingly, many philosophers have long argued that free will and **determinism** are perfectly compatible. These so called compatibilists argue that free will is about the ability to cause our behaviour with our minds in the right kind of way and not about further questions of whether our minds themselves have causal antecedents. If compatibilists are right, then the simple fact that our minds are determined by our brains does not in any way show that we are not free.

Compatibilism is probably the most philosophical contemporary position in philosophy. Not everyone agrees with the compatibilists, however. A number of philosophers think that freedom of the will and determinism are not compatible. These so called incompatibilists come again in two flavours: So-called hard determinists, who believe that determinism is true and that because of incompatibilism, this means that we cannot be free. This is a minority position in philosophy, but it seems very popular among many of the scientists who developed the empirical challenges (e.g. Haynes or Wegner). The majority of incompatiblist philosophers tend to be Libertarians. They agree with the hard determinists that freedom of the will and determinism are incompatible, but they also believe that determinism is false and that we are free.

The debate between libertarians and compatibilists is far too complex to be discussed in any detail here, but what is important to note is that nearly all libertarians accept that the compatibilist conditions of what it takes to be free are real and necessary conditions on libertarian free will as well. For incompatibilists, however, these conditions are just not sufficient. Given that compatibilism in this respect is, as it were, the baseline of philosophical accounts of free will, we will concentrate here on compatibilist accounts of free will and how they fare with regard to the science challenge.

The compatibilist philosopher Richard Holton (Holton in Clark et al. 2013) even has an explanation for why we intuitively find it plausible that free will and determinism are not compatible that allows us to disable our first challenge. According to Holton, the confusion stems from a muddling of two concepts that sound similar, but are actually very different: Namely determinism and **fatalism**. If determinism is true, our minds can still cause our actions, but our minds in turn are caused, while if fatalism is true, then our minds would not make a causal difference. According to Holton, we are worried about predictability, because on one reading predictability implies fatalism. This would be the case if the prediction made it impossible for the agent to act otherwise, even if the agent wanted to. We have no reason to believe that the kind of predictability that science might make possible would be of that kind, however. Instead, all that science might be able to predict is how we would act, if we could act as we wanted to act anyway. This kind of prediction does not in any way seem to be in conflict with the idea that the mind can have causal powers.

The right mesh

Once we accept that freedom of the will and determinism might be compatible, the mere fact that we are determined by our brains clearly does not rule out that we might have free will. However, so far we have heard very little about what compatibilists mean when they say that we are free when our actions are caused in the right kind of way. There are a great number of compatibilist positions on this, and it would be impossible to discuss even most of them in this context. So instead, we will focus here on one of the most prominent positions in the field: So-called **reason responsiveness** accounts. On these accounts, what makes us free and responsible moral agents is the ability to detect and act on moral reasons.

Reason responsiveness accounts are very popular because they seem to get right what we intuitively value about free will, and they explain our moral practices very well. They explain why animals and to some extent children are not moral agents, because they can't understand moral reasons at all or not well enough. They also give us a sense of why we blame others when they do the wrong thing: Because we assume that they were aware that an alternative course of action would have been better supported by moral reasons and that they would have been capable of acting on these reasons.

If reason responsiveness is what makes us free, then it seems we do not need to worry about the truth of determinism. All that matters is that we have the ability to detect and act on reasons. It does not matter if this ability is caused by a brain, determined by its chemistry and physics.

The zombie challenge

Armed with the compatibilist reason responsiveness account of free will, it might now seem that there is no challenge from the sciences and free will is safe. We don't need to be worried any longer, even if we are determined by our brains as long as our behaviour is reason responsive. But this would be too hasty. While it is right that the truth of determinism is not a problem for a compatibilist, there still is an elephant in the room that has not in the past played a major role in philosophical discussions of free will. This changed with the arrival of the scientific challenge, however, and the elephant in question goes by the name of consciousness.

The worry that is not addressed by the conceptual footwork on what free will consists in is that free will might require that our reason responsive behaviour is caused by our conscious deliberative **agency**, and that the scientific results might show that the actual psychological story of behaviour production bypasses conscious agency. This is what Vierkant and colleagues call the **zombie challenge** (Vierkant et al. 2013). Additionally, it might also be the case that the reason responsiveness of the unconsciously produced behaviour is too context dependent to be responsibility enabling. We will take each of these worries in turn below.

Pre-theoretically, we assume that our conscious deliberation plays an important role in the control of our behaviour. We are responsible for our doing, because we can consciously evaluate reasons for or against a particular course of action. If it were the case that the real decision of whether to act or not happens behind closed doors in our unconscious brains and we were not even aware of the reasons that make us act, then it seems that we do not have the right kind of control over our deciding behaviour and thus it seems unfair to make us responsible for it. It does not seem enough here to point out that the behaviour was not just a simple reflex, but quite responsive to reasons, as long as the reasons are not our (conscious) reasons. Whether or not science really does give us any good reasons to think that our conscious deliberation might be so detached from our behaviour is hotly debated, as is the question of whether it might not be the case that reason responsiveness is good enough for responsibility, even in the absence of conscious control.

It is in this latter discussion, and in particular the worry that seemingly reason responsive unconsciously triggered behaviour might not be responsibility enabling is of the highest importance. Manuel Vargas (in Clark et al. 2013) calls this the worry from **sphexishness**. The common digger wasp (sphex ichneumoneus) always puts its prey down in front of its burrow and then checks the burrow before pulling prey in. This seems at first glance to be immensely rational – after all, there could be danger down there – until one learns that the wasp will reboot this process indefinitely if one simply moves the prey a couple of inches away from the entrance. The checking behaviour clearly is not down to a deeper understanding on the part of the wasp, but is simply instinctively triggered whenever the wasp approaches the burrow with prey. Perhaps humans are like the wasp? Perhaps our moral behaviour is also dependent on a large amount of morally irrelevant factors that we are not aware of?

Studies like the one about pictures of eyes being present, discussed before, might suggest such a picture. Again, there is no agreement about the seriousness of the threat amongst philosophers, and we don't know to what degree our moral behaviour is determined by these irrelevant facts. One obvious problem with the studies is that they are very rarely about serious moral problems. So it is quite possible that we are influenced by non-moral factors only when the decision does not have very high moral significance. That this might be true is also supported by another of the findings that we discussed: The choice blindness paradigm was also used to see whether subjects could be fooled into justifying a moral decision they did not make. Again, the researchers found that that was possible, but they also found that it only worked if subjects did not have a firm view on the dilemma posed before participating in the experiment. On the other hand, as Vargas (Clark et al. 2013) points out, there are studies like the famous Milgram experiments, in which normal people were willing to seemingly torture someone as part of a fake scientific experiment. Such findings should make one careful to be too sure about what it takes to change ordinary decent human beings into immoral monsters.

So we simply don't know yet how serious the zombie challenge is. But we can already say one thing: It seemed at first as if science and free will were two different poles that could not mix. The new knowledge that the sciences of the mind have made possible seemed incompatible with our traditional notion of free will. But this first impression rests on a mistaken and simplified understanding of how we ought to understand the notion of free will completely independently of the progress of science. Thus, once this conceptual confusion was out of the way, it emerged that the scientific results still have the power to change our conceptions of what it is to be free, but the question now has moved from a simple yea or nay to a much more subtle discussion of the exact role of conscious and unconscious reason responsive mechanisms for the production of behaviour. Science and philosophy here are not enemies but partners in a quest for a better understanding of human nature.

Chapter summary

- Some cognitive scientists have argued that we might not have free will, but the scientific arguments often lose power because they are conceptually unclear. Once we are conceptually more careful, a less radical but more subtle and nonetheless revisionary challenge emerges.
- Haynes and Libet show that scientists are in principle capable of predicting our behaviour before we know about it, simply by looking at the brain.
- Wegner and others show that we can be deceived about our own choices.
- A wide range of social psychology experiments show that we very often do not know why we made the choices we make.
- Experiments show that the belief in free will is important for a range of cooperative and cognitive tasks.
- Philosophical analysis shows that the truth of determinism might not be incompatible with free will.
- One of the most important compatibilist positions in philosophy are so-called reason responsiveness accounts. They hold that free will consists in the ability to detect and act on moral reasons.
- Compatibilist accounts do not have to worry about the predictability challenge, if all it shows is that our behaviour is determined.
- The zombie challenge argues that even compatibilist accounts are threatened by the scientific results, because they often assume a causal role of consciousness in behaviour production and this role seems threatened by the experiments.
- The results can also be read to show that humans are sphexish to a responsibility undermining degree.

Study questions

1. What are the three scientific challenges to free will?
2. What is moral dumbfounding?
3. What is choice blindness?
4. Does the belief in free will matter even if it turns out that we do not have free will?
5. What is the difference between determinism and fatalism?
6. What is compatibilism?
7. What are the conditions of moral agency according to reason responsiveness accounts of free will?
8. What is the zombie challenge?

Introductory readings

Mele, A. (2007) Free Will: Action Theory meets Neuroscience. In C. Lumer (ed.) *Intentionality, deliberation, and autonomy: The action-theoretic basis of practical philosophy*. Farnham: Ashgate, 257–272. [This is a great introductory text to the philosophical issues around Libet's seminal experiments and an interesting compatibilist interpretation of the findings.]

Wegner, D.M., and Wheatly, T.P. (1999). Apparent mental causation: Sources of the experience of will. *American Psychologist*, 54, 480–492. [This is a very accessible text by one of the most famous conscious will sceptics in the cognitive science world, which also includes one of his most influential experiments.]

Vierkant, T., et al. (2013) Introduction. In A. Clark et al. (eds.) *Decomposing the will*. Oxford: Oxford University Press. [This text is a comprehensive introduction on a wide range of issues in the burgeoning field of free will and science.]

Kane, R. (ed.) (2011) *The Oxford handbook of free will*. Oxford: Oxford University Press. [This is a great introductory reading on the traditional philosophical free will debate.]

Advanced readings

Baumeister, R.F., et al. (2009). Prosocial benefits of feeling free: Disbelief in free will increases aggression and reduces helpfulness. *Personality and Social Psychology Bulletin*, 35(2), 260–268. [This study shows how the belief in the absence of free will makes people behave less morally.]

Clark, A., et al. (eds.) (2013). *Decomposing the will*. Oxford: Oxford University Press. [This is a collection full of cutting edge work on the issues in the free will and science debate. There are papers on some of the most surprising empirical findings by eminent scientists like Haynes and Johannson as well as work by philosophers like Holton or Vargas that evaluates the relevance of the findings for the philosophical free will debate.]

Nahmias, E., et al. (2005). Surveying freedom: Folk intuitions about free will and moral responsibility. *Philosophical Psychology*, 18(5): 561–584. [This essay provides a good introduction on the empirical work on the importance of the belief in free will.]

Ernest-Jones, M., et al. (2011). Effects of eye images on everyday cooperative behavior: A field experiment. *Evolution and Human Behavior*, 32(3): 172–178. [This is an impressive study demonstrating the effect of eye pictures on moral behaviour.]

Sinnott-Armstrong, W., and Nadel L. (eds.) (2010) *Conscious will and responsibility: A tribute to Benjamin Libet*. Oxford: Oxford University Press. [This is a great collection on Libet's seminal experiments on free will.]

Internet resources

Haidt, J., Bjorklund, F., and Murphy, S. (2000) Moral dumbfounding: When intuition finds no reason. *Unpublished manuscript, University of Virginia*. www.faculty.virginia.edu/haidtlab/articles/manuscripts/haidt.bjorklund.working-paper.when%20intuition%20finds%20no%20reason.pub603.doc. [This is the original famous incest moral dumbfounding study.]

BBC Radio. The Libet Experiment: Is Free Will Just an Illusion?www.youtube.com/watch?v=OjCt-L0Ph5o [This is a great little introductory video to the Libet experiments.]

14   What are the ethical implications of the science-and-religion debate?

Jeremy H. Kidwell

Introduction

The extended reflection that stretches across this book might be considered an interesting intellectual exercise, but does it have any real world consequences? As you will have found, many of the authors here are well aware of the significant implications that result from ways that we narrate the relationship between science and religion. In this chapter, I'd like to explore some ways that this is the case, specifically with regards to ethics. This is no small undertaking in my view, as the religious implications for science and vice versa do indeed have serious consequences for ethical reasoning.

First, however, it's important to clarify what I mean by "ethical reasoning", as this can have many possible meanings. For example, on the one hand, there are many professional ethicists who are often affiliated with a particular sub-field of science, and who may even work for a specific laboratory. They provide oversight, particularly where there may be some risk to human subjects involved in research, but also may call attention to unanticipated risks and dangers which will be generated by a programme of research. In this kind of ethical work, ethicists serve as a resource for front-line scientists who may not always have the time or training to reflect on and respond to the ethical implications of their work. A more technical term for this kind of reflection is **casuistry**. Casuistry focusses on what can often be relatively minor procedural questions, and these issues can be embedded in very specific contexts. On the other hand, there's a second form of ethical work, often called **normative ethics,** which concerns itself with big-picture questions which may transcend a specific context. As we shall see, there are important normative consequences which result from debates in science and religion as well. It's also worth noting that within the domain of **normative ethics** there are a range of secular and theological approaches to moral quandaries. A non-religious approach to ethics might take up the emphasis on **virtue** pioneered in the work of Aristotle, the emphasis on **duty** which was first commended by Immanuel Kant, or the argument by thinkers like Jeremy Bentham and J. S. Mill that **utility** should be considered the best arbiter for ethical decisions in seeking the greatest good for the greatest number of persons. Theological approaches to ethics are generally thought to rely upon sacred texts as a source for moral norms, alongside theologically conceived concepts such as **natural law** and **justice**. However, in recent years scholars have observed that "religion" may also involve a host of other factors: historical traditions to be sure, but also personal experience, commitment to community, and **non-propositional** forms of cognition including **aesthetics**, self-transcendence (e.g. any experience of "the sublime"), emotion, and intuition. With this in mind, it would be difficult to argue that any of the supposedly secular philosophical traditions are wholly non-religious (that is, devoid of any account of the divine, or of human **aesthetics** or experience of transcendence) or that any of the resources explicitly located within religious moral philosophy are off-limits to a non-religious ethicist. On the basis of this more complex definition of "religion" and its relation to ethics, I won't aim to respect the boundaries of an **essentialised** "religious" or "secular" normative ethic, but will instead cast my net more broadly, exploring some specific ethical questions which have arisen recently, in order to explore ways that the science-and-religion debate might illuminate or trouble those issues.

Professional ethics

Let's look first at some examples of professional ethics, and note possible ethical contexts and quandaries that may lie there. Though ethical issues are often in the foreground with the medical and engineering professions, ethical issues are also relevant for researchers in the experimental sciences, especially biology. Take, for example, the need to test and regulate new pharmaceuticals. Experimenters need to respect the **agency** of the persons they are working with in their studies (particularly surrounding informed consent), and there are specific aversions to modes of treatment or intervention which are rooted in religious belief. Many religious traditions take issue with the drawing or transfusing of blood. Other religious traditions have theologically specific reasons to resist the intentional harming or killing of animals. The ways in which we maintain or resolve conflicts between religion and science have significant implications for the level of importance we'll afford to objections by religious persons, and the importance we'll place on the religious inclusiveness of experimental science.

On the basis of these kinds of contexts and quandaries, many sub-fields of science have developed professional codes of ethics. For example, the American Society for Clinical Laboratory Science (ASCLS) has a code which includes a duty to (1) the patient, (2) colleagues and the profession, and (3) society. Generally, the codes present an account of the researcher or scientific practitioner as being virtuous in their conduct, applying rigour to their work, being honest in their representation of data and disclosure of conflicts-of-interest, fair in their work with the public, and careful in their treatment of animals used in research. It's interesting to note that what tends to be the sole mention (if any) of religion or theology among these codes relates to the desire to avoid conflict of interest and deal fairly with other persons, that is, to conduct science in a way that is blind or neutral with regards to religion. In 2007, Sir David King, the former Chief Scientific Adviser to the British Government, produced a "Universal

Ethical Code for Scientists", which presented these duties as "Rigour", "Respect", and "Responsibility". Across all these codes of ethics, including the document by King, religious dimensions are notably lacking, presumably stemming from the widespread practice in public policy matters of regarding one's religious beliefs as a "private" matter which shouldn't impact on the "secular" public space. But this tidy separation of public and private, secular and religious is difficult to maintain in practice. What if, for example, scientific research involves working with subjects whose religious beliefs feature prominently? Can researchers authentically represent themselves in ethical conversations if their values are constituted on religious grounds? Particularly in light of the global expansion of religion, a range of scholars now argue that the twenty-first century should be marked by *post*-secular public discourses. In this configuration, scientific practitioners might be encouraged not to suppress their religious practice, but rather to be candid about the ways in which religious convictions provide the underpinnings for their support of values such as "respect" or "rigour". Moreover, as I have noted above, the secular accounts of duty and responsibility have a significant historical link to theological accounts of justice, human wellbeing, and virtue. Navigating this balance is difficult to be sure, but participants in any current debate over science and religion need to be aware of this changing perspective on the nature of the public sphere.

Hinting towards a more civil and constructive relationship between science and religion is the presence of religious leaders, priests, and theologians on a variety of official consortia in scientific ethics. Islamic theologian and scholar Prof Mona Siddiqui sits on the present Nuffield Council on Bioethics, and she was preceded by other British theologians such as Robin Gill, Richard Harries, Duncan Forrester, and Gordon Dunston. The same is true for the official German Ethics Council, which is currently chaired by a German theologian, Peter Dabrock, and the official body in France, the Comité Consultatif National d'Ethique, which has statutory representation by theologians.

Whatever perspective one may have about the inclusion of religious representatives and perspectives within these normative discussions about scientific practice, it's important to note that influence usually works in both directions. Religious representatives may bring theologically specific insights which influence discussions about scientific ethics, but by their participation in this kind of secular public body, theologians may also alter the way they think about theology. And there are questions, too, about whether the levels of participation and influence are adequately balanced. In surveying the significant representation by American theologians in professional medical ethics, Stanley Hauerwas notes:

> Though religious thinkers have been at the forefront of much of the work done in the expanding field of "medical ethics," it is not always clear that they have been there as religious thinkers . . . often it is hard to tell how their religious convictions have made a difference for the methodology they employ or for their response to specific quandaries. Indeed, it is interesting to note how

seldom they raise issues of the meaning or relation of salvation and health, as they seem to prefer dealing with questions of death and dying, truth telling, and so on.

(Hauerwas, 546)

We find a similar critique coming from Ted Peters just over 20 years ago in his book *Science and Theology: A New Consonance* (Oxford: Westview Press, 1998), where Peters observes that there's an encouraging level of conversation emerging between science and theology, but that this conversation can often be one-sided with science leading the way and theology rarely occupying a leadership role.

When attempting to construct a bridge between two scholarly conversations, it's unavoidable that this work will involve some level of translation and adaptation to your dialogue partner. In Hauerwas' (and Peters') diagnosis, this kind of work, which brings together the broad public of medical practitioners or scientists with theologically minded scholars, is important work, but it carries at least two possible risks. First, there's the risk that the work of translation will be imbalanced, and here both our writers worry that religious thinkers may leave behind their particular frames of reference far more than the scientists they seek to dialogue with. The second risk is that as a result of this imbalance, the theologians involved may fail to bring an important contribution, namely the more fundamental discussion of moral good and human flourishing which provides a cloth into which we may weave more specific ethical casuistry. In particular, the worry here is that the emphasis in these professional bodies on "issues" and specific ethical questions can sideline more fundamental reflection on the notion of good science and the practice of medical care.

There are significant tensions here which cannot be resolved in the space of this brief chapter. For now, I want to highlight the way that these two different ways of framing ethical reflection, casuistry and more fundamental normative ethics, may exist in some tension. Different parties to this debate between science and religion may naturally lean towards either "professional" or "normative" ways of framing ethical deliberation, and risk some kind of imbalanced thinking. It's also interesting to note that it was much easier to assume earlier in the twentieth century that science and theology were intellectually stable ways of interpreting the world, that is, that a person working "scientifically" or "theologically" could assume there were well-established ground rules for how such reflection was to take place, or what resources were important (whether this was the scientific method, the Bible, empirical observation, or mathematics). This is far less the case in the twenty-first century. Increasingly the modes of enquiry across a variety of scholarly ways of "knowing" the world are blurring together and overlapping. Keeping this in mind, it may be a mistake to draw too tidy a categorisation of either "science" or "religion".

Normative accounts of ethics and science

Turning away from the role of religion in professional ethics, I would like briefly to examine some of the ways in which the engagement of science with religion may also invoke more fundamental moral claims. It goes without saying that there are many well-noted disagreements between science and religion on "big issues". Generally, bioethics has been an area where there has been recurring and very public conflict between religious authorities and scientific disciplines. One example can be seen in the 2001 decision by American president George W. Bush to restrict federal funding for research on stem cells obtained from human embryos. In his words, "At its core, this issue forces us to confront fundamental questions about the beginnings of life and the ends of science". Bush's move towards this policy decision was encouraged and celebrated by many religious leaders in America and ran in direct opposition to the formal recommendation by the American NIH (National Institute of Health) embryo research panel in 1994, which encouraged the federal government to fund a range of research involving human embryos. As Bush strove to make clear in subsequent interventions, there were other accessible pathways towards scientific research into adult stem cell lines which were eligible for federal funding, but as his critics observed, the plasticity and thus potential for research within these lines was greatly diminished. While some observers of this policy debate have suggested that this is an instance of conflict between religion and science, or perhaps even a "culture war", it's not necessarily safe to assume that there's an unambiguously "Christian" position, at least within the relatively specific space of stem-cell research regulation. Towards this end, it's worth noting that in America, Bush's successor, also himself a professed Christian, Barak Obama, lifted the ban in 2009. One can also find accounts by theological scholars which argue both for and against embryonic stem cell research. Further, England (which has an established Christian Church and representation by religious leaders in the upper House of Parliament) has permitted embryonic stem cell research, albeit under closely regulated conditions, since 1990.

I have argued in the previous section that the roles of religious representatives and scientists within ethical discussions are far more blurry than we might initially think: scientists may be religious, religion may be scientific (i.e. oriented towards empirical reality or working towards positivistic claims), and each individual may work out the role of religion in generating ethical clarity in different ways. We may find that professional ethics and the casuistry which happens there can be individualistic. This stands in some contrast to the public policy context which is usually by necessity corporate. Given the broad implications of a policy decision to regulate some area of scientific practice, or the appropriation of public funding towards the development of new technologies (as was the case with Bush's ban), policy work seeks to find consensus and so must reach for a more fundamental moral ideal or an adequately encompassing pragmatism. Is there a right way to configure the relationship between religion and science on the matter of ethical reflection? Before I provide an answer to this question, I would like to turn to a second example to further highlight the complex dynamics of religion and science in ethical debates.

A more unexpected example can be found within the domain of contemporary climate science. Many authors who write about climate change, including those who write without any particular religious association, emphasise the fragility of the earth's systems and their vulnerability to anthropogenic (human caused) impacts. To be fair, among religious leaders and communities, there has been a polyphony of many different voices bringing a range of perspectives on climate change, sometimes less-than-harmonious, with some religious leaders describing climate change as one of the key moral issue of our time, and others dismissing it as a distraction from more central ethical concerns. Polling data shows a mixed picture, but at the very least, the level of consensus among climate scientists that climate change is a serious issue is often not shared by the religious public. While many observers of this debate have been quick to dismiss the so-called climate "sceptics" and sometimes religion more broadly as anti-science or even anti-intellectual, I'd like to suggest that there's more than meets the eye to this debate as well. One reason that some of the latter group have expressed concern with the idea of climate change as a moral issue isn't merely generic protest against the encroachment of science on daily life. Instead, it relates to a more specific concern that this claim regarding the vulnerability of the earth to human impacts can stand in some tension with the claim that the earth was created by God and as such has a level of durability and purpose which should not be easily thwarted by human misuse.

One of the most famous paintings by the Italian Renaissance artist Raphael is a fresco set in Athens (the title is *The School of Athens*) which depicts a range of famous ancient Greek philosophers standing and interacting in various ways. Of particular note are two central figures: Plato and Aristotle, who are shown to be in conflict. Plato is pointing up to the heavens, presumably towards "pure reasoning", while Aristotle is pointing towards the earth, emphasising the importance of empirical observation informing our **axioms**. This is a caricature of these two famous philosophers and their positions, of course, but serves to illustrate the point that what we might be tempted to see here on the issue of climate change is a simple conflict between "realist" climate scientists, who are informed by empirical observation, and "idealist" religious spokespersons, who are informed by free-standing axioms. We might even be tempted to pick sides, as has been (in)famously done by some scientists who have argued for the priority of reductive materialism against supposedly "superstitious" religious ideas.

However, it's important to appreciate that there are potentially two fundamentalisms which are being mobilised here, and particularly inasmuch as a resolution of the religion and science debate on climate change may involve the silencing of sceptical religious voices, much stands to be lost. This is illustrated by the resonant suggestion put forward by other scientists that some of the framing of the issue of climate change by climate scientists, and in particular the suggestions for public policy which have resulted, may not fully capture the relationship between earth and humans. That humans are having an unprecedented and often negative, and potentially disastrous impact, on a whole range of specific ecological systems and many of the earth's systems (climate, oceans, soils, etc.) is agreed on both sides of the scientific divide. However (especially given their focus on places which humans and other creatures co-inhabit), an urban ecologist may observe that climate and conservation scientists are not simply passing along their own objective

empirical observations. They have their own filters and axioms, and potentially work within a specific understanding of political authority and action.

The point here is that the human response to an issue like climate change cannot be reduced to a binary choice between assent and dissent. Furthermore, our characterisation of the religious and scientific voices involved in debates surrounding policy responses to climate change must take into account the central role played by **axioms** and filters for both religious persons and scientific practitioners. If we take a step back and look more broadly at perspectives on fragility in environmental science, the role played by perspective comes into sharper relief and we can see that there is actually an array of responses among environmental scientists to the problem of earthly fragility. To provide two examples: first, some conservation biologists argue that "environmental change" is inherently undesirable, and they characterise all signs of change as degradation. We might characterise this perspective as drawing on the past to form norms for the present. However, in a second example, we can look towards the "novel ecosystems" concept, which has been floated by a range of environmental scientists over the past decade. Here, ecologists point out that the health of a current ecosystem may not necessarily be related in obvious ways to its state 11,700 years ago at the start of the current geological epoch, the "Holocene". Ecosystems may reconfigure in response to impacts and changing circumstances and arrive at new and unexpected forms of equilibrium and integrity. Thus, we can see how the past-focussed perspective of conservation stands in some tension with a present- or future-focussed perspective represented by "novel ecosystems" ecologists.

Of course, the choice of past, present, and future to anchor our norms for ethical discussion isn't a neutral choice: many humans may fear and seek to avoid change, while others may rush hastily to embrace novelty. Meanwhile, other-than-human creatures adapt and evolve while we sort out the details. My point here is not that we must choose between these two narratives, that it must be either novel ecosystems OR fragile systems, but that there's a plurality of perspectives on global ecological health *among* scientists. Even more to the point, these different perspectives may lead to different kinds of policy perspectives. Do we seek to create carbon-sinks and preserves which are fenced off from human interaction? Or should our strategies work alongside urban development? The dialogue over these two questions has often been contentious, and there's no uniform answer coming from within either science or religion.

There isn't adequate space here for me to present all these positions or to argue for my own preference on either embryonic stem-cell research or on climate science. For our purposes, I'd like to observe that the role of ethicists and philosophers is not to try and referee these arguments from behind an imaginary intellectual fortification. Not only do debates in religion and science generate ethical quandaries, but there's also an ethical shape to the way one *participates* in these debates. Put simply, both science and religion need to engage with the big constructive questions (what is life? how does it have value?), and they both also need to participate in empirical observation of the world, including human social politics.

I'll elaborate on both of these suggestions, but let's first take up the details of my second suggestion (that both religious and scientific thinkers need to participate jointly in empirical observation of the world). What I'm arguing here is that part of the work of ethics must also include the hard work of public communication. In fact, I'd go so far as to say that one of the responsibilities of the moral philosopher (or theologian/scientist for that matter) is to form an understanding of the landscape of public opinion before intervening in a debate with a public and constructive voice on issues like these. Some contemporary ethicists like Robert Frodeman have argued that philosophers should be willing to take up philosophical "field experiments", and other field-philosophers have also begun to engage in more nuanced empirical research. In a way, this is a return to a form of moral philosophy which was common before the twentieth century, among modern pragmatists and empiricists, and among patristic and medieval theologians such as Augustine of Hippo, who considered the work of engaging theological reflection with social "reality" to be paramount.

Returning to my first suggestion (that both scientists and religious persons take seriously the normative underpinnings of their work), I want to argue that there's good reason for both religion and science to appreciate how there's a richly metaphysical basis for both these modes of understanding the world. Appreciating this diversity of opinion, and the nuance which may lie behind religious perspectives, can help us to see that it may be unwise to dismiss out of hand the claim by some religious persons – returning for a moment to the example of climate change – that the earth is durable, even in the face of anthropogenic impacts. Perhaps this claim may actually carry a level of wisdom regarding the functioning of the earth's systems. If we assume that there's a simple and irreconcilable conflict between scientists who simply communicate their observations regarding climate science and religious persons who express anxieties regarding the normative (if concealed) underpinnings that come along with this communication, we may miss out on the possibility of a valuable conversation. Of course, many climate scientists are quite aware of this fact, and to a certain degree what I'm problematising isn't the work of scientists but rather the way the discourse has been configured in public. However, it's also important to appreciate that different framing of our empirical inquiries, whether on a global scale (earth climate systems) or local one (specific creatures in their natural habitat), can close down our ability to consider some ethical positions. What ethics calls for in this situation is an awareness of the limits of our own perspectives and a willingness to see possible value in the claims of others – whether scientific peers or religious practitioners. Taking this seriously might lead us to conclude that the title for this chapter should be concerned with the ethical implications of the debate underway between sciences and religions.

So what is the role of ethics in this debate? In the first instance, looking for ethics in these debates between science and religion may drive our attention in a pragmatic direction, that is, towards an enhanced awareness of the way that our descriptions of the world can enable or prevent certain forms of moral action. We never approach an ethical quandary with our minds as a blank slate, ready to consider any possible option and its merits. Rather, moral reflection requires a high level of critical self-awareness precisely so that we may understand the intellectual limits of our own starting points – the work represented in each scientific discipline, whether algorithmic design in computer science, the engineering of genomes by biologists, or speculation about cosmology by physicists, is situated within a culture. In one case, precaution and uncertainty may be preferable, and in another, we may find someone particularly willing to tackle a problem through innovation and design. I would like to suggest that, in order to negotiate the tensions that exist between individual scientists, philosophers, and theologians, and in order to negotiate the way that these are represented in the public sphere, we must jointly pursue an ever-increasing measure of wisdom. This seems like an appropriate common ground on which to set what is a challenging but ultimately very rewarding task of cultivating the common good.

Chapter summary

In this chapter, I survey a range of different ways that the debate between religion and science might be described as ethical. I suggest that within the space of professional scientific ethics there has been a tendency to sideline or absorb religious ethical perspectives. I then turn to more constructive "big issue" ethics and examine two specific cases – embryonic stem cell research and climate change – in order to highlight ways that science and religion can be reduced to essentialised stereotypes: that scientists work with the real world and religion deals with ideas (and not reality!). I argue that looking more closely at the range of perspectives represented by scientists and religious leaders in both cases presents a much more complex case and that this in turn commends a kind of ethics which should be jointly pursued by both science and religion.

Study questions

1. How might religious persons contribute to professional scientific ethics? Consider kinds of input that might be provided towards specific case studies.
2. What are the possible hazards presented by the involvement of religious representatives in professional ethics bodies and panels for scientific practice or theological reflection?
3. Consider the cases of animal testing and blood transfusions. In what ways might scientific ethics accommodate the particularities of religious belief and practice?
4. Are there ways that an experimental scientist or medical researcher integrates their own religious beliefs into their professional code of ethics?
5. Come up with a list of 3–5 fundamental moral issues at stake in embryonic stem cell research. Can any of these be identified as unambiguously belonging to "religion" or "science"?

6. What is the role of scepticism and caution in interacting with scientific discoveries?
7. How might scientific enquiry be framed as participating in a common pursuit of wisdom?
8. Consider how an emphasis on "wisdom" (as above) might provide an account of ethics that is different from one which emphasises "justice" or "knowledge". What impacts might any of these three emphases have for specific debates on moral quandaries represented by new scientific discoveries and technologies?

Introductory readings

Deane-Drummond, Celia, "How Is Theology Inspired by the Sciences?", in *Conceptions of Truth and the Unity of Knowledge*, ed. Vittorio Hosle (South Bend: University of Notre Dame Press, 2014), pp. 300–323. [In this chapter, Deane-Drummond explores ways that theology is influenced by science, and considers ways that theology might provide leadership in this conversation.]

Hauerwas, Stanley, "Salvation and Health: Why Medicine Needs the Church". in *Theology and Bioethics*, ed. Earl Shelp (Dordrecht, The Netherlands: D. Reidel Publishers, 1985), pp. 205–224. [In this brief chapter (which I have quoted from above), Hauerwas explores the tricky task of engaging professional ethics with theological reflection.]

Northcott, Michael S., *A Moral Climate: The Ethics of Global Warming* (Maryknoll, NY: Orbis, 2007). [Northcott provides an introduction to some of the challenges facing theological engagement with an issue like climate change. The book provides a model of how theologically minded persons can benefit from scientific understanding of this phenomenon, and some ways that theological reasoning might offer resources for grappling with the spiritual challenges of climate change.]

Tachibana, Chris, "Responsibly Conducting Research". *Science Magazine* (Jan. 29, 2016), www.sciencemag.org/careers/features/2016/01/responsibly-conducting-research. [This article provides a helpful overview of professional ethics in science, and some of the different kinds of questions that are considered "ethical" in current practice.]

Advanced readings

Demeritt, David, "The Construction of Global Warming and the Politics of Science", *Annals of the Association of American Geographers* (June 2001), 91(2), 307–337. [Demeritt focusses on the ways that scientific discourses (such as climate science) have been imagined as working independently of the political sphere. He provides a brisk survey of possible ways of appreciating the social construction of scientific knowledge, which may open up some shared epistemological space between religion and science.]

Latour, Bruno, *An Inquiry into Modes of Existence : An Anthropology of the Moderns* (Cambridge, MA: Harvard University Press, 2013). [In this challenging text, Latour attempts to provide a new basis for narrating the relation between science and religion (among many other things).]

Peters, Ted, Karen Lebacqz, and Gaymon Bennett, *Sacred Cells?: Why Christians Should Support Stem Cell Research* (Lanham, MD: Rowman & Littlefield, 2008). [In this book, the authors provide a contrasting account of stem-cell research ethics, and comment on the involvement of theologians in this scientific enterprise.]

Internet resources

Full text of George W. Bush address on stem cell research (August 9, 2001): http://edition.cnn.com/2001/ALLPOLITICS/08/09/bush.transcript/index.html?_s=PM:ALLPOLITICS

Harrison, Peter, "Scientific Expertise in a Time of Pervasive Scepticism: Enlightenment Values Cannot Help Us Now" blog post hosted by *ABC Religion and Ethics* website: www.abc.net.au/religion/articles/2017/03/22/4640640.htm [Comments on issues raised in this chapter. The ABC website also contains a wide array of other articles by scholars and leaders in various fields on scientific ethics.]

King, David, "Universal Ethical Code for Scientists": www.gov.uk/government/uploads/system/uploads/attachment_data/file/283157/universal-ethical-code-scientists.pdf

Nuffield Council on Bioethics, "Interesting Links" hosted at: http://nuffieldbioethics.org/about/links [Provides a huge index of professional scientific and ethical bodies.]

Glossary

Aesthetics   While aesthetics can refer to the study of beauty, it can also refer to a branch of ethics which attempts to broaden out the sources we rely upon for moral deliberation, including factors which may be highly evocative but not easily described in propositional terms: taste, intuition, and a sense of the sublime are all possible aesthetic concerns.

Agency   Ethicists use the term 'agency' to refer to a person's ability (or disability) to function as a moral agent.

Agent detection   The cognitive tendency for humans (and other animals) to attribute events or activity to intentional agents, regardless of whether or not those events or activities are actually caused by agents. It's thought that agent detection serves an evolutionary purpose by making individuals hyper-aware of potential danger; assuming the activity of sentient agents allows one to take precautionary measures. Some scientists think that religious belief is at least partly a result of hypersensitive agent detection in humans, suggesting that humans have a natural inclination to attribute natural phenomena to divine agency.

Agnosticism   Typically defined in terms of a *lack* of belief (or some related positive epistemic attitude) toward the existence of God or other deities. *See also* **atheism**.

Apologetics   The attempt to offer a defence of religious faith using the concepts and vocabulary prevailing in the society with which it is interacting.

Arational   A belief or viewpoint is arational if it lies beyond the proper scope of rational assessment; if something is arational, it is neither rational nor irrational.

Aristotle (384–322 BCE)   Philosopher who made foundational contributions to metaphysics, physics, ethics and the philosophy of biology. Codified a theory of causes and biological explanation that remained essentially unshaken until Darwin.

Atheism   The denial of theism. *See also* **theism**.

Axiom   A basic or fundamental assumption which is taken to be self-evident and serves as the basis for other secondary arguments.

Cognitive biases   Errors in thinking that lead to irrational inferences and conclusions when processing information.

Cognitive Science of Religion An interdisciplinary field concerned with the cognitive and evolutionary bases of religious beliefs and behaviours. CSR researchers utilise the methodology and findings from a range of disciplines, including evolutionary psychology, anthropology, the various cognitive sciences, and neuroscience.

Compatibilism A position in the philosophical free will debate that argues that free will and determinism are compatible.

Conciliatory view On the conciliatory view of the epistemic significance of peer disagreement, rationality requires that you adjust (to some degree) your confidence about the target proposition upon finding out that someone you regard as an epistemic peer on the matter disagrees with you.

Confabulation Subjects confabulate when they are not aware of the true causes of their behaviour and sincerely believe the reasons that they invent to explain their behaviour.

Cosmologies/Cosmology Any way of describing the entire universe in a meaningful manner; until the modern period cosmologies often incorporated astronomy, physics, metaphysics, ethics, and theology in the same account.

creatio ex nihilo Latin for 'creation out of nothing'. A religious doctrine describing the concept that God created the world from absolutely nothing, and entailing spiritual and moral consequences for human beings.

Darwin, Charles (1809–1882) Naturalist and biologist. Codified the theory of evolution by natural selections, after years of detailed observations and biological theorising, in his *Origin of Species* and subsequent works. Acknowledged debts to Alfred Russell Wallace, Lamarck, his grandfather Erasmus, and others.

Darwin, Erasmus (1731–1802) Grandfather of Charles. Offered an important forerunner of evolution by natural selection and proposed gradual modification of species in his *Zoönomia* (1794–1796).

Deduction A deductive inference is one where the premises logically entail the conclusion. This means that if the premises are true, then the conclusion must also be true. *See also* **induction**.

Determinism The claim that all events are determined. In the philosophical debate on free will, determinism is important because some philosophical positions hold that free will is compatible with determinism (compatibilists), while others think that it is not (incompatibilists).

Divine hiddenness The divine hiddenness argument is an argument for atheism; the argument represents a case where religious disagreements can have first-order epistemic significance.

Divine sufficiency The traditional idea that the existence of God, unlike everything else, requires no further explanation since it is necessary, complete, and self-causing. This is sometimes described in terms of divine 'aseity'.

Doxastic involuntarism The view that our beliefs are not subject to our direct control.

Ecumenical Seeking unity amongst Christian churches.

Efficient cause   The event, process or object that brings about an effect; the primary source of the change produced.

Electroencephalogram (EEG)   A procedure to measure brain activity. Little sensors are attached to the scalp and are able to measure electrical signals produced by the brain. EEG has a high temporal but a low spatial resolution.

Empirical   That which can be established by experiment, observation, and testing, as opposed to claims of logic, definition, and pure hypothesising.

Epicurus (341–270 BCE)   Ancient philosopher. Offered a purely materialistic explanation of complexity as arising through endless recycling of indivisible particles through otherwise empty space.

Epistemic peer   An epistemic peer, relative to whether some proposition *p* is true, is someone who is equally cognitive capable and well informed as you are with respect to the truth of *p*.

Epistemology   A field of philosophy that is concerned with the nature of knowledge and rationality, and related notions such as truth, understanding, wisdom, and so on.

Essentialised   An approach to reasoning which assumes that certain categories can be universalised on the basis of inherent, stable and common traits.

Evidentialism   A view about the epistemology of religious belief that demands that such belief be based on appropriate evidence. As the view is usually understood, the evidence required needs to be sufficiently independent of religious belief itself, which is why evidentialism often focuses on the kind of evidence putatively offered for religious belief by proofs of God's existence.

Evidential problem of divine hiddenness   An argument against the existence of God. In sum, if God is perfectly loving, he would make it so that anyone capable of having a personal relationship with him would be able to reasonably believe that God exists. Given that some such people do *not* believe in the existence of God, then such a perfectly loving God does not exist.

Evolution   Originally, any process of gradual development, but usually used to mean specifically the process whereby organised biological complexity and species arose through gradual incremental change.

Exemplar account   According to the exemplar account of the epistemology of religious belief, we are not to compare religious belief to perceptual belief (as, e.g. reformed epistemologists do). We should rather focus on other domains that have very different properties, such as ethics. The point is that certain domains – like the ethical and the religious, but unlike the perceptual – incorporate a special role for expertise, wisdom, and a distinctive kind of experience. One consequence of this account is that there is an important function for religious exemplars to play in one's religious epistemology (just as ethical exemplars play an important role in our ethical epistemology).

Existential problem of divine hiddenness   The angst generated by (i) the belief that a personal relationship with God is incredibly important *for general* *human flourishing* and (ii) the perception of God as hidden or silent – potentially resulting in a view of the world as uncaring and/or inhospitable.

Falsificationism According to falsificationism, science proceeds by postulating bold conjectures and then seeking out counterevidence which would decisively show these conjectures to be false, and in the process falsifying them.

Fatalism The idea that all events are inevitable. The doctrine is stronger than determinism, because it assumes that our minds cannot exercise any causal influence over future events.

Fideism Holds that religious belief is not to be rationally evaluated in the way that ordinary belief is, in that it is a kind of belief that is essentially arational. On this view, religious belief can be completely lacking in supporting evidence even while being not subject to rational criticism as a result. *See also* **quasi-fideism**.

Fine-tuning The observation that the laws of nature and physical constants of the universe are very finely-balanced, such that tiny differences from what we currently observe would have resulted in an entirely different kind of universe. The interpretation of fine-tuning is contested in both theology and scientific cosmology, though its origins lie in the latter.

First-order evidence Directly concerns the truth of some target proposition.

Functional Magnetic Resonance Imaging (fMRI) A neuroimaging procedure. Subjects are put in a scanner and the researchers are able to measure brain activity by detecting changes in blood flow. fMRI has a very high spatial but a low temporal resolution.

Fundamentalism Involves strict and dogmatic adherence to a specific belief or set of beliefs, and an insensitivity to countervailing evidence.

General relativity A theory of gravity put forward by Albert Einstein in 1915 to replace Newton's ways of calculating and explaining gravitational force. Relativity introduced the concept that the force of gravity can be understood as the result of distortions in the fabric of spacetime by mass and energy concentrations in the universe.

Genotype An organism's genetic composition or traits; the DNA an organism inherits from its parents.

Higher-order evidence Higher-order evidence doesn't bear directly on whether some target proposition *p* is true but rather on the matter of whether one has *rationally assessed* the relevant first-order evidence. *See also* **first-order evidence**.

Hume, David (1711–1776) Empiricist philosopher and historian, who sketched an alternative, modified 'Epicurean' explanation for apparent Design in his posthumously published *Dialogues Concerning Natural Religion*.

Inclusive metaphysics A harmonised system of thought, combining the insights of both science and religion.

Incommensurability Two scientific theories are incommensurable when there is no basis that is common to both theories on which they may be assessed (because the two theories lack common conceptual, methodological, and experimental resources, among others). Where there are only two competing scientific theories available, it follows that each theory is assessed relative to the other in a theory-relative manner.

Induction   An inductive inference is one which provides strong evidence for a conclusion, but which doesn't logically entail it. For example, that the sun has risen every day in living memory is a good inductive basis for believing that it will rise tomorrow, but it is at least logically possible that the sun won't rise tomorrow. *See also* **deduction**.

Inductivism   The view that identifies the scientific method with the inductive method. On this view, scientific knowledge would proceed from many positive instances (with no negative instances) to a universal generalization about the phenomenon under investigation. *See also* **induction**.

Intellectual virtues   Traits or qualities associated with intellectual flourishing, such as open-mindedness, intellectual courage, curiosity, and intellectual autonomy.

Lamarck, Jean Baptiste (1744–1829)   Naturalist and biologist. Offered a theory of species-change in which advantageous adaptations acquire by organisms are handed on to their offspring. Nature thus moves from simple to complex organisms via a *pouvoir de vie* or 'complexifying power'.

Literalism   In creationism, the belief that the Bible contains the actual words of God, and should therefore be taken as the literal truth, whatever the subject matter.

Logic   The study of the validity of arguments. Today, logic is a branch of mathematics that makes use of formal languages in which the validity or invalidity of arguments can be proven using mathematical methods.

Logical empiricism   According to logical empiricism, a claim is scientific if there is a way of empirically verifying it (i.e. if there is a way of finding positive empirical instances confirming that claim or statement). On this proposal, the scientific method is induction, and thus the view is wedded to inductivism. *See also* **induction, inductivism**.

Metaethics   The branch of philosophy concerned with understanding the nature of morality (as opposed to normative ethics, which concerns questions about what *is* moral).

Metaphysical   That which cannot be tested empirically; usually concerned with the fundamental nature of reality.

Metaphysics   The study of the fundamental structure of reality (exploring e.g. philosophical issues related to identity, space, and time).

Methodological naturalism   The working hypothesis at the heart of all natural sciences, that the natural world can be explained entirely on its own terms, without recourse to the supernatural.

Modal logic   The study of the validity of arguments that use modal terms such as 'possible' and 'necessary'.

Monotheism   The position that there is only one God; notable examples of monotheism include Christianity, Judaism, and Islam.

Multiverse   The idea that there are many universes in addition to our own. Some multiverse scenarios claim that every conceivable physical scenario can thereby exist somewhere.

Naturalism   The philosophical doctrine that in principle everything that exists can be explained without reference to supernatural cause or agents.

Natural selection   The process whereby better-adapted organisms tend to survive and to enjoy greater reproductive success than less-adapted organisms.

Natural theology   The attempt to draw conclusions about the existence and nature of God from observations of the natural world.

Neural correlates   Patterns of brain activity that correspond to specific mental experiences. Scientists generally affirm that neural correlates in the brain are required for any given subjective experience. Applied to religious experience and belief, there's some disagreement over whether neural correlates actually *cause* religious beliefs and experiences, or whether they're instead neural responses to a supernatural reality.

Neuroplasticity   The brain's ability to alter its structure and functioning in response to experience. As individuals repetitively engage in certain behaviours or experiences over time, the neuronal connections associated with those activities become stronger – this is how habits are formed. Applied to religious belief, some scientists suggest that religious rituals and habitual practices condition the brain to be neurologically disposed towards religious belief.

No-fault assumption   The assumption that someone can sincerely and honestly consider the question as to whether or not God exists and non-culpably maintain non-theistic belief (agnosticism or atheism).

Non-belief   Abstaining from theistic belief; atheism or agnosticism regarding the existence of God.

Non-culpable   Not subject to blame. If someone was non-culpable in their atheistic or agnostic belief regarding the existence of God, then that means that they cannot be blamed for their belief (or lack of belief) – that they have sincerely and honestly looked into the issue and made the best decision with the evidence they had.

Nonoverlapping magisteria   Subject matters that are not in principle in conflict with one another.

Non-propositional   In contrast to 'propositional' forms of knowledge, which rest on factual description, non-propositional claims and knowledge do not rest upon 'facts' and cannot be proven or disproven on the basis of logic. They often seek to explain subjective experience.

Normative ethics   A branch of philosophy which seeks to define possible norms for human action. This can often include arguments which seek to classify actions as right and wrong, and result in a set of rules which can govern human conduct.

Ontological arguments   Arguments for the existence of God from the concept of God. Ontological arguments differ from other arguments for the existence of God in being purely conceptual. They do not appeal to broadly empirical premises, which is to say they do not appeal to anything that we know through experience or observation.

Ought-implies-can principle   This philosophical principle, attributed to Immanuel Kant, says (roughly) that if it's true that we *ought* to do something then we must at least be capable of doing it.

Perfect being theology   The academic study of God considered as the greatest possible being. A greatest possible being is usually understood to have all the perfections *maximally* (i.e. to be perfectly good, perfectly powerful, perfectly knowledgeable etc.), to have these perfections *essentially* (i.e. it is in its very nature to have these perfections), and to exist necessarily.

Perfectly loving assumption   The assumption that because God is perfectly loving he would make his existence sufficiently manifest to everyone or at least everyone capable of having a relationship with him.

Phenotype   An organism's observable (or macroscopic) physiological or behavioural characteristics or traits, as determined by interactions between its genetic constitution and its environment

Philosophy of science   Focuses on the nature, methods, logic and implications of science.

Possible world   A comprehensive way things could have been. Possible worlds are usually understood as being complete descriptions of a possible universe, leaving out no details. The idea of possible worlds can be used to explicate modal claims, and to check if arguments involving modal claims are logically valid.

Problem of auxiliary hypotheses   This problem concerns how no scientific hypothesis is tested in isolation, but only in conjunction with other relevant theoretical hypotheses and auxiliary hypotheses. This means that when we discover counterevidence we can't be sure which element is the problematic one that should be rejected.

Problem of induction   This problem concerns the fact the induction cannot be deductively justified, and any non-deductive justification would be circular, since it would presuppose prior inductive inferences. There is thus no justification for induction.

Quasi-fideism   Maintains that our most basic religious commitments are essentially arational, but that this is no barrier to our non-basic religious commitments being nonetheless rational. This thesis is defended on the grounds that our non-basic everyday beliefs, which we typically hold to be rational, have basic commitments at their heart that are essentially arational. By parity of reasoning, if these non-basic everyday beliefs are rational, then we should think the same about non-basic religious beliefs. *See also* **fideism**.

Realism   Belief in an objective external world existing beyond the human subjective consciousness.

Reason responsiveness   A compatibilist position that argues that free will and responsibility can be ascribed to agents that have the ability to recognise and act on moral reasons.

Reductionism   Belief that the physical properties of a multi-component system can be explained in terms of the physics of its most basic components.

Reflexivity, transitivity, and symmetry   A relation is reflexive if and only if everything bears that relation to itself. For example, the relation *is the same size as* is reflexive, as everything is the same size as itself. A relation is transitive if and only if, if one thing bears that relation to a second thing, and the second thing bears that relation to a third thing, then the first thing bears that relation to the third thing. For example, the relation *is taller than* is transitive. If person one is taller than person two, and person two is taller than person three, then person one is taller than person three. A relation is symmetric if and only if, if one thing bears that relation to a second thing, then the second thing also bears that relation to the first thing. For example, the relation *is a brother of* is symmetric. If person one is the brother of person two, then person two is also the brother of person one.

Reformed epistemology According to reformed epistemology, our religious beliefs are no less rational than other forms of belief, like perceptual belief, that are typically regarded to be rational. In particular, just as our perceptual faculties can, in the right conditions at least, generate rational perceptual belief and perceptual knowledge even when we have no supporting evidence (and certainly no independent supporting evidence), so the same can apply in the case of religious belief. In this regard, proponents of reformed epistemology appeal to a religious faculty, known as the *sensus divinitatis. See also* **sensus divinitatis**.

Replicator An entity which replicates (makes copies of) itself or, more generally, any entity which is capable of being copied.

Schellenberg, John The leading figure in the divine hiddenness literature. His 1993 book, *Divine Hiddenness and Human Reason*, is often pointed to as the seminal work on the subject.

Scientific realism Holds that well-confirmed scientific theories are approximately true and that the aim of science is to give a literally true account of the world.

Scientific relativism The idea that any scientific theory could be valid from within its own point of view, with no way of comparing the relative validity of competing scientific theories.

Scientism The view that we can only gain knowledge through the natural sciences. Restricted scientism applies this view to one particular area, which unrestricted scientism applies it to all of reality.

Self-referential incoherence A position is self-referentially incoherent if holding it to be true entails the falsehood of the position.

Sensitivity A belief that p is sensitive if and only if, were p false, the agent would not believe that p.

Sensus divinitatis This is a religious faculty, or divine sense, which is held by proponents of reformed epistemology to enable us to acquire, at least when functioning appropriately and in the right conditions, rational religious belief, and religious knowledge. *See also* **reformed epistemology**.

Sophisticated falsificationism According to sophisticated falsificationism, counterevidence cannot falsify a theory. Scientists may instead accommodate anomalies by modifying their theories with the addition of auxiliary hypotheses. If the new version of the theory is theoretically progressive – i.e. makes novel predictions – it qualifies as scientific and its proponents may keep working on it.

Sphexishness   Seemingly reason responsive behaviour that on a closer look turns out to be highly context dependent and merely instinctive.

Steadfast view   Denial of the conciliatory view. *See also* **conciliatory view**.

Teleology   Explanation of traits or parts by means of the goals or end-states that those traits/parts serve.

Theism   The belief that there is one, and only one, God; who combines omniscience, omnipotence, and omnibenevolence with a personal interest in all created things.

Theory-ladenness of observation   This refers to how one's previous training and experience, and thus one's theoretical commitments, can inform one's experiences, such that one's observations are not completely theory-neutral.

Validity   An argument is logically valid if and only if its conclusion follows logically from the premises. More specifically, the premises and conclusions of an argument include both logical vocabulary (e.g. 'and', 'or', 'not', 'if . . . then', 'for some', 'for all') and non-logical vocabulary. Replacing the non-logical vocabulary of a premise or conclusion with dummy placeholders reveals the logical form of a premise or conclusion. An argument is logically valid if, and only if, the conclusion follows from the premises in virtue of the logical form of the premises and conclusion (i.e. no matter what non-logical vocabulary we plug into the placeholders).

Worldview   The entire set of beliefs that determine an individual's orientation towards the world.

Zombie challenge   The worry that we might not have free will because consciousness might not be involved in behaviour production in the right way.

Index

Page numbers in *italics* indicate a figure on the corresponding page.